KNOW IT ALL

FINDING THE IMPOSSIBLE COUNTRY 🍁

ALSO BY JAMES H. MARSH

The Fishermen of Lunenburg

The Fur Trade in Canada

The Discoveries

New Beginnings
A Social History of Canada,
co-authored with Daniel Francis

Alberta
A Story of the Province and Its People

Beginnings
From the First Nations to the Great Migration

Co-editor and author of
Alberta: A State of Mind

"Alberta's Quiet Revolution: The Early Lougheed Years"
in *Alberta's 2005 Centennial History*

KNOW IT ALL

FINDING THE IMPOSSIBLE COUNTRY

JAMES H. MARSH

A MEMOIR

DURVILE &
UpRoute Books

Calgary, Alberta, Canada

Durvile & UpRoute Books
DURVILE IMPRINT OF DURVILE PUBLICATIONS LTD.

Calgary, Alberta, Canada
durvile.com

© 2022 James H. Marsh

LIBRARY AND ARCHIVES CATALOGUING IN PUBLICATIONS DATA

Know It All: Finding the Impossible Country
Marsh, James H., author

1. Canadian Studies
2. Memoir | 3. Canadiana | 4. Toronto Junction

Reflections Series. Series editor, Lorene Shyba

978-1-988824-84-0 (hardcover)
978-1-988824-90-1 (ebook)
978-1-988824-91-8 (audiobook)

Cover design, Lorene Shyba based on
the generative art work *Glyphs* (2019) by James R. Parker.

Durvile Publications would like to acknowledge the financial support of
the Government of Canada through Canadian Heritage Canada Book Fund
and the Government of Alberta, Alberta Media Fund.

Printed in Canada. First edition. First printing. 2022.

We acknowledge the traditional lands upon which we live, work, and play.
The Indigenous Peoples of Southern Alberta include the Siksika, Piikani,
and Kainai of the Blackfoot Confederacy; the Tsuut'ina; and the Chiniki, Bearspaw,
and Wesley Stoney Nakoda First Nations. Also the Region 3 Métis Nation of Alberta.

All rights reserved. No part of this publication may be produced,
stored in a retrieval system or transmitted in any form
or by any means without prior written consent.
Contact Durvile Publications Ltd. for details.

FOR LOUISE, REBECCAH, AND CHARLOTTE

*The truth becomes a landscape of many layers
in an ever-changing light;
the details depend on whose memories illuminate it.*

— Denise Chong, *The Concubine's Children*

CONTENTS

Prologue   xi

1. The Door Opens   1
2. Shadows on the Sand   7
3. As Fugitive as the Years   20
4. The Ruins I Mapped   36
5. My Father's War   49
6. Streets, Laneways, and the Games We Played   70
7. Life in Toronto's Junction   84
8. Huntsville, Muskoka   95
9. School Days   108
10. Turning the Pages   122
11. It's a Fucking Miracle, James   141
12. Unity in Diversity: A Centennial History for Canada   152
13. Becoming Canadian   169
14. Place Where the Light Enters   190
15. On to Ottawa   204
16. A Gift to Canada   219
17. To Shine a Light on Canada   234
18. A Nation in a Nutshell   249
19. Who Is Powlisik?   266
20. Into the Digital Age   276
21. Bookends   290

Acknowledgments   303

PROLOGUE

ONE SPRING DAY in 1979 I was scrummaging around the National Archives in Ottawa, researching a book that I was editing. I loved the atmosphere there—quiet, serious, a sense of importance. At frequent intervals I headed to the sixth-floor coffee shop to meet friends, most of whom were graduate students from Carleton University. On this day, my friend and future co-author, Dan Francis asked me if I had seen an ad in the *Globe and Mail* for an editor in chief for a new national encyclopedia of Canada, an epic publishing project underway in Edmonton, Alberta. Dan told me that I should apply. I never did see the ad but I found Hurtig Publisher's address in Edmonton. I wrote them a letter, not knowing that over three hundred other people had seen that ad and had already responded.

I had met Mel Hurtig on a few occasions at book publishing meetings and was always impressed with his energy and fervent advocacy of Canadian publishing. I had never seen anyone so at home on a podium, so perfectly dressed—by the great Edmonton haberdasher Henry Singer as I later found out. His speeches were full of impressive anecdotal evidence of how corporate America was destroying Canadians' ability to publish their own authors. In response to my application, Mel sent me a note scribbled with a large black Sharpie telling me to write him a letter, no more than a

xi

page and a half long, telling him who I was and what I had done to qualify for such a significant job.

What should I say? I really was not at a stage of my life where I was comfortable summing up. I had an eventful editorial career, I thought, with several Canadian publishers. I had written a number of books, including a two-volume *Social History of Canada*, and I was currently on a joint appointment between Carleton University and publisher McClelland & Stewart, where I had edited almost a hundred scholarly books on Canadian history and social sciences. Several other applicants had, I was sure, as much or more experience. What other qualities might Mel be looking for in a candidate to lead the grandiose project of a new, comprehensive encyclopedia of the entire country?

My family and friends encouraged me, but I had serious doubts about my prospects, particularly about my lack of knowledge of the French language in a national endeavour. I also had reservations about my ability to be "chief" of anything, as I had no managerial experience. I eventually received a note from Mel, telling me that he was headed to Ottawa and that we should meet. This letter to me had been lost in the Carleton University mail system for two weeks and I'd only received it two days before Mel arrived. He was in Ottawa to be interviewed on the radio. After a hasty phone call, we arranged to meet afterward at the restaurant that was in those days located in the basement of the Château Laurier hotel. I listened to the CBC interview on the car radio. Mel was having a terrible time speaking, apologizing for his persistent cough.

Prologue

At brunch with Mel at the Château Laurier, he recounted anecdotes of customers to his bookstore, of his authors, of his golf game, or of his victories over hapless opponents in debates. Mel's charm and earnestness always tempered his ample self-importance. After considerable time, he finally asked me about my background in publishing. Almost with a sense of naiveté he asked me if I was a "generalist." I was prepared for that question and responded that I had a little knowledge about a lot of things: literature, classical music, sports, art, social science, philosophy, biography, and history. Above all, I told him that the driving force, almost the redeeming force, in my mental life from the time I was a boy was my curiosity and my love of books. How much of our lives is determined by these encounters, in which each person tries to evaluate the other, guessing, interpreting, and either trusting or evading our instincts? Mel persuaded me that he was an accomplished, ambitious man, but what did he think of me? As long as I knew him, he never said.

So, who was I? And what had I done to deserve such a significant job?

CHAPTER 1

The Door Opens

*"There is always one moment in childhood
when the door opens and lets the future in."*

– Graham Greene, The Power and the Glory

NUMBER 4 NORFOLK was said to be the oldest house on one of the shortest streets in Toronto. Annie and Charlie Radford had raised two daughters and a son in that house, before they adopted me. Across a cinder lane that separated the house from Shirley Street, a house that was torn down years ago, was Mrs. Mitchell's baby refuge, where my mother Ada had left me while she sorted out her life as a 19-year-old unwed mother, recently arrived in Toronto from domestic service in Bracebridge, Muskoka. In December of 1942 Ada met a young soldier on leave, John Harley Marsh, and I was born nine months later.

Annie Radford was a short, vibrant woman, pretty in her youth. She had a nervous melancholy about her that suggested a sad resolve from some loss. She was on speaking terms with the many Scots and Irish immigrants in the neighbourhood after the war. Annie particularly loved babies. She could not let a baby carriage pass on the street without enquiring about the name, gender, and age of its passenger. She would lift the infant out of its blanket into the air, chirping cheery words in baby talk. She treated small dogs much the same way, patting them firmly on the back, as if she were burping them. Annie volunteered to help daily with the feeding and changing of the half-dozen or so abandoned children consigned by Children's Aid to Mrs. Mitchell's care in her house on Shirley Street. When the babies reached 8-months old, Mrs. Mitchell either returned them to mothers who had managed to patch their lives together, or she sent them to foster care. When Ada did not come for me, Annie took me across the lane. What a remarkable idea for her to adopt a baby, with her own children grown and her son Jack flying bomber missions over North Africa in the Royal Air Force. She saw me take my first steps and heard me speak my first words: "ice cream," as she later told me.

I passed the next two years, to age 3, with Annie. What would my life have been like had I stayed with her? Jack left this modest house to become a decorated flyer in the RAF, an engineer, and a vice-president of one of the largest construction companies in Canada. The younger daughter, Jean, married a TransCanada Airline (Air Canada) mechanic and raised three daughters. The elder, Grace, fared less well, being thwarted by Annie in her ambition to go to nursing school, and in her love life, for she had a son, Donald, fathered by a man of whom Annie did not approve. Was he married? Neither Annie nor Grace would say, but Donald seemed lost without him. Grace raised the boy on her own in a two-room attic apartment on Earnbridge Street, a few blocks south of Norfolk, just north of Queen. She settled for being an assistant to Dr. Robert Braiden, who later navigated me through several childhood illnesses.

Annie said that her husband Charlie adored me when I was a baby, but if that were true, the affection did not survive this awkward adoption. If his sentiments were not quite hatred of me when I grew into a fractious boy, they contained ample resentment, which he expressed in sullen silence. He had a heart attack—"mild" Annie liked to say, dismissively—in the late 1940s and retired early from his job as chief electrician at the Ontario Legislative Building. He grew reclusive as he spent the next thirty retirement years, friendless, profoundly alone in his garden and his workshop in the dirt floor basement,

In the backyard shortly after my arrival at 4 Norfolk Street, with a cat named Sassy.

surrounded with rusty garden tools and tulip bulbs amid the dark smell of loam, fertilizer, and seeds. He and Annie barely spoke to one another. Annie was strong-willed and Charlie had little influence on what she did, even bringing a young stranger into their home.

There is a photograph of me about age 9- or 10-months old, sitting on the grass in the backyard at 4 Norfolk Street with wet pants, contemplating my fingers under the scrutiny of a fluffy cat who stands in a pose of detached curiosity, her tail rising above her like a puff of black smoke. Around us in that yard were Charlie's rose bushes and lilac trees.

"No crying," were the first words that I remember Annie Radford or anyone saying to me, words that ignited my conscious life. "You must not call me 'mommy' anymore. Your real mommy is coming to get you," she said. I was standing in hard, polished shoes on the red corduroy sofa in the Radford's living room, overlooking the narrow garden and picket fence on Norfolk Street. Annie fumbled with the buttons on my shirt and roughly brushed my hair. I stomped petulantly on the couch cushions. I hated when she fussed over me.

Whatever did those first words mean, that another "mommy" was coming to take me away? "No crying," Annie repeated, with an impatient shake of her head. "Jimmy, you must try to show your real mommy that you are a good boy." She lifted me down from the sofa and I ran across the room to the piano, an old rosewood Heintzman with cracked varnish, which Annie played each day, smiling at her own fumbling, grasping for chords, singing in her gruff alto voice, hymns from a dog-eared music anthology. Light streamed in bands through the fake ivory Venetian blinds into the room in still, dusty shafts. I crossed the floor and banged the chipped keys of the piano, unaware of what it meant that another, "real" mother was coming to take me from a comfort where no memories or fears had impeded the flow of the day.

The doorbell rang and the surrender was swift. "C'mon," Ada commanded at the front door of 4 Norfolk, as she tugged and pinched my arm. I heard but do not remember further words exchanged between the two mothers. A car waited on the street, motor running. Ada prodded me into the back seat, climbed in next to me and slammed the door. I lost sight of Annie standing forlorn behind the screen door. Ada stopped my flailing with a slap, stinging my face, ringing my ears.

From Norfolk Street to Perth Avenue would be today a twenty-minute car ride, up Brock and left on Dundas Street, north along Lansdowne, past the house where the streetcars slept, then under the subway at Royce Avenue, then left beneath the steep hill at Davenport. The final left is at the "T" at Perth Avenue. Occasionally, the car would jar in and out of the steel streetcar tracks, stop for a red light, and then start up again. Where were we going? I could not tell.

Number 567 Perth Avenue, "your real home," Ada announced, was one of many identical houses on that street, each a narrow duplex attached to its twin by its spine. For me it was the gate to a dark world, with a peeling green door and shaky verandah, a dim, papered front hall leading to the narrow dining

The Door Opens

Age 3, 1946, in the backyard of Norfolk Street days before Ada came to take me away. I seem to have a worried look on my face in every childhood photo.

room with a bare metal stovepipe from floor to ceiling, too hot to touch in the wintertime. I was past rescue now. Each passage confirmed my internment. Ada did not release her grip on my aching arm, as she dragged me into the kitchen and shouted down the basement stairs: "Harry!" I could hear him pause as he shoveled the ashes. "Harry!" He ignored her. "Aren't you going to say something to your own fucking son! ... You're the one who wanted him here." The words are as clear to me today as the Lord's Prayer or *God Save the Queen*.

"I don't want to be ... here," I thought but could not say. "I want to go back, to get back, to drink the cold milk and to eat the honeyed toast and to have Annie scrub me gently in the zinc tub next to the electric heater; to go to bed on cool sheets, and to hear Annie say in her kind voice, 'Oh Jimmy, you are the limit,' and to have her pull a soft woolen blanket over me as I spoke my prayers, 'Now I lay me down to sleep. God bless Nana. ...' And then to wake the next day anew with her, with no need of memories."

I shut my eyes to repel the hallucinations of the alien world. Harry awkwardly hopped up the basement stairs, a crutch under one arm, grasping the banister with the other hand. He loomed over my bowed head, but he did not speak. Ada dragged me like a marionette up the stairs to the second-floor bedroom and pitched me onto a small mattress in the corner by the door. I lay motionless in a daze, my eyes shut, my ears hearing only echoes. I pulled my knees tightly against my chest, my face pressed onto the rough blanket as I fell into a dark, placeless sleep, in vain hope that Ada would not find me. As darkness fell, she grabbed my arm and shook me. "For Christ sake, leave the kid alone," were the only kind words I ever heard Harry say.

CHAPTER 2

Shadows on the Sand

"Consciousness converges with the child as a landing tern touches the outspread feet of its shadow on the sand."

– Annie Dillard, American Childhood

AMONG THE RUINS of the broken and scattered people and things of the distant past, tangled threads of memory still link us to the struggles of our unformed selves. In the end we know that we cannot reveal all the secrets that we hid in order to survive, or ultimately cannot understand why we were here or why we could not have chosen to be better, happier, or other than we were.

Still, we try to connect, to explain, to solve time's mystery, with the few tools that we have: a kaleidoscope of images without words, voices without names, all retrieved in a half-sleep of aching loss. My remembrance of childhood is less an episodic narrative as a sense of conflict between two worlds, one of violence and disarray, and another of hope and love. My identity mirrored the two prevailing women in my life. In Ada's view, I was a sullen, ungrateful boy who had wrecked her life with my presence. I reacted to her in fear and even hatred. For Annie, I was her lost child, the reawakening of meaning in her life, an antidote for her empty marriage. I loved and longed for Annie Radford. It was my great release that, at least partially to be rid of me, Ada sent me to visit Norfolk at least one weekend a month,

*Family portrait, circa 1947–48, with
Ada, Marian, Harry and me.*

and for Christmas, Easter and summer holidays. I waited for Annie's call.

The photographs that survived in shoe boxes and wrinkled albums from those years that followed my passage from Norfolk to Perth Avenue when I was a boy of three, ignite flashes of memory from their commonplace subjects, like the tiny chemical burst of light that made them. They are jarring in their insistence on a ghostly physical presence in that world.

A family portrait dating from 1947–48 was taken in our narrow Perth Avenue backyard. It is at first glance a conventional picture of a mother and father with their two children. My father Harry is dapper, his black hair swept back from his forehead, his light windbreaker is zipped to the neck, the slipper on his wounded left leg is set up from the dirt and stones onto a piece of wood. Ada shows some weight gain from her recent pregnancy, but she still appears young, with her hair pulled back to the sides of her head. She holds my restless younger sister

With Marian and my kitten Cuzio on the front verandah at 567 Perth.

Marian on her lap. Behind us is a row of shrubs and stalks of rhubarb, where I spent hours with a shovel digging a twisting raceway for my two Dinky Toy cars, a red Maserati and a green Ferrari that Annie Radford had passed on to me from her son Jack. In the background is the tail end of a dog, her head hidden, likely one of the many mutts Ada successively named Princess over the years. The sun brightly lights the figures, like an overhead studio lamp, highlighting my father's black hair. I stand in my dirty overalls and a striped shirt, my arms hanging, untouched by my father's hand, squinting quizzically at the unknown photographer. This photograph provokes in my mind a nostalgic illusion across time, a "normal" image of a family, masking what I know of the drunken furies of my father, the helpless desolation of my mother, and the crushing void of my childhood.

A photograph of me, in dirty, torn overalls, standing on the verandah of 567 Perth Avenue has a stronger resonance to me now. Likely on order, I have put my right arm awkwardly around my sister Marian. Pressed into the cradle of my left elbow, pulling down my shirt with its little claws is a kitten.

My Aunt Muriel Marsh gave that kitten to me, naming it after a compelling character in Shakespeare's *Romeo and Juliet*, which she was studying in high school. My contraction of Mercutio was "Cuzio," and I loved that cat. Once again, the posed charade of sibling affection belies the fact that we look like two forlorn kids in a Dorothea Lange portrait from the Great Depression.

A photograph that conjures a haunting reminiscence of my presence in that ephemeral world when I was six or seven years old was taken from across the road towards 567 Perth. My father is talking to the coal delivery man, who is crouched tightly on his knees at the back of his delivery truck. Harry is dressed in a shirt, vest, and tie, leaning on his right leg, with his damaged left leg slightly bent. In the 1940s and 1950s, coal, ice, and newspapers were brought to our door regularly and the coal man returned to collect the furnace ashes. The popcorn man, ice cream vendor, Fuller Brush man, postman, and the rag-and-bone collector were also regular visitors to our street. The popcorn and ice cream vendors pushing their carts lured me onto the street with their bells and the scent of popping corn. I could stare at the buckets of flavoured ice cream, but I never had any money to buy these treats. The Life Boys and Boy Scouts gathered at Davenport Church on special occasions and marched through the neighbourhood banging drums and blowing trumpets. At Christmastime the Salvation Army Band paraded right past our house in uniforms, playing "Onward Christian Soldiers!"

We even had doctors visit our house occasionally. Once a nurse pinned a Quarantined! sign on our door after my younger sister Sally and brother John were diagnosed with contagious whooping cough. We were forbidden to pass the barrier of the front door. I peered through the letter box to watch my friends pass on their ways to school and to wait for strangers to arrive on the verandah with groceries. One day the nurse returned and administered a new wonder drug, sulfa, to my sister and brother.

My father Harry and the "coal man"
Uncle Charlie Jenkins on the street, at 567 Perth.
My spying head is visible in the upper window.

In this photo of the coal man, I recognize a face in soft focus staring through the second-floor window. This image of myself as a boy pierces me now, like an arrow shot through time. It reminds me that I often secretly used that perch over the years in my parents' bedroom to kneel at the window and spy on the street below. Under the main window was a cedar chest, in which my mother kept hidden, under the musky blankets, pages of love letters, cards, envelopes, and photos that my father (and another man) had sent from overseas during the war—all lost now. "Two Dutch girls who loved the chocolate I gave them," I read on the back of one photograph taken by a fellow soldier of two pretty young girls sitting with Harry. Who took this photo of the coal man and my father talking casually on Perth Avenue? I guess that it was my mother, since the delivery man was her brother, my Uncle Charlie Jenkins.

KNOW IT ALL

However these surviving images suggest an awakening of consciousness and a dawning of a sense of time, they fail to mend the broken narrative of my life. I wonder why they were taken. Do they show a care for a family life on my mother's part that I did not feel? Did she resent the darkness in me, the helplessness and dejection—the longing for Nana Radford? I blamed myself for being a disappointment to her, for failing to stir in her a mother's love.

I insulated myself from the strangeness and fear of being alive in those early days at Perth Avenue, from a peripheral world of noise, yelling voices, profane insults, violent assaults, denunciations and fights. "Kiss my ass!" was a favourite expletive from my mother; my father would respond "It looks too much like your face!" When called to the arborite table for meals, I hunched in my ripped vinyl chair, head down, and shuttered my eyes, like a prisoner avoiding guards in the Gulag. My senses sharpened most at bedtime, homing in on the voices, huddling in the closets, peeking through the cracks in the doors to spy on my drunken uncles or my father's war buddies hoisting beer bottles, fist fighting or lying passed out on the floor. In a relentless panic, I feared that at any moment my father would descend on me again, shred the protective veil I had drawn over my eyes, pull me into the fray, humiliate me and hector me with questions I could not answer. During the day, I could flee the chaos and darkness and break into the freedom of the streets and lanes and playing fields, where I met friends, ran with gangs and played whatever game the streets had crafted. With friends, I laughed, risked danger, learned to compete and to peer into a wider world and feel brave. I could forget the darkness of night, the odours of alcohol, smoke and urine in the house on Perth Avenue, and the fear of shadows.

WHEN I WAS AGE 6, Ada asked Annie to take me back to Norfolk temporarily while she was in the hospital giving birth to my younger sister Sally. Annie arrived at Perth, packed a few of my clothes, and as we left the verandah, she took my hand. In my mind, it was all my dreams come true. We walked to the streetcar without the drama that erupted on that day three years before when Ada came through the door at Norfolk. Annie enrolled me in Shirley Street public school, around the corner from her house. I tried to make friends at recess in the school playground but ended up in shoving matches, chase downs, ridicule and rejection. In class a teacher asked me to complete the phrase "as black as...?" I answered "shit," and was sent to the principal's office and then home carrying an envelope for Annie. Charlie Radford's comment was, "What else would you expect from that kid?" I pretended that I did not know that "shit" was a bad word. Annie apologized to the principal and her pleas got me back into class. At first recess on my return, I was suddenly befriended by several boys and I sensed that a band of girls was watching me. It was an unplanned and risky lesson in how to be noticed and to gain attention—do something that others were afraid to do.

With Annie Radford on Norfolk Street there was a religious overtone completely alien to my life on Perth Avenue. Annie's adherence to the High Anglican Church was at odds with her working class, everyday world—one might have expected Methodism or the Gospel Hall—but Anglicanism was part of her undying Imperial devotion to Queen and Empire. She observed the High-Church rituals with conviction; hers was an all-seeing interventionist deity, as concerned with maintaining the proper social order as with commanding righteousness. At home she prayed by her bed on her knees and read the books of the King James Bible daily in order, starting over again at Genesis when she completed Revelations. She would read to me random phrases, like an itinerant preacher. "And he shewed me a pure river of water of life, clear as crystal, proceeding out of the throne of God and of the Lamb."

Annie paid the weekly tithe in glue-lipped envelopes at St. Anne's Anglican, that idiosyncratic miniature Hagia Sofia on Gladstone Avenue, contributed a wobbly alto in the choir and was on a first-name familiarity with the successive ministers over the years. Her religious fervour remained solitary in her own family, none of whom, including her husband Charlie, who grumbled weekly about the donations, bothered to go through even the pretense of belief.

Annie's missionary zeal might have succeeded with me, a little heathen boy, had I not been a born skeptic in my divided world. On my weekend visits from Perth Avenue, she brushed my hair, ironed my shirt, and marched me along Dundas Street to Gladstone on Sunday mornings. She sat me under the gilded dome, holding the sealed donation envelope while she went behind the pulpit to join the choir. I felt self-important sitting there alone as the cool silver plate made its way along the pews; I proudly dropped the coins or envelope onto the plate and passed it on humbly to the tolerant smiles of the worshippers next to me. After the sermon, she left me in Sunday school for another hour of indoctrination. She begged me to behave and gave me an imploring look, hoping that all this pomp and instruction would turn me into a little Christian. It was not going to succeed at the level of storytelling and belief, but events take on their own significance in a child's mind. For me, sitting in St. Anne's, under the frescoed dome, with the melodious hymns echoing around the piers and the kneeling parishioners drawing me down, invoked a nascent feeling of the numinous, which as it evolved in me tended more to a sense of aesthetics than of religion. I felt eerily insignificant in that open space and had a profound visceral reaction to the great fresco of the Virgin Mary above me on the arch of the dome, with her long blue dress draped over her knees and the baby Jesus perched on her lap. Above her were inscribed those mysterious words, "And the word became flesh!" If I craned my neck, I could read the beautiful invitation inscribed around the starry dome: "Come unto me all ye that labour and are heavy laden and I will bring you rest."

I did for a time harbour a suspicion of a benevolent other, a glow beneath the darkness. I was awed by the care that was promised in return for belief and expressed in the tender words we sang in Sunday school. I remember them still: "God sees the little sparrow fall."

The fresco in the opposing arch of the robed, bearded Christ riding a donkey to his doom evoked disquiet; I did not believe

Annie's Anglican refuge, St. Anne's, the miniature Hagia Sofia on Gladstone Avenue.

that Jesus loved me "because the Bible told me so." He clearly had other things on his mind. If I had a spiritual sensibility, it was an awful fear of my own existence. I resisted kneeling and earned stern sidelong glances when I remained upright during the invocation "let us pray." To Annie's shame I performed some now forgotten transgression (likely swearing, though I prefer to think it was some skeptical wisecrack) and got myself expelled from Sunday School, just as I had from the Lifeboys, for going AWOL from a picnic, and from the Boy Scouts for locking up the Girl Guides by propping a lawn mower against the latch on the church door, and from Oakwood Collegiate for refusing to read the Bible in front of the class.

Annie never gave up. She later counted on Billy Graham himself to save me. How she reconciled her passion for the handsome preacher with the liquid Southern American accent with her Anglican affiliation I could not say—her own Anglican minister admonished her for it. She took me to one the evangelist's "crusades," along with her Scots friend Peggy Macinley. Peggy worked as a cook for one of Billy's wealthy Canadian benefactors who lived on the swanky Bridal Path and perhaps shared the preacher's snide anti-Semitism. The gathering was at a packed Exhibition Stadium, where my Uncle Don Marsh had once taken me to the chaotic stock car races. I was intoxicated by Graham's intonations and chastened by his warnings about the impending punishments for my sins. I was moved by the sonorous singing of the hymn "How Great Thou Art" by the bass George Beverly Shea, but nothing Annie could do would make me go forward to the stage to be "received" by the invisible Christ, even with the unwelcome tears in my eyes—how I wanted to be part of something, to believe that I was special, while knowing that I was not.

Back on Perth Avenue, I would walk out some evenings a few blocks along Davenport Avenue and into the tiny, dark Gospel Hall. There were no glittering frescoes in this simple space, as at St. Anne's, and the members themselves, not a robed priest, provided the reading and led the singing. I felt humility there as I sat in the beautiful darkness and warmth, out of the winter air. No one questioned me as I entered, and I was anonymously handed a hymnbook. We sang unaccompanied and were encouraged to be a community and to live better lives. No one asked for money. It was a solitude and promise of love that I could accept.

The minister of Davenport United Church bungled the last attempt to make a Christian of me. I joined the Lifeboys there (we wore little sailor suits and aspired to graduate into the Boys Brigade). I loved the chaotic floor hockey in the church gymnasium, played with broom handles and a felt ring, that ended each meeting. As part of our instruction, which was focused on tying naval knots and marching in order, the Reverend Mr. Ferry invited us into the rectory for little talks about God ... and sex. God's presence in our world he explained was made evident in miracles. During the war Mr. Ferry told us, his son, plummeting to earth from a stricken aircraft with an unopened parachute over France, prayed earnestly. God saved him by opening the soft welcoming boughs of a tree. Again, those beckoning arms. What more proof did we need? We knew he was lying.

I don't remember being troubled by the powerful "urges" that the devil tempts us with until Mr. Ferry warned us. He cautioned us particularly about the temptations that we would soon face to "touch" girls, who possessed a vulnerable spot that if touched even accidentally would render her helpless. I of course passed along this information to all my friends, many of whom were less shy than I was in trying to locate that magic spot. So, it was, growing into puberty in the 1950s, that the arcane relics of Christian sexuality were still there to confuse the minds of young boys and to establish firmly the connection between sex and guilt.

These talks continued with select boys in Mr. Ferry's living room by a fireplace and there was a perhaps unconscious romancing to his revelations. But his greatest admonishments were saved for what he and the warnings of the time called "self-abuse." He acknowledged that it may feel good—he believed that his credibility would increase with candour—but he warned that the practice could have dire consequences. In addition to somehow offending God, he warned that the practice would destroy our ability to make babies. He explained that there were tiny nodules located around the sacred head of the penis. Vigorous masturbation, he declared, would rub these particles off and leave us sterile and cast us out of God's grace. He overestimated a thirteen-year old's concern about making babies.

Mr. Ferry never touched me, even though I was alone with him several times. Once he called me to his house at Christmas time and gave me a gift from under his Christmas tree, a small metal airplane whose wheels and propeller spun. But he was disgraced by accusations of sexual misconduct, against boys or girls I never knew, and (not fired of course) was exiled to a church in Owen Sound. As for his unveiling the particulars and dangers of sex, his views had far less effect than the more detailed information provided to me by my friend John Hunter, who was not only a fund of information about the sexual roles of men and women, but who was able to provide visual evidence in the pornographic cartoon books he stole from his grandfather's garage. (All men and boys, it seemed, had to conceal their curiosity about sex.) This "information" only intensified my intense dread of girls and heightened their power to dissolve me into a flaming blush with a mere glance.

I have always had a skeptical nature, driven as much by distrust of authority as by curiosity. Who could believe in the Santa, I declared as a mere boy, when there was one sitting on a throne in Eaton's department store and another on another throne across Queen Street in Simpson's? A child easily senses the smirk behind the explanations, and they fail if he has no motivation to suspend disbelief. By the time I got to high school I was in trouble again for refusing to bow my head for the Lord's Prayer that began each day or to take my turn reading Bible passages to the class. I nevertheless saw Annie less as an example of what we all failed to believe, and more as someone who somehow understood things better than the rest of us. She was an isolated figure, Christ-like herself; though her beliefs remained alien to me, she was the best person that I ever knew. "Faith, hope, and charity," she would say, "and the greatest of these is charity." Though indeed saved by her charity and belief, I could not acknowledge it and I was troubled by my ingratitude. I taunted her with the paradoxes—her prejudices against Jews, Blacks, and Catholics; her loving a God who callously struck down her beautiful granddaughter with meningitis; the fate of stillborn children (like her dead baby's portrait in her photo album) forced to roast in purgatory; the inanities of the literal words of the Bible and her endless incantations about the immanent end of the sinful world. I saved a particular mockery for her question, "If there is no God, then who made you," to which I replied, "Then who made Him?" "You don't worry me," she said with patient kindness, "you will end up with more faith than any of us. It is God's way to test those he has chosen. You will realize this when it is your turn to die. You will recant and Jesus will take you in his arms." I did sense the power of her beliefs and from time to time saw that they were deeply felt and a comfort in her unhappiness. I remember her rebuke of Jehovah's Witnesses who came soliciting to her door. "Have you no shame?" she scolded them, "that God has given us the brains to find ways of saving the lives of children and you ignore his gift and endanger the lives of innocents so that you can feel secure that only you are chosen? Get away from my door!"

In retrospect, I was no more than a reflection of the culture of the 1950s itself, clutching for belief but losing faith. My proud skepticism, fueled in my later teens by reading my first inklings of philosophy—Bertrand Russell, Frederic Nietzsche and Baruch Spinoza—dimly understood, but providing comforting support and devastating critiques from the "rational" world, did not prevent me from brokering with the unseen and unproven. "God! Let me pass school this one year," I feigned in prayer; I know that I have been lazy, but I promise that next time I will work if you intervene and let me pass. "Miraculously," I did pass. And still the literature of belief echoed in my mind: "suffer the little children." The search for that feeling that I felt sitting in St. Anne's led me to art and beautiful depictions of sweet love: Fra Angelico's *Annunciation*, the promise of hope tinged with regret, that lily across the Virgin's breast, just like the ones Charlie grew in the backyard on Norfolk Street.

CHAPTER 3

As Fugitive as the Years

"The reality that I had known no longer existed ... remembrance of a particular form is but regret for a particular moment; and houses, roads, avenues are as fugitive, alas, as the years."

–Marcel Proust

Perth Avenue runs south from a T on Davenport Road, a single block down to where the railway tracks crossed at Kingsley. Then it re-emerges on the north side of Dupont. That whole northeast corner of what is still called the Junction in Toronto was defined by railway tracks, from a time when the entire prosperity and pulse of the city was driven by steam. The tapering rail lines traversed a broad, desolate, windswept backdrop to our lives, an alien landscape of smoke, ties and iron that still disturbs my dreams. We boys crawled under, cut through or climbed over the fences enclosing the forbidden rail yards. We hopped the slow-moving freight trains, climbed atop the couplers and broke the seals on the refrigerator cars to steal watermelons, or to scoop and suck the crushed ice on a hot summer day. We collected pop bottles from the factories that lined the tracks, and (my friend Danny, not I) climbed high on the girders of the black-iron, riveted bridges. The tracks were flanked by flat-roofed, brick warehouses and factories, docked to the expectant boxcars. Through the thousand-paned glass windows, flares of furnaces or flashes of electricity evidenced the industries within. Surrounding them were the grimy yards, where the locomotives would shunt back and forth, coupling and uncoupling, spewing smoke and grit, cobbling together the next convoy to Collingwood, London, Kitchener, Owen Sound, Stratford, Buffalo, Windsor and beyond. There was the almost mythical nation-building Canadian Pacific Railway, of course but, before that, the Grand Trunk Railway of Canada crossed Davenport at Caledonia, a few blocks northeast of Perth Avenue. Ontario's very first railway, The Ontario, Simcoe and Huron Rail Road, scuttled a little to the east across Davenport on its way from the Lakeshore to the port of Collingwood on Georgian Bay, to fetch the grain that had shipped from the head of Lake Superior and was stacked in the high silos at Owen Sound.

Though I was living on Perth Avenue with Ada when I turned five, and would be attending nearby Davenport School, it was Annie Radford who fetched me and registered me on my first day. Davenport Elementary (later called Osler, then Carleton Village, and now a police station) is a red brick edifice that rides imperiously on a hill above Davenport Road, like a modest cathedral, with the kindergarten classroom projecting out on the south end, like a cathedral apse. Annie coaxed me through the arched portal entrance, which felt so vast that I dared not look upwards. I lifted my knees high to make each stair. Annie held my hand tightly, but I knew that she would leave me there.

When school started, Ada would wake me with a shout to "Get Up." I picked a pair of trousers and a t-shirt from a damp pile in the corner of my room, put an apple in my pocket and walked off across the street. I made sure that I walked directly under the majestic oak tree opposite 567, whose amber leaves I pressed and taped into a scrap book when autumn came. In my dreams at night, I imagined that great oak was the master of the neighbourhood and that it made the wind blow.

When I began kindergarten at age 5, I was expected, as all kids were in those days, to walk back and forth to school on my own. I turned the corner west onto Davenport Road, following its ancient northwest curve, echoing the footpath of the Anishinaabe Nation who stamped it, past the hardware store and candy shops, the gospel hall and the Polish Orthodox

Church, to Osler Street where the kindergarten apse of the red brick school rode high above the street. Over the years, I ventured there alone on weekends or at night and shot or threw a ball hundreds of times towards a chalk strike zone on the brick wall. "Strike! Ball! Or Goal!" I shouted.

When John Hunter became my best friend, I altered my route, cutting through the Davenport United Church yard to the tiny street Hibernia, where he lived. We walked on together to Connolly Street past Wadsworth Park. John always had stories prepared for me, about his beautiful mother Elsie, of his bullying uncles, his chemistry experiments, the books he read or the movies he had seen. He never raised a topic that did not stir my curiosity, from science fiction to cars, the military, or sex. John was a handsome boy, with thick black hair who spoke in a confident narrative as we walked, always looking ahead. He never explained to me why there was no father in his life; he never questioned me about my parents.

I often dodged through traffic as a boy, ignoring all the safety rules drilled into us at school. Once I ran right into the door of a moving car, escaping with only a few bruises. I saw a small boy killed by a car at the corner of Perth and Davenport amid the screams of his horrified sister. He broke away from her hand grip and ran into the metal onslaught and then lay lifeless like a soiled rag on the curb. The distraught driver banged his hands frantically on his head. We had a sad memorial assembly at school a few days later; Elmer the Safety Elephant's flag was solemnly lowered to mark the blemish on our record. I never spoke a word of being a witness, lest some blame fall on me. Every day that we arrived at school and saw Elmer still forlornly at half-mast, we dipped our heads in shame.

When the bell rang on my first day in kindergarten, I flew into the street and ran home to Perth through empty streets. My puzzled mother sent me back telling me angrily that it was only recess. I felt like a sheep in kindergarten, forming and reforming circles, sitting cross-legged staring out the window, mouthing songs I did not know, completely baffled by what I was doing there.

From kindergarten to grade 6, the days dragged relentlessly, agonizing constraint in the classroom broken by wild escapes into the schoolyard at recess and into the streets and lanes and hockey rinks at the end of the day. Most days, there was nothing that could be said by a teacher or written on the chalkboard that could compare with the liberty of running free.

I hardly knew what I was doing in the early grades to annoy the teachers so much or to cause the frequent meetings to discuss my punishments. There were reprimands, detentions and suspensions of privileges, such as being forced to sit alone in the classroom at recess (proving to me that they knew that it was a punishment to be confined to class). The most common accusations against me were talking back, fighting and fidgeting. The authorities first administered the strap to my hands in grade 1. It was not the full, flaming palm punishment of later years but the ritual humiliation of lofty authorities commanding, "hold out your hand!" that struck me in the gut. In grade 4, the teachers skipped me forward a grade, perhaps with some idea that I was misbehaving because I was bored (I was), but I acted so badly in the new class and fought so much with my new classmates that the grade 5 teacher sent me back down.

"Tell the truth and shame the devil," was one of the few things that I remember hearing my father say. I knew that was a lie. Telling the truth had no rewards, since I always seemed to be on the guilty side of whatever arbitrary rules were transgressed. By my calculation, lying seemed at least to reduce the chance of punishments at school or home. My mother was so suspicious that she struck me even when she knew I was innocent, pronouncing, "That is for when you are lying." Most of my life was lived in imagination anyway, where only fragments of "truth" survived. We boys expected one another to lie about our accomplishments, gaining praise at least for our narrative abilities: the winning goals we scored, the girls who spoke to us, my father's imaginary war heroics, the phantom uncle who played in the NHL, the toys I owned, even my name, which I often said was really Radford. It took years to overcome the shame of all this lying and the gravity of the secrets that I kept, which became too daunting ever to reveal to anyone else.

I experienced an unexpected diversion from the dreary world in grade 4 or 5 at Davenport school, an inexplicable obsession for a pretty black-haired girl named Gloria, one row over in my class. I furtively glanced at her pleated skirt, soft across her white knees, her black hair gathered and tied with a ribbon, red perhaps, though I can't be sure. I could not sleep for thinking of her. One day, she startled me when she rose up and spoke my name "Jimmy." It was some occasion, Halloween perhaps, and she was dressed as a ballerina, distributing homemade cookies to her classmates. I was too piteously shy to look or reply. I stared at the floor and her soft pink slippers, my face flushed with a frantic crimson, like a bludgeoned animal, shrouded in blood. She placed a cookie on my desk. I wondered where she lived and was jealous of everything she did that excluded me. I remembered her for years. Now and then, the spark of her memory would ignite an imagined tenderness, though I was sure in the light of day that, should I approach her, I would disappoint her.

With a lifetime passed, the memories of young girls drift like floating cherry blossoms in the spring, vanishing in their brief, perfect beauty. Gloria was the first in a pattern of "crushes" on girls that I conjured anew each school year. They may be pretty or plain, but they were girls, empowered by my own imaginings to constantly possess and pass judgment on me.

I was a poor student by any measure; I was reported lazy, inattentive, fractious, "fidgety," and disobedient. There was no awareness in my teachers of my father's nighttime abuses, the persistent sarcasm and slaps from my mother, or of the untended, rotting teeth that sent me to bed sobbing. I accepted the school's judgment that I was a useless distraction to the rest of the school. The only thing for which I might have mustered some pride was that I stood up against school bullies—one of the few qualities I imagined that I had gained from my father. Arriving at Perth (the first "Junior High" of its kind in Toronto), with my friend John, the only two students chosen to be sent from Davenport (as we were later chosen to attend "collegiate"), I was an outsider without allies. Neither of us knew why we had been chosen, though despite my spotty record at Davenport, I had taken home a certificate of excellence in grade 6, perhaps out of the sympathy of a teacher at the end of the year rather than any real accomplishment.

John managed to blend in peacefully at Perth. I was picked as the outsider, punched or kicked every time I changed classes by a gang of boys led by George Lefebvre and Johnny Guest. George was an older, bigger, stronger boy who had been failed a grade. He loitered in the bathrooms and made fun of other boys' dicks and punched them hard with his knuckles on their shoulder. He was not one of those bullies who turned coward when confronted. He bullied anyone, even our teachers, especially our social studies teacher Mr. Byers.

Since I liked history and geography, I always knew the answers to Mr. Byers' questions and he once announced to the class that I was his best student. This did not go down well with the Lefebvre gang. George himself one day got up in the middle of class and started systematically to break the items that Mr. Byers had collected in a little museum at the back of his class. I remember in particular a stuffed baby alligator, which Mr. Byers had brought back from Florida. George held it up blatantly and snapped it in two. Poor Mr. Byers stood there helpless and repeated "Oh dear, oh dear."

Johnny Guest sought me out in the school halls, punched me, called me an asshole, sent me threatening notes, and challenged me to fight him at recess in the schoolyard. I could hardly sleep worrying about the harm that he threatened me with daily. One day I could not avoid the dare he made to fight him in the schoolyard at recess. The word spread and a circle of Johnny's allies formed around him in the middle of the school yard.

Ashamed of my fear, I approached him and shouted frantically for him to "Leave me alone!" As he advanced, jumpy and menacing, I kept dodging him, retreating, ducking his swinging fists. He stumbled, practically crying in frustration. Suddenly I lunged forward and rammed him to the ground. I had learned from almost daily street fights that if I could ignite my anger and attack, inflicting pain as suddenly as possible, it would be worth the risk of being hit hard in return. Johnny was shocked by my unexpected aggression. A teacher drawn to the fracas broke up what had deteriorated into a snarled wrestling match, in which it appeared to the teacher that I was the aggressor. He demanded to know what was going on. I said, "We're playing tag." Next day we both were brought to the principal's office and strapped for fighting. Johnny nodded to me afterwards in the hall, stifling his own tears. Whatever had driven his animosity to me had passed. George Lefebvre, however, shoved me and said that I would have to deal with him next. He said that he was going to wait for me at the end of the day in the yard, and that he was literally "going to kill" me. He was a much bigger, angrier boy. I realized that I was going to have to run away, but Ross Morelli, my neighbour and sometime partner in raiding our local grocery store, had overheard the threat. "Just show up. I will take care of it," Ross said.

Another circle of boys formed in the yard, with a line of smirking girls to the side. Lefebvre's buddies pushed me forward. There was no teacher to save me now; it was end of day. Lefebvre slapped me and my eyes flared as I wrapped my arms protectively around my head. The circle parted silently. Ross pushed me aside and grabbed Lefebvre by the neck, pulled his sweater over his head, drove his fist into his nose, tossed him to the ground and kicked him in the ribs. It was over. Lefebvre lay on the ground, nose bleeding. Ross strode away contemptuously. I tried to run after him to thank him, but I could not keep up. Soon he disappeared over the railway fence on his way to his home on Symington, behind his father's Morelli Cleaners.

Ross wasn't the only fighter in the Junction. One day at Davenport United Church an older boy by the name of George Chuvalo came with his boxing coach to talk to our Life Boys class about the success that was possible if we could stay out of trouble. (We Life Boys wore shorts, a naval cap and a lanyard across our shirt.) Chuvalo was no stranger to the tough life in the Junction in those days. His father worked on the killing

*The famous Heintzman piano factory (left), one of the many factories along the Junction railway lines.
(City of Toronto Archives)*

room floor at Canada Packers, where my mother had worked as a meat packer briefly. George sat there sheepishly as his manager described his success in the boxing world. I never forgot the time he spent with us. I much later listened spellbound on the radio to his epic fight against Muhammed Ali at Maple Leaf Gardens in March 1966. The announcer was breathless as Chuvalo had Ali on the ropes in the 14th round. Ali won on points but declared of Chuvalo that "He's the toughest guy I ever fought." Junction boy, I thought.

As afraid as I was of the bullies at school or of my father at home, there was still more to fear from the teachers and principals. Punishment and humiliation were part of the daily school routine and I spent most of every day in anxiety for the threats of school as much as I did at night for the menaces of home. The main instruments of punishment at home were my mother's hands and my father's belt. At school there was a constant barrage of ridicule, criticism, detention and the *sine qua non* of institutional power, the strap. The weapon itself was advertised in school supply catalogues, along with desk blotters and brass hand bells, as a "regulation strap," 15 inches long and 1.5 inches wide, constructed of "good quality rubber." Most straps were made from 3-ply industrial transmission belting, and of course it had a hole at one end so that it could be hung threateningly from a wall hook in a class cloakroom. It was known even in the United States as the "Canadian strap." We boys called the burning flares the strap inflicted "the slugs."

Davenport and Perth schools used the strap frequently, though never in my experience on girls. I hated it and was ashamed when it made me cry. I first got "the slugs" in grade 1 for a forgotten reason, then again and again for swearing, fighting, lateness and giving lip. I sensed a small reluctance on the part of some of the teachers who administered the punishment but not Mr. Mortson, the vice-principal at Perth Avenue School, who clearly enjoyed his work and his domination.

In grade 8, showing off, I threw a knife across a classroom and lodged it successfully in a lump of clay, just as the art teacher came through the door. He dragged me to the office and Mortson telephoned my mother to discuss an appropriate punishment for throwing a knife. "Give him the strap?" she suggested helpfully, and he did. I hated holding out my hand, not only for fear of the pain but almost more for the submissive gesture that acknowledged the abuser's power over me. I tried to avoid the blows, but every one that glanced bought me two more. I went to pieces. In a fury I screamed at him, anything not to cry. As much as any pain in my hands, I felt the cruelty in my stomach, as if I had swallowed burning acid. The art teacher grabbed my arm and Mortson had him twist it over so that he could strike the back of my hand, and that indeed made me cry.

He calmly wrote in his report that I was given twelve strokes on each hand, an understatement. When I went back to class I sat sullenly, red faced, in the very last seat. My enflamed, swelled hands throbbed for hours. I could not hold a pencil. I could not endure the pitying looks, grabbed my books and walked out, wandering the neighbourhood for the rest of the day. Unfortunately, these ritualistic punishments dominated my imaginings every night drifting into an uneasy sleep, as I tried to muster in my mind the courage and resilience that failed me in the world of bullying teachers.

An old cherry tree papered with curled red-purple bark dominated the backyard of 567 Perth. Like everything else in that dilapidated house on Perth Avenue, that tree was dying, broken and diseased. Still, I loved to climb its branches, peel and roll its fragile bark, spy on the world and watch for something to happen in the backyards I could see over the fences, down towards where the Parks and the Morrisons lived. On a lucky day Mr. Morrison might emerge onto his back porch in his green tartan kilt, brilliant red jacket and white sash to practice the wailing bagpipe that he played in the 48th Highlanders marching band. That shrill skirl carried my imagination off to some costumed parade or highland battle. When the red-green cherries appeared, I would collect them in a bucket. They were so sour that I could not eat them, but my mother would bake them into pies. Trees often provide us with hopeful scents of our youth, landmarks of longevity, but I remember that now torn-down cherry tree more in sadness, as a departed friend.

I always carried an arsenal of hand-made weapons wherever I went when I was a boy: darts made from flowers and needles, arrows with "poison" (flour and water) tips, a tomahawk fashioned from a pointed stone secured to a wooden handle with hockey tape, or a sling shot made from strips of rubber bicycle tubes suspended from a Y-shaped tree branch, which I used to propel metal staples. The neighbours' yards were in stark contrast to our overgrown junkyard, with their mowed lawns, clipped bushes and neat rows of tulips and roses.

The small shack that my father built as a clubhouse below the cherry tree helped to provide me with a shortcut to the lower branches, but we seldom entered it. It was typical of the peculiar constructions that Harry would build in fits of energy, from scavenged lumber and rusty, recycled nails. Huge, crooked timbers completely out of scale, one tiny glassless window, a hinge-less door, and a leaky asphalt roof made the little dank hut more like a mouldy cave than a clubhouse.

The back porch was my father's madcap masterpiece,

a magpie's delight of rummaged lumber, broken windows, jammed doors, busted appliances and tarpaper. It was crammed with cases of empty beer bottles, mouldy rags where the neighbourhood cats lay and gave birth, a broken old icebox and near the kitchen door, bushels of fresh, tart apples Harry bought at the St. Lawrence market. In the corners, he piled the loot we collected from the neighbours' garbage. He made me go ransacking with him the night before garbage day. I dreaded that one of my friends would see me picking through their trash and cast-offs, looking for rusted tools, bent utensils and broken toys. Harry tried to fix what we collected, but he never could make things work; they accumulated in the porch or were strewn across the yard. Once collected, he could not discard them. Many years later, when my father was released from the asylum and died alone in an apartment, he left a long row of scavenged broken toasters, stacked neatly above his kitchen cupboards, not one of them in working order. This was pretty much all he left behind from his life, except for a small bank account of $10,000 that he had inherited (and had not spent) from his father, recorded in a bankbook my brother-in-law found carefully hidden behind the moulding in his bedroom.

In contrast to Perth, the Norfolk house was clean and orderly. Annie did a laundry every Monday and ironed the bed sheets, tea towels and shirts on Tuesday. When I visited on weekends, I played mock hockey on the linoleum floor with a yardstick and a ball of yarn against the wall in the kitchen. I sat for meals at the table facing the back window with Annie always on my right and Charlie always on my left, dodging one another like boxers bobbing before the bell. In the dining room was a table with thick, carved mahogany legs. There was a sideboard where Annie kept the China and some old 78s of excerpts from Handel's *Messiah* and a tenor rendition of that sentimental old-country song "Danny Boy." Annie always cried when she heard "And I shall hear, though soft you tread above me /And all my grave will warmer, sweeter be." Most important to me was a mahogany barrister's bookcase filled with books: *Alice in Wonderland*, the Hardy Boys and many others. I loved every one of those books. I took them out carefully and pretended to read them. That bookcase and a plain green glass vase are the only artifacts that fell to me when 4 Norfolk was razed to provide parking for the expansion to Shirley Street School.

In the living room was the upright Heintzman piano, the famous piano brand made nearby in a Junction factory. The piano bench was my favourite spot on which to play with the Minibrix that once belonged to the Radfords' son Jack. I loved those Minibrix more than any toy I ever owned. The secret to the Minibrix was the strong yet flexible rubber, which was originally invented for shoe heels and was diversified into a range of goods that included bath brushes, nonslip in-bath mats, various medical items and, ultimately, Minibrix. The set included longer, white "concrete" pieces, and numerous small brown rubber bricks with two pips on the bottom, which fitted into holes in the top of the bricks. In this way, brickwork walls could be constructed into houses or (in your dreams) into super-models of London's Tower Bridge or the Empire State Building depicted hopefully in the manual. (This method, later copied in hard plastic, became Lego.) I could never build proper models and was bored with constructing houses or plain office buildings. I used the bricks to construct hockey players and used them to play out endless games on the bench, shooting a crokinole puck with the long white Minibrix stick. The whole sense of the house on Norfolk, when I was playing and when cookies were in the oven and the radio was turned on, was of peace and refuge. It was a garden between storms where roots could grow, and wounds might heal.

CHARLIE RADFORD was a retired electrician who had worked as foreman at the provincial Legislature building on University Avenue. Annie often said that Charlie's father was the grumpiest "louse" (her strongest word, which she also applied to Montreal Canadien star Maurice Richard) that she ever met. An earnestly religious woman, she could not muster regret that a streetcar killed the old man at the age of 92 while he was on one

31

of his long walks around old Toronto. In contrast, she insisted on showing me the picture of a dead baby, rigid, wrapped like a mummy, with its eyes forced shut, from the family album. That picture never failed to make her cry. Perhaps the dead child had been hers? It must have been, I thought, for she would never say. In her mind, was I that boy?

Charlie had a heart attack and had quit working in the early 1950s. There was also some reason why he did not fight in the First World War and I always suspected that Annie's lack of respect for him came from his seeming complete lack of activity or ambition. He had no interests or hobbies, except puttering in the garden, as Annie would call it, or secretively in the basement in the winter. Once a day, every day, he would go for a long walk, like his father, and once a week he would come home with a loaf of raisin bread from the A&P—the only shopping that he did. I was forbidden to touch it. Annie was glad to have him out of the house and I wondered more than she did where he went. One day on one of my own walks I saw him, standing at a construction site, dragging on a cigarette and talking to the workers. Annie had no idea that he smoked—she never would have allowed it. If I happened to be at home with Charlie when Annie went out, he transformed into a completely different human being. When Annie was home, he looked at me with hopes that the earth would open and swallow me.

At night I would lie with my ear on the bathroom grate and hear him berate her to "get rid of that kid." But when we were alone, he would reach into the back of the dining room bureau and retrieve a mickey of whiskey, take a sip, and tell me stories of his work days, of how he was a foreman on the job of rewiring the Parliament Buildings in Ottawa, after they burned down in 1917. I listened and nodded, marveling at how a single body could contain two completely different people. In all the years I knew him I never saw him speak to a friend or to any of Annie's friends and rarely even to his own family. Charlie particularly detested the dreaded widow, Carrie McGee. She lived directly across the street and would once or twice a week set sail, blown by the ill wind of her sad life, and arrive to gossip and complain about her ungrateful, negligent family to Annie. Charlie watched the front window like a sentry and would with a groan announce the pending arrival of the "bag of woe." Annie would listen attentively, feed Carrie biscuits and tea, and repeat "Oh dear, oh dear" to her sad tales.

I did not know when Charlie and Annie stopped talking to one another, a silence broken only by his grunts of disapproval and directives to get rid of me, which always occasioned another comment by Annie about how Charlie reminded her of his old man. She was a tiny woman, bald except for a few wisps of gray hair, barely topping five feet, who lived on tea and bread soaked in warm milk. At dinner she might eat a tiny corner of a pork chop and a few peas. She tried for months to wear an awkward, tightly curled wig, but she could never keep it straight, luckily, for it was ridiculous. Yet her energy for life, particularly as it meant other people's business, was boundless. Annie sang in her church at St. Anne's and her rare low alto was in demand across the city. She kept up frequent gossiping sessions with the neighbours and spent hours every day talking on the phone with her two daughters, Grace and Jean. Grace was petulant and critical; Jean recounted cute anecdotes of the latest malapropisms of her three daughters. Annie was active in the Shirley Old Girls, an organization that sent knitted sweaters and socks and baked goods to the soldiers overseas during World War II. After the war, the Old Girls evolved into a euchre club and a network of gossip and recipe exchange. I still have recipes for Old Girl Clarisse Halsey's hermits and ice-box cookies, in her own handwriting, in my recipe book. When I got a little older, I called Annie "Nana"; when my mother shamed me for wanting to see my "na na," I called her "Granny."

I hardly know what to think about Charlie's life in retrospect. I think now that he was the loneliest man I have ever known. He and Annie slept apart and I heard him pleading with her for "something." She refused him by telling him that "it would wake the boy." No wonder he hated me. When a television arrived, Annie insisted that he let me watch "Maverick" and "Air Power" (he detested anything that had to do with the war), and he mutely conceded. His own interest in sports was tempered by Annie's fanatical adherence to the Toronto Maple Leafs. He had at one time attended the hockey games at the Mutual Street Arena when the Toronto team was called the St. Pats. But at the time of my visits to Norfolk, he had no interest in the hockey Leafs or music or religion or anything that Annie did. He did however take me once, perhaps at her insistence because this time he would not talk to me, to a sandlot baseball game along Dundas Street.

Charlie held to the dictum that every game, every boxing match, every sporting contest was "rigged." It was his way of not having to take sides or to care the way Annie did about the beloved Leafs. The one sport Charlie did care about, as Annie had no interest at all in it, was baseball. He listened religiously to the broadcast games on the radio station 590 CKEY. The Toronto Maple Leaf baseball team played in the International League and I would sit by and listen to the reports from far-off Syracuse, Buffalo and Havana, Cuba (whose Yo Yo Davalio had my favourite name). I was confounded years later when I learned that these "out-of-town" broadcasts were bogus. Apparently, the announcer Joe Chrysdale sat by a ticker tape machine in the Toronto radio station, read the tape sent from the out-of-town ballpark and called the plays, pressing buttons to simulate crowd noise or the crack of the ball on the bat.

While Annie introduced me to live hockey at Maple Leaf Gardens, Don Radford took me to watch the Maple Leaf baseball team, which played in one of the largest minor league stadiums. It was located strategically on the south side of Lake Shore Boulevard. I loved watching the ships pass through the Western Gap as we called it, past the towering silos of the Canada Malting Company. The Maple Leafs were an independent team, owned not by a major league team but by Canadian media baron Jack Kent Cooke, so they tended it to have more stable rosters than farm teams. Some major league stars played there, notably Elston Howard and Rocky Nelson, but I remember cheering outfielders Archie Wilson, Sam Jethroe and the perennial minor leaguer Lew Morton.

Years later when Charlie lay dying at Toronto Western Hospital from prostate cancer, Annie refused to visit him. I went to see him just before he died, and we just looked at each other across a great chasm. His daughter Grace never forgave Annie for not visiting him and for making a phony scene of grief at the graveside. She told me that it meant so much to Charlie that I had gone to visit him and to talk to him at the end. We reminisced about the old baseball Leafs.

CHAPTER 4

The Ruins I Mapped

"These are the ruins I mapped onto my body so that I might always be lost."

– Traci Brimhall

SATURDAY ON NORFOLK was bliss with buttery ice-box cookies in the oven, peach preserves brought up from the larder, real, not powdered, milk, butter, not margarine, and pork chops for dinner. This is how I learned that I might exist: an ironed shirt, homemade plum jam on toast, butter tarts with currents, and chocolate cake with raspberry jam filling and chocolate icing. Saturday night Annie and I walked north on Brock Street across Dundas to College Street and took the Carlton streetcar to Maple Leaf Gardens to watch the hockey Leafs. We could not get there fast enough, though I loved the rocking movement and vinyl odours of the streetcars. Annie handed her single subscriber's ticket to the attendant at the arena, who would nod and let us both through the turnstile.

Sunday evening Annie sent me back to Perth Avenue. I suffered the return like a prisoner on weekend leave returned to jail. Ada would not lift her head from a romance magazine she was often reading when I arrived. Harry would have spent the day in bed recovering from a Saturday drinking binge. When I was around, he sent me to Middleton's store on Davenport to buy Player's cigarettes, Kik cola and a *Flash* ("No Fear, No

The Ruins I Mapped

Favor—the People's Paper") or *Tab* magazine. I tried to run there as fast as I could so that I could linger on the way back and absorb the sexy covers and lurid exposés. Sunday night, Harry turned on the radio in the bedroom. I sneaked into the clothes closet outside his door to listen to "Boston Blackie," "Amos and Andy," "The Shadow" and magically, "The Greatest Story Ever Told." Whether he heard these programs or slept through them I could not tell, but I was gripped by the dialogue, humour and romance.

Ada would not let me into the house when I came home on school days. No matter how cold it was she made me stay outside, telling me to "go and play." Eventually she would relent, feed me left-overs from the adult supper and send me to bed. In the first few years, I woke up crying and wet the bed, trying desperately to hide in some closet or under a bed or behind the sofa. When she hit me, it was always with cupped hands aimed at my ears. She threatened that my father would beat me harsher when he got home, but he showed little interest in her battles with me.

On weekends my father's war buddies would crowd into the little kitchen to drink and play poker: Jim, for whom I was named; "Buff" Ransom, a big, handsome man with a beautiful wife; and Elmer, a chubby affable man who always seemed to get the worst of every fight. Harry's brothers Reg, who had also served in the Lake Superior Regiment, and Don, who had been too young to enlist, were often present for these bouts, as were Harry's sisters Pat and Muriel with their husbands.

I watched, mesmerized, through a crack in the doors between the front bedroom and the living room, for fragments of the predictable violence. I never knew why the men fought but the more they drank the more likely it would be. The evenings always started with humour and banter and sexual innuendo, often over a game of poker. As the men drank beer and reminisced and carped or bragged about their experiences in the war, the shoving, shouting, and punching erupted. Despite his injured leg, Harry dished out as much punishment as he got; he had been an amateur boxer. In one brawl he knocked his younger brother Don through the second-floor bannister and down the stairs, breaking his arm. The wives and girlfriends tried to keep Harry from "the hard stuff," which they knew accelerated his rage.

Except when I was summoned out of bed by my father to be made a spectacle in front of his friends, I only experienced these alcoholic bashes peering through the crack in the living room doors or from the dark hall closet or stairs. I was mesmerized by the figures flickering in and out, like hand shadows, leaning, rising, falling, disappearing. Often, they just sat, as they do in a Cezanne painting, stone-faced, reading their hands of cards through a cloud of cigarette smoke. The jargon added to the mysterious puppetry, with incomprehensible mutterings and mysterious outbursts of "Hold'Em" or "Seven Card Stud" followed by barks of "call!" or "hold." After a muttering of calculations of pairs and straights and Aces high, the losers would utter a stream of obscenities. According to my mother, Harry was too drunk to play effectively and always lost all his money. He would get angry and the arguments would escalate into punching matches, spilled beer and broken bottles. When the guests left and Harry climbed the stairs to bed, I sneaked into the kitchen and scoured the floor for stray coins.

Jim had been in Harry's platoon in the Lake Superior Regiment. He stopped coming to our house for a while and one night he showed up in a new suit. He announced that he had gotten sober and had a new job. Harry ridiculed him, got him to take a drink and then so many more that Jim passed out. I watched that night through the crack in the doors as my father dragged my namesake, using his neat new suit as a mop through the puddles of beer on the floor. I could sense the hopelessness in rescuing anyone from the drunken miasma of life after the war, and the anger of my father that his friend would even try. As a witness to these bouts, I learned how men interacted. Though having shared war and family, they quickly shed their loyalties and attacked one another.

When Ada brought my baby sister Marian home, I was sent back to Perth and moved away from the downstairs room with the sliding doors and into the upstairs back bedroom. Marian was in the bottom of the iron bunk bed and I was in the top. Our uncle Don now rented the upstairs front bedroom and his steady stream of girlfriends aroused my first prurient interest. One night I saw one of his girlfriends on her way to the bathroom naked, and I lost much sleep, spying for that to happen again.

When my second sister Sally was born, Harry was out all night in the bars, more fuel for Ada's resentment. As part of the turmoil, she complained loudly that he was too drunk "to be a man." Harry directed his anger towards Ada and she deflected hers onto me. The police were summoned several times to warn him, but they seemed helpless to prevent Harry's abuse. The police would try to reason with him and he conned them with charm. Ada ended up with bruises and black eyes from his punches, but she fought back. One night after Harry struck her, she waited until he passed out drunk in bed. She took his boot and struck him repeatedly with its heel. Always when he woke up sober, he retreated into his shell of silence and pain. On his paydays, Ada would send me to steal money from his pockets so that she could buy groceries. Once he was drunk it was not hard to do, but I lived in dread that he would catch me. Once I stole $10 from one of Harry's friends, who was passed out drunk on the kitchen floor. He told me later that he knew what I had done, and he warned me that he was not going to forget it. I lied whenever I was caught stealing. I took it seriously and managed to hide my gains and to take the punishments when they were meted out. It was all worth it if I could buy candy or a water pistol or a model airplane kit.

When they were not fighting at Perth, Harry and his buddies stormed the local bars, ending up in so many fistfights that only the Brunswick and the Legion had not banned them. The names of those bars—Embassy, Silver Rail, Brown Derby, Friar's, Horseshoe—were so etched on my mind, like the names of foreign countries, that when I came of drinking age, I could not bear to enter them. The smell of beer and cigarettes made me sick to my stomach. I did once enter the Brunswick lounge with a friend and drank a beer in what seemed to me a cell of unbearable boredom.

Our grandfather "Ned" and grandmother Marion Marsh visited Perth Avenue only a few times. I was on the verandah when our grandmother dropped my baby sister Marian. Ada came flying out of the house to see the baby lying on the ground, crying and bleeding from a gash across her nose. She accused the old lady of carelessness and after a row, the grandparents left, never to have anything to do with Ada again. It was fine with her.

My strategy for survival while living at Perth was to hide, conceal, lower my eyes and to long for those visits to Norfolk. Our family almost did not, literally, survive. Ada had little to brag about when it came to her husband, but she did say that he proved an excellent marksman with a gun in the war, that he was officer material, too lazy and too drunk to advance himself. He came back to Perth one day from a hunting trip carrying a friend's shotgun. Needled by Ada for his inadequacies he went into a rage, loaded the gun and shouted that he would kill us all. It was late in the evening but as usual I was spying, anticipating. I had never heard Ada speak as she did that night, pleading. "Come on, Harry, you don't want to do that. C'mon put the gun away." "I am going to kill the fucking kids first and then you!" I heard him bark. I opened the second-floor bedroom window over the very alleyway where my cat Cuseo had fallen to his death. I grasped the metal drainpipe with the crazy idea that I could escape into the night when Harry came looking for me. I heard a gun blast and then another. Silence, but I was too terrified to climb down or to jump.

Then, I heard two voices approaching, slowly up the stairs. Ada was cooing, "C'mon Harry," as they passed my bedroom door. She had persuaded him to fire those two blasts into a wooden basement support post. The story of the shotgun was never spoken. Whenever I went to the basement to shovel ashes, and sometimes just in curiosity, I would run my fingers over those gunshot holes and pick at the shattered wood slivers. When I hear stories of domestic murder-suicide, I remember the fury of my father and the blind chance that Ada's resolve had saved us.

I was six or seven when I met Danny Stranhagen. He lived with his single mother on the second floor of a semi-detached house two doors east of Perth on Davenport. It was Danny who introduced me to my next two friends, Jimmy Devlin and John Hunter. Danny was my first "best friend" but he and his mother soon moved away. He was a daredevil. If we passed a billboard on the street, he would climb up the angle shafts on the back and tightrope across the top beam above the advertisements for Export "Canada's Finest Cigarette" or Lux Toilet Soap. Most astonishing to me was to watch him clamber up onto the iron girders of bridges, and stand arms spread triumphantly on the railing, precariously balanced above the tracks far below. I never had the bravery to follow Danny and would simply wait below in wonder.

Jimmy Devlin lived with his mother behind the laundromat on Davenport Road. She was separated from her husband, Jim Sr., whose parents owned the small grocery store some three or four buildings east of Perth. I was often sent out by my mother to shop but wondered why she never sent me to Devlin's. When on occasion I entered the store looking for Jimmy there seemed to be no one there and the groceries amounted to a few canned goods, loaves of bread and bottles of milk. Jim Sr. regularly disappeared for months at a time. Ada gossiped that he was a bookie, whatever that was. I always thought that young Jimmy Devlin was so privileged. His mother was a devoted, caring person, who for years supplied me with his castoff clothing—he was a year or so older than me.

On Saturday nights, Jimmy would invite me to the movies. He would first ask his mother for money and then ask his father—the two never spoke—and then he would pay my ticket and share his popcorn. Jimmy knew that I had no money and he was kind and generous to me—the first of many friends who treated me this way. He spent much of his time at Middleton's confectionery store, squeezed between the laundromat and Devlin's grocery. The two spinster Middleton sisters gave Jimmy free candy and pop and they let him watch TV on a comfortable sofa in the back room where they lived.

Jimmy's mother got an idea that I was smart and since he struggled in school, she asked me to tutor him, even though I was a grade behind. I would sit with him at the kitchen table and read his textbooks with him. When he broke his arm tobogganing down Davenport Hill in Earlscourt Park, I took him home and went to the doctor with his mother and him. Another time he caught his finger in a gearbox in behind the Guerney foundry. His mother thanked me for these rescue missions, though I felt partly at fault in each since he was following my roving habits. My reward was great, for Mrs. Devlin got one of the first television sets in the neighbourhood and encouraged Jimmy to invite me over on Friday evening to watch the affable William Bendix in "The Life of Riley." The first television entered our home on Perth when my uncle Don Marsh, who was on and off renting a room at our house, bought a tiny black and white tube set. I was invited by him to watch the hockey on Saturday night when I was not at Norfolk. The first thing that we watched was a hazy, ghostly black and white picture, gathered by a pair of rabbit ears, of a playoff hockey game between the Boston Bruins and Montreal Canadiens, which as far as I can determine was likely in April 1953. Despite my hatred of the Canadiens, fueled by Annie Radford, and my fascination for the player names on the Boston Bruins—Fleming MacKell, Jerry Toppazzini, Real Chevrefils and Bill Quackenbush—the Canadiens prevailed with a goal by Elmer Lach in overtime. We were barely aware of the profound change to our lives that television would bring.

The main east-west streets in our neighbourhood, Davenport, St. Clair, Dundas and Bloor were dominated by streetcars, which survive till this day. Though Annette, Ossington, and Lansdowne were converted to bus routes, I always subscribed to the apocryphal theory that Toronto alone resisted the corrupt payoffs by which Detroit motor works persuaded city councils across North America to tear out the streetcar lines and replace them with their buses, which moved so many fewer people and which created so much more pollution. Streetcars were a potent symbol of Toronto, with their dedicated rails set in brick, their trolley poles reaching up for power into the overhead wires, sparking whenever it rained. I loved when I was aboard and the car "threw the trolley," banging frantically to and fro. I would rush to the window to watch the shower of orange sizzling electric sparks against the hot wire. The driver had to stop, open the folded door, walk around to the rear and deftly pull the trolley rope like a halyard to set the wheel back on the power line.

As we got a little older, we boys ventured farther and farther out of our enclosed world. We defied the warnings not to intrude on the territory of nearby gangs. There were apocryphal stories of boys being beaten or even killed. But we kept a watchful eye and to be truthful never encountered these nasty spectres, despite stories in the tabloids about gangland killings. There was always an older boy in our group who had been somewhere noteworthy and who promised to lead us back if we dared to follow him. At Perth I always had to be outside the house, roaming, loitering, and exploring, partly because Ada insisted and partly because I wanted to be far away from her and Harry. At Norfolk I wanted to be inside, to stay, to be close to Annie. When I did go outside at Norfolk, it was always on my own. I had no friends there. I would walk southward down Brock Street to Queen Street, which seemed to me the lower backbone of the city. I knew the shop windows that ignited my appetites, particularly the hobby shops displaying plastic models of destroyers, Spitfires, or German panther tanks. I had no money so I could not buy things or eat or drink along the way, but I felt an intimate connection to the vendors and promised myself that one day I would manage to buy things that I dreamed about.

In my last two weeks of summer staying with the Radfords, I would walk from Norfolk east on Queen Street to Dufferin Street and then south through the Dufferin Gates to the Canadian National Exhibition, where I would spend a day clambering over the AVRO CF-100 Canadian fighter or North American Sabre aircraft on display, inspecting the latest television sets and Canadian-made—my friend John proudly informed me— Electrohome stereos in the impressive Manufacturers' Building, listening to concerts, eating samples in the Food Building and roaming endlessly through the crowded Midway. Once when I attended the Ex with Annie, she sent me to an attendant at the gate to get a nametag in case I got lost. When the terrifyingly pretty girl asked my name, I mumbled shyly and apparently made no more impression when she asked me to repeat what I had said. As a result, I spent the day with a nametag on which she had written "Marsh Marsh." I could never muster the courage or the funds to get on the Ferris wheels or roller coaster and I felt even more isolated watching the screaming participants. Later, when I managed to persuade a girl to go with me to the CNE, she abandoned me in boredom. The only bravery I could manage was to climb the glass-enclosed stairwells of the Shell Tower to the observation deck. This impressive glass and steel structure was twelve storeys high. I first climbed it with Annie Radford encouraging me, as she had with Brock's Monument at Queenston, counting the steps. Its huge clock above the observation deck was visible from anywhere within the CNE grounds—it was the Eiffel Tower to me. From the top observation deck, there was a panoramic view directly down onto the dense crowds shuffling through the Midway, and outward to a vista across Lake Ontario or the downtown skyline. The distinctive Shell Tower was lost to Toronto when a beer company demanded its destruction to make way for the deafening bore of its Indy car race. *Lost Toronto* is one of the saddest books I own.

One summer day in our neighbourhood, an older boy declared that he knew where we could go fishing. Fishing always seemed to me to be a fascinating activity, filled with promise, the barbed hooks, line reels, and rods. The boy declared that we could improvise some fishing rods and bait when we got there. About six or seven of us set out with hope, trusting him. We walked south on Symington, over the railway tracks to Dupont and then west on Annette to High Park Avenue. From there it was straight south to High Park. Walking through the High Park neighbourhood with its prosperous brick houses and leafy backyards was a stark contrast to our grubby working-class housing, only a 30-minute walk away. We felt a mixture of trepidation that we should not be there and defiance that we could not be caught if anyone objected. More than once in Toronto when I was an

The climb up the switchback glass stairwell of the 12-storey Shell Tower at the CNE was harrowing for me, but the view was well worth the climb. The glass curtain walls, and steel frames were innovations in Toronto in 1955.

unkempt kid, police removed me and my friends by force from neighbourhoods where wealthy residents had reported us as undesirable. We were told never to return because we did "not belong." Once I mouthed off that I had a right to be anywhere in a public park, where we were playing touch football. A policeman placed his boot on my running shoe and crushed my toes. He then pushed me into the police car, deliberately knocking my head on the car roof. I was made to sit for hours in the police station waiting room and briefly in a cell before another officer told me, without explanation, that I could leave. These experiences of a lower-class kid being bullied by police left me with no illusions about the shibboleths of class equality and the rule of law.

High Park itself has always seemed to me a perfect refuge, with its pathways, ice rink, tennis courts, zoo and sculpted gardens, though once again there were warnings about the violence that threatened if you were not careful, or if you were in the wrong place or in the dark. One rumour of an "attack" and murder of a young girl, or was it a boy, hung over the park for years. Somehow our self-appointed leader managed to get us to our fishing goal, the legendary Grenadier Pond. We all of course believed that the bones of numerous drowned Grenadiers rested at the fathomless bottom.

In the 1950s there were still remnants of rich wetlands at the south end and eastern bank of Grenadier Pond. We waded through the cattails, grasses and shrubs, soaking our shoes and socks. We watched men fishing in high rubber boots, casting and waiting. The pond was stocked each year and some of the fish were tagged with cash prizes for those who caught them. We had no success improvising a rod, much less a hook or bait. But we passed the day in the sun, balancing on slippery logs, tossing flat stones across the water and chasing and shoulder punching one another in a scramble of boyhood. I did not know all the boys' names, but we felt a strong bond of camaraderie. We were tired and silent on the long walk home.

There was yet another world to explore beyond High Park. On the same trek past Catfish Pond and Camel's Hump hills and the marshes of Grenadier Pond, you could cross Lake Shore Boulevard and reach the boardwalk alongside the magical world of Sunnyside amusement park. Tens of thousands walked the boardwalk in their finery in summertime in the old days. Annie Radford first took me there as a young boy on the streetcar via the famous many-pronged Queen/King/Roncesvalles/Lake Shore intersection. The billboards on that corner dazzled, trumpeting British American Gasoline, Old Chum tobacco, Neilson chocolates and a one-dollar taxi service. Off the streetcar, Annie coaxed me patiently across the high traffic bridge, for I was deathly afraid of heights. I closed my eyes and held the guardrail. At the western end of the bridge, we descended gingerly down a steep, iron staircase into the fairground. I grew in confidence the lower we stepped. Sunnyside was famous for its roller coaster Flyer and its large merry-go-round, called the

Derby Racer, enclosed in a huge circular building. Riding that merry-go-round took all the courage I had as the life-sized mechanical racehorses pranced, forged ahead, "trotted," and fell back imitating an actual horse race. My favourite ride, the stuff of my dreams, was an oval track around which you could drive small electric cars. Annie insisted that she squeeze in with me at first, but I eventually succeeded in persuading her to let me drive alone around the track.

When the Sunnyside amusement park was dismantled in 1955 to make way for the disastrous Gardiner Expressway, the Derby Racer was shipped to the new Disneyland in Anaheim. Once, when I was eight or nine, I visited Sunnyside with my friend Danny Strandhagen. Still the daredevil, he climbed aboard the Ferris wheel, while I waited below. He told me when the ride was over that a man had grabbed him in his pants and that they had fought for the rest of the ride. Neither one of us knew what to make of this, why this man acted this way or what we should do about it. I was shocked that the brave Danny was so upset.

Sunnyside became a ruin before it was finally demolished. The rides broke down; the battered old boardwalk splintered and fell to pieces. Three suspicious fires broke out near the roller coaster. Toronto can be ruthless when it trades its latest version of "progress" for history. When it comes to its history and architecture, it is truly a "lost city." Sunnyside was wiped clear in February 1956. Only the Palais Royale, swimming tank and bathing pavilion are left as reminders of when hundreds of thousands of Torontonians found time to play games, dance, boat, canoe, bathe, swim, stroll, and ride the Carousel.

Many nights of my life I have dreamed that I am lost in ruins, be they razed by firebombs or flooded by storms. My destination is obscured by rubble. I don't believe that dreams necessarily mean something, though it is not just coincidence that I plummet to a nightly death when an elevator cable snaps. My father was an elevator operator. Inevitably, my memories and present geography grow apart and the ghostly images in the mind no longer resemble their origins. The Guerney Foundry on

Davenport where I jumped into the sand pits is now Off the Wall Films. Davenport United where I joined the Boys' Brigade is now a drug rehabilitation centre. The parallel tracks and rolling stocks of the marshaling yards were torn up years ago for scrap metal. The branch line to the old A&P Bakery, where we poached cherry pies, has been replaced by row housing. The tall poplar trees that lined Connolly (now Wadsworth) Park, the hockey cushions and the baseball diamond have been replaced with a single concrete basketball court. Davenport (Osler) School is now the 11th Division Police Station. The Canada Packers stockyards are now Banana Republic, Old Navy, Home Depot and sports grills. As for Norfolk Street, there are only memories of a haven with Annie and Sassy the cat, and the gladiolas, the Heintzman piano and the picket fence. Number 4 was demolished long ago to make way for a school parking lot.

CHAPTER 5

My Father's War

"War is unlike life. It's a denial of everything you learn life is. You are exposed to horrors you would sooner forget."

– Robert Graff, USN

BOTH MY GRANDFATHERS and all but one of my many uncles (Uncle Don Marsh was too young) were in either the First or Second World War. My father joined up at age 19, which seemed inevitable since the defining moment of his father William "Ned" Marsh's life was being injured at Vimy Ridge. The old man's lifelong declaration of his own significance was "Vimy Fucking Ridge!" which he expected would end all arguments in his favour. But this was not as part of that Canadian offensive that military enthusiasts have foolishly claimed made Canada a "nation." Ned took part as an English volunteer with the Duke of Cornwall's Light Infantry, which fought at both Vimy and at the second battle of Passchendaele, where my maternal grandfather Andrew Jenkins was injured by shrapnel in his back and hip and invalided home. My father's serious injury at the end of the Second World War destroyed his life and almost destroyed his family.

Recent and threatened world conflicts hung over us in the 1950s in Toronto like an impending storm, unsettled our daily lives. Returned veterans, traumatized or injured in the Second World War, were supposed to rejoice in a valorous victory, but many were disillusioned and sorely disappointed in the hopes

49

they had of adventure in combat and of the anticipation they had of a prosperous life returning home. Thousands of families were left to deal with the deaths of sons and daughters. Now there was the Korean War from 1950-53, which was in the headlines of the newspapers and discussed at school. Some 26,000 Canadians were engaged again in war in that distant land. The Cold War that threatened our daily lives with nuclear nightmares and the evils of "communism" loomed closer than the wars of the past.

I absorbed this atmosphere as a young boy, first-hand from my damaged father, and by obsessively reading books on the military campaigns on the Eastern Front, Normandy and North Africa. I poured over endless descriptions of the killing machines: fighter planes, bombers, warships, and tanks. I sat for hours in a dizzying cloud of airplane glue, assembling plastic models of the fighters and bombers, the battleship *Bismarck*, the aircraft carrier *Ark Royal* and dozens of others. I remember clearly the first model I made, of a "Fletcher Class" American destroyer, which I had purchased at a hobby shop on College Street. I was thrilled by the shape of its hull and its movable gun turrets. I collected cereal box tops and sent away for a plastic submarine, which I filled with baking soda, placed in the base of the bathtub, waiting for it to fizz, bubble, and rise to the surface. "Run silent, run deep!" I declared after it had discharged its imaginary torpedo. My interest in war was ridiculed and discouraged by Ada and Annie and by my schoolteachers.

Neither my father nor his army buddies, who had served for years in Europe, fought and were injured, spoke of the grand principles of the war. Their experiences had little connection to the lofty tomes written about campaigns, like the volumes I read by Winston Churchill. Harry returned from the Second World War broken and resentful, unappreciated and abandoned in his injuries, physical and mental. When sober, he was sullen and quiet. He might unexpectedly launch a project to build a telephone shelf from ridiculously oversized lumber and spikes, or to paint the kitchen pink; inevitably he would leave the job undone. When he was hungover, he would lie in bed and summon me to fetch him a Kik Cola (a Canadian alternative to the two American colas), a *Flash* tabloid, and a McCormick's Molly-O chocolate bar from Middleton's Confectionery on Davenport Road. When drunk, he was angry. The object of this anger might be my mother or me or his brothers or friends, and he expressed it with sarcasm and violence.

As a result of his shattered leg, Harry wore a boot with a three-inch heel on his left foot. He walked with an awkward tilt, lurching from side to side. When he stood, he leaned uncomfortably on his good leg. The photographs he brought home from the war showed razed houses, flooded fields, and mangled bridges where he served in Holland—even some of the girls he met. He had two medals for his service overseas, as I suppose every soldier did for participation, which I retrieved from his uniform when he lay in his casket. That maple leaf on his shoulder was proof that Canadian soldiers were different, but disrespected, that the sacrifice they made in saving "Blighty's ass" was not recognized. He and his army friends had particular scorn for the ex-British military who brought their snobbery to Canada as immigrants after the war. Never did I hear a word spoken between Harry and his war buddies about saving democracy or sacrificing for Canada so often described in solemn ceremonies, by military historians, or in the media, or in schools on Remembrance Day. Harry and his fellow soldiers joined the Army for escape and adventure; they fought for their own survival, and for one another. That is what being Canadian and being a soldier meant to them.

The soldiers formed tight friendships in the war, as much over drink and engaging women as in battle. Among Harry's war buddies after the war were Buff Ransom, Elmer, Tom, and Jim. The drunker they got the more their camaraderie rallied not so much around an idealistic pride as in a sense of being exploited and of "not being," in particular of not being British. If they had doubts about their participation in the war, they were more about why they fought, and many were injured or died, to save Britain when the British so clearly disdained them. (They acknowledged no context for this animosity, such as the

British soldiers' jealousy over the Canadians' superior pay and their dalliances with the pretty home girls while they were off in North Africa or the Far East fighting.)

Charlie Radford had been exempted from service in the First World War for weaknesses in his heart or his feet; though his son Jack had been a navigator in the RAF, he would not tolerate talk of the war. Ada implored Harry to "shut up about the damn war! Nobody wants to hear about it." Was it something that men did, without women, among themselves and then were supposed to keep secret? Would anything else they ever did in their lives live up to those intimate experiences in combat with other men? Would they ever fall in love again with such beautiful, eager girls?

I simply did not know enough about my father to identify what he actually did in the war, or what he was thinking about his shattered life, or what if anything he might have thought of his son, or of being a father. Very early on, the one thing about him that gave me any pride was that he had been a soldier, that he had been part of what the popular culture pronounced the defining episode of our lives. Through the 1950s, movie theatres weekly showed heroic films about the Second World War: *The Halls of Montezuma*, about an attack on a Japanese island in the Pacific, *The Desert Fox*, about Erwin Rommel's combat in North Africa, *Run Silent Run Deep*, about submarine warfare, *From Here to Eternity*, about the Japanese navy's attack on Pearl Harbor, and the epic *Bridge on the River Kwai*, about a Japanese prisoner of war camp in Burma, directed by David Lean. None of these films, of course, were about Canadian soldiers—we were ignored by both the British and American narratives. Our own historians did little to speak up for Canada's "contributions." My father and his fellow soldiers never spoke triumphally of their experiences, only about confusion, error and the incompetence of their officers. There were no anthems or regimental hymns on my father's harmonica, only the sad ebb of "Lilli Marlene" and "We'll Meet Again."

I doubt that I took the patriotic lessons intended in these American or British movies, often cheering for the enemy,

Harry at the wheel of his Jeep in an unidentified Dutch town. He drove anything that would move.

sympathizing with the Alec Guiness character about saving his bridge over the Kwai River, and daydreaming about how to save the *Graf Spee*. Why "scuttle"? Why not fight? Why not slip out into the dark night and sink those British cruisers one by one? Of course, this was before most of us knew about the terrible atrocities committed by the Japanese and Germans in the war. It was long before any of us had even heard the word "Holocaust."

Mainstream television did even more to glorify the military accomplishments, of Americans that is, in winning the war. I had to tussle Charlie Radford for TV time to watch "The Silent Service" (1957-58), remembering to this day the opening "Tonight, we bring you another thrilling episode of Silent Service stories, of warfare under the sea." "Air Power" (1956-57), narrated by Walter Cronkite, was to me a gripping documentary series on the supremacy of the US Air Force, which was a partner in the production, in winning the war single-handedly—air force propaganda never to be spoken in the presence of my father. It was no doubt potent marketing for increases in military spending. (I wrote letters to aircraft manufacturers in the United

States, such as Lockheed, McDonnell and North American, asking for photographs of their warplanes; they always responded with free 10x12 glossy photos, which I pasted into an album with notes about each plane's climbing rate, armament and speed.) I still remember dramatic episodes on "Air Power," of the drone of the Liberator bombers over the Ploesti oil fields in Romania and the Schweinfurt ball-bearing factory in Germany. These episodes never explained how the Germans were able to keep on fighting, despite these "decisive" raids. Nor was there any hint of introspection about the terrible inefficiency of Allied bombing or the morality of simply killing German or Japanese children because you failed to hit the supposed targets. (We also learned later that Albert Speer actually increased military production through the bombing campaign.)

"Victory at Sea" (1952-53) provided the same victorious narrative for warships, plunging their bows into the swell of heavy seas, but with more impressive music. Meanwhile, at Oakwood Collegiate, an ex-colonel was principal and another injured officer with a "wooden leg" was our guidance counsellor. Cadet training was mandatory for all the boys. Most of us were bored by the chatter and grandiloquent rhetoric of the solemn Remembrance Day ceremonies. We boys were far more drawn to the actual violence. We fired live rifles in a shooting range built into the back of the school. The "fighting spirit" spread onto the streets, as we were armed with various "weapons" (sling shots, spears, and flimsy bows and arrows) and were always looking for a battle. We did not need video games to incite our aggression.

GRANDFATHER NED MARSH carried a cruel warrior spirit into his private life, as many ex-soldiers did, ruling his house on Keewatin Avenue like a tribal chieftain, dominating his children and tormenting his wife with an open affair, at least my mother claimed. To punish my father, Ned locked him in a broom closet, too small for him to sit down, for hours, and then would beat him with his belt. In the Japanese film *Vengeance is Mine*, directed by Shohei Imamura, the father of a serial killer on death

My grandfather William "Ned" Marsh in a photograph taken on Queen Street, Toronto, in the 1930s to illustrate a report in the Toronto Star *about his revelation of a political scandal at Toronto City Hall.*

row confronts his son with derision, telling him that he killed strangers because he was too cowardly to kill the man he really wanted to kill—him. I thought immediately of my father and his aggression against his wife, children, neighbours, "Limeys," and members of the navy or air force, or even against soldiers from the wrong regiment. As far as I knew, he never had the courage to confront his father.

I only saw my grandfather Marsh in person two or three times. Once, my father packed me into his '49 Mercury and drove recklessly up Lansdowne Avenue and across St. Clair Avenue to Mt. Pleasant Road and east to his parents' place on Keewatin, by the Mount Hope Cemetery. I suppose he thought that he was still careening through the ruins of wartime Holland in his Jeep. I could see when we arrived that Harry's bond with his mother was a common rage at his father. She seemed a kindly person and it was said that she played the piano well. Harry stayed in the kitchen to talk with her and told me to go up the stairs and "say hello" to the fearful despot. I had no sense that my father had spent his youth in this house.

Grandfather William Marsh was born in Westhoughton, Lancashire, near Wigan, in August 1894. He arrived at Quebec City in 1921 on the Cunard liner *Ascania*, which made over two hundred voyages across the Atlantic, bringing passengers to Canada. Hundreds of immigrants shared giant, open steerage decks or tiny steel cabins dominated by stacks of bunks and bare bulkheads. William reported in the immigration log that he had come to Canada with $100, his pregnant wife Marion, and his two sisters to join his brother John Frederick Marsh of 383 Helmsley (now Sorauren) Avenue, Toronto. Grandmother Marion Forsyth was born in Roughcraig, Scotland, outside Glasgow, in February 1893. Her mother was a Macdonald. After my father John Harley was born in 1922, William and Marion had two more boys, Reginald and Donald, and four girls, Rita, Patricia, Jean, and Muriel.

Grandfather Marsh held court from his bed in the front, second-floor bedroom of the Keewatin house—an affectation my father later tried to emulate. I remember my father telling me to climb the stairs to visit him. Grandfather asked me who I belonged to, flipped me a quarter and told me to "get the fuck out" and leave him alone. There is a photo of Ned from the *Toronto Star* newspaper looking dapper in an overcoat and hat, striding down Queen Street in downtown Toronto. It was taken after he made the city news when, as an auditor for the City of Toronto, he uncovered some financial scandal among the politicians at City Hall.

MY FATHER's birth certificate read "John Harley Forsyth Marsh," born at Toronto, 27 August 1922. He was occasionally called by his first name, but never Harley. He never included the name Forsyth on any of his military forms. His friends generally knew him as Harry, or Moe. Once or twice in his war record he scratched out "Harley" and inserted "Harry." In his enlistment interview, Harry gave his education as two years completed

Grandfather William "Ned" Marsh ringing the bell on the Ascania, *on his way to Canada, 1919.*

at Northern Secondary School. He claimed that he left school because "financial aid was needed at home," which seems unlikely as his father was a senior auditor for the City of Toronto. He worked as a store delivery boy, a candy machine operator at Rowntree Chocolate, a shipper at Hunt's Pastry, two years as a parcel delivery truck driver, and four months as a "labourer." He often added on his forms that he was also an "assembler," but gave no definition or specifics for this occupation.

Harry was about to turn twenty years old when he enlisted in the Canadian Army at Toronto, on December 8, 1942. He was not asked why he wanted to join, but the fact that he had been involved in an accident that had injured a pedestrian with his delivery truck and that he was being pursued in court by the victim's insurance company likely had something to do with it. The army interviewer described him as

> a pale, erect, immature lad of good build and intelligence. He is talkative, though not boastful, seems alert and frank. He is very careful about his personal appearance, possesses good manners. He is particularly interested in sports, having played hockey, rugby, softball, hardball, lacrosse and soccer. He especially enjoys boxing and can play the harmonica. He has a brother in the Royal Regiment, but has no desire to join the same unit.

(As it turned out, both he and his brother Reg ended up being transferred later to the Lake Superior Regiment and both ended up recuperating in the same Toronto hospital after the war. Nothing brought them together in a family sense. They were similar, violent drinkers but hated one another.)

Harry always listed his mother's name as next of kin. Sometimes he omitted, and once crossed off, his father's name in his war records. He was variously measured to be 5'10.5" or 5'11.5" and 145 pounds, with dark hair and brown eyes. He swept his thick black hair back over his forehead. He smiled in his many portraits in uniform, so I assume that he was happy to be a soldier.

Harry expressed a wish to join the Toronto Scottish Regiment (after 1938 also called Queen Elizabeth The Queen Mother's Own), perhaps as homage to his Scottish mother. Her Majesty visited the Regiment in Canada in 1940 and 1943. Because the Toronto Scottish Regiment had been designated as a "machine gun battalion," it did not fight as a coherent unit during the war. Members of the Regiment took part in the disastrous raid on Dieppe in August of 1942. From D-Day until 1945, the Toronto Scottish was in Europe supporting units of the 2nd Canadian

Division. On December 19, 1942 Harry was transferred to Unit 44 at St. Jerome, Quebec. Less than a month later, on January 7, 1943 he was admitted to Notre Dame hospital in Montreal. He explained that he had met a girl and "exposed himself" in Toronto on December 18 (ten days after he enlisted), 1942. He was diagnosed with "acute urethritis." When asked why he did not use a condom, he replied, "Because none was available." It is rare when we know the exact day we were conceived; I was born nine months later.

In February 1943 Harry was transferred for training to Trois-Rivières, Quebec. In March he was transferred again, to Aldershot, Nova Scotia. He was on furlough May 5, 1943 and on special leave May 19 to May 22. One assumes that this is when he met Carrie Veinote of nearby Waterville, King's County, who later wrote plaintively to the Army that she had not heard from Harry in a long time, though they were "very close," and that he had promised to marry her. He qualified as Driver Class III on June 19, 1943 and was given an increase in pay to $1.40 per day. On July 21 he was sentenced to 168 hours detention for being AWL after being "duly warned." Perhaps he took off to see Carrie. He must have "exposed" himself again as he was back in hospital November 2-11, 1943, this time in the Halifax Military Hospital. He was diagnosed with gonorrhea and was put on 14 days sick leave.

However he was carrying on with Carrie and others, Harry must have gotten a letter from Ada and must have known that she was pregnant. Either persuaded by Ada, or instructed by the Army, he "was granted permission to marry Miss Ada Jenkins on or after December 23, 1943." He was on furlough December 23, 1943 to January 5, 1944. (Their son, myself, was four months old. They borrowed me from Mrs. Mitchell, where Ada had left me, and took a number of pictures of the "happy family" before returning me to the orphans' care home and Harry to the army.) The marriage took place on January 2, 1944 at the Salvation Army, 14 Vaughan Road. Harry overstayed his furlough and was convicted of yet another AWL violation; sentenced to 28 days detention and docked another 38-days' pay. There is no official record of what he was up to when he skipped duty.

Harry complained of the boredom of training in England, and it did not take long for him to be convicted again, in his new regiment, of being AWL in France (no doubt partying with girls in lieu of Germans). He was sentenced to another 60 days detention, but was released after 40 days, as the Army was reluctant to keep men locked up when the unit was going into action.

The Lake Superiors did not take part in the initial Normandy landings in June 1944. The regiment's vehicles and men landed at Red Beach near Graye-sur-Mer on the morning of the 26th of June. The Winnipeg Rifles Infantry, Canadian Scottish, 6th Armoured and II Grenadier had suffered heavy losses there during the original invasion on June 6. By the time my father joined the Lake Superior Regiment in October 1944, it had already seen action at Caen and in the failed Allied push to close the Falaise "gap" and surround the Wehrmacht's 7th Army. Harry was in action driving armoured personnel carriers and Jeeps when the regiment advanced into Belgium and Holland, where the Germans had opened the dykes, blown up the bridges and flooded the country for miles around. After the first hectic months of pursuit, the Lake Superiors' role changed to standing occupation, with daily patrols and minor offensives. When the regiment abused the privileges of dances, music, public baths, and chasing girls, the city of Bruges was declared out of bounds. For the next several months determined German resistance in Holland tied down the Superiors. This was not all bad for the soldiers, as leave was available to visit Hertogenbosch, Antwerp and Brussels for shops, beer parlors, nightclubs, dances, and brothels. On 20th of December the men moved south near Boxtel and enjoyed Christmas dinner. Each soldier received a parcel of cigars, cigarettes, and chocolate. In down time the men played hockey, football, and held boxing competitions, in which Harry took part.

The next big regimental maneuvre began on February 24, 1945 with an armoured thrust through the Hochwald Gap. The fighting was bitter but by daybreak on March 1 the Canadians

Harry in uniform, 1943.

held possession of both shoulders of the Gap in some of the toughest fighting of the war. Patrols crossed the bridge over the Twentekanaal. There are several photographs of my father taken in Holland, sitting by the ruins of a canal or bridge. Sadly, he sent home a photo that he had taken of the grave of a friend Pte. J.J. Batyski of the Lake Superior Regiment. On the cross it notes that Batyski was killed in action 28.4.45. There is no notice of his age when he died. He was no doubt a young man, like my father, and died only a month before the cease-fire.

The last two weeks of the war saw intense combat as the Lake Superiors advanced towards the banks of the Küsten Canal in Germany. The German surrender agreed to on May 1st took effect at 8 a.m. on the 5th. The LSR were the last Canadian troops to be in combat. They were dismayed to learn that their demobilization would be delayed; those with longer service overseas were going home first. The men were kept occupied with concerts, dances, guard duty (there is another photograph of Harry on guard duty), and sightseeing tours. On one of these tours, Harry found or purchased an elaborate album of an unknown German family's extended family, their celebrations and vacations in the German countryside. On May 8 the regiment moved to Varel in northwest Germany and then back to Hengelo in Holland and then to repatriation depots in England. The last men of the Regiment did not leave Europe until a dull, drizzly day on January 21, 1946, aboard the *Île-de-France* at Southhampton. Unfortunately, only nine days before that departure, Harry's life changed forever.

ON JANUARY 12, 1946, at the #7 Canadian Repatriation Depot in England, Harry suffered the accident that would demolish much of the rest of his life. In an early interview, he stated that he was standing in front of a vehicle when a Jeep backed up into him. His left leg was caught between the vehicles. He did not fall and was helped by the other men and taken to hospital on a stretcher in great pain.

Later, at a formal enquiry, Harry's report of the accident was that at 1500 hours on January 12 he was "standing in front of my CWT vehicle (a truck dubbed the "gin palace" in the Canadian army) with the hood of the engine up fixing the fuel pump. A Jeep suddenly backed out of the garage and caught me between the two vehicles crushing my left leg. I did not know any of the people who were there."

The differences in the two reports may have had something to do with the various forms that had to be filled out in order to establish that the injury occurred in the performance of Harry's military duty. The report found that no one was to blame, and that the accident occurred on a military premise, #1 Canadian repatriation Depot (even though Harry was stationed at #7). The X-Rays showed a "supracondylar fracture" with anterior fracture fragments displaced laterally. The injury caused great distress and the patient was reported as very miserable, nauseated, groaning, and crying in pain. Harry was finally discharged, still on a stretcher, from the hospital April 19, 1946 for repatriation.

Harry at "Bazooka Bridge" by a ruined canal in Holland.

He left England on the hospital ship *Letitia* on April 29 and arrived in Canada May 8. He was transported to Toronto from Quebec City on a hospital train, arriving at Union Station, and then was taken to Chorley Park Military Hospital (where his brother Reg, also severely injured, was taken for rehab). He had his cast removed September 3 and was honourably discharged, on crutches, from the Army September 24. He wrote and asked that any medals be sent to 567 Perth Avenue. He was sent the 1939-45 Star, France and Germany; and the Star, Canadian Volunteer Service Medal and Clasp.

While I only saw the violent anger and unpredictable cruelty of my father, he managed to act charmingly to outsiders, particularly to women. He was a tall, handsome, athletic man. Despite this, there was often a vacant look on his face, echoes perhaps of his disturbed childhood. His only consolation, aside from alcohol, was his time in the war and the girls he had known. When he drank alone, he would take out his harmonica and play the plaintiff song he had learned in Germany, "Lilli Marlene," eyes closed, over and over again.

It is hard to tell how much of the fighting action of the Lake Superior Regiment Harry saw. War records say nothing of the time or place of a soldier's action in battle. The regimental history (written by historian George Stanley) rarely breaks the combat down by companies. Harry wrote Ada sentimental letters and cards from Holland and sent her a picture of himself sitting next to some pretty Dutch girls (whom he declared loved the chocolate that he gave them). When I was a boy, I loved to snoop around in the cedar chest where my mother kept these letters, cards, mementos, and pictures. I stared in wonder at that photo, but it disappeared from my mother's collection.

Shortly after Harry was released from the hospital, he used what was left of his modest pay (less all the deductions for his fines) to put a deposit on the house on Perth Avenue. We shared it briefly with Harry's younger brother Reg and his wife Ruth. At some point Harry decided to retrieve me from Annie Radford. He told a reluctant Ada to go and get me; this was how my life was changed.

Harry's expectations for a job were certainly thwarted by his injury. On his discharge from the army he told the vocational interviewers that he would like to set up a mechanic shop. He was forever adjusting the carburetor or fan belt or replacing the spark plugs on his own cars but never found employment as a mechanic as he had hoped. The last note in his file was that he would get a job with the Toronto civil service, as he "might" have a contact there. (His father was a senior auditor there.) But he was in constant pain and had taken refuge in alcohol. His left leg was now significantly shorter, and he had difficulty walking without an awkward wobble. He ended up operating an elevator at Sunnybrook Hospital. Even as a young boy, I was so embarrassed by his lowly vocation that I lied about it to friends and teachers, claiming some grander avocation for him, such as firefighter, or I just said that he was dead. I was deeply ashamed, as he seemed to be, of the name that I shared with him: Harley. In first-year high school at Oakwood Collegiate, I was called

My father Harry Marsh's photograph of the fresh grave of his friend J.J. Batyski, killed in action, in Holland. The war ended only a month later.

to Principal Vincent Tovell's office and instructed to insert my middle name on the school register. "I know you have one" he boomed at me. Even after I was given a series of detentions, I refused to reveal that name Harley. I felt that ridicule would rain down on me should the humiliating name leak out.

That small house on Perth Avenue was always crowded with relatives and boarders. My mother tried to earn some money in childcare but was soon found unfit. Once, one of the mothers asked me, "Why is my baby crying when I come to pick her up?" I answered that it was because Ada slaps her. I disappeared for the rest of the day, but Ada was waiting for me when I crept home. Ada's preferred slaps over my ears left me with lifelong ear infections and extreme tinnitus. Once, when Annie called to talk to me, I took the phone sobbing. She took a taxi to Perth Avenue, scooped me up without any protest from Ada, and took me to a doctor. He treated me for two serious ear infections, which Annie speculated were caused by Ada's blows. She took me to Norfolk to recover but returned me, despite my begging, when my father called demanding my return.

The most enraged Harry ever got with me was when I burned a pot of beans. It became a sad family story that focused on my inadequacies rather than the beating that I took. From my youngest years, I was expected to shovel coal, cook, shop, and babysit. (My oldest sister Marian arrived when I was five. Sally then John followed.) One night when I was only eight, my parents left me to babysit. My father gave me grim instructions to watch over a pot of beans that he left cooking on the stove. I had no idea what to do. Turn up the heat and risk burning them? Turn off the heat and leave the beans uncooked? When Harry arrived home, he broke into a fury when he saw that the beans had charred at the bottom of the pot. He dragged me into the backyard by the arm, clubbing the back of my head with his fist. As he let go to pull off his belt, I broke loose. He tried to chase me but his injured leg disadvantaged him. In my own mixture of fear and rage I picked up stones and began flinging them at him. "I hate you, I fucking hate you!" I screamed. I ran up the Perth lane towards Davenport Avenue and begged carfare from a stranger (I can still recall his worried face, a young Italian whom I had seen in the neighbourhood) and found my way by bus and streetcar to Norfolk. Annie let me in. Charlie demanded that she send me back immediately as he could see no physical evidence of a beating and accused me of lying. She put me in a bath and kept me for the night but explained that I must go to school the next day and then straight home to Perth. My father was sitting at the kitchen table when I arrived at Perth Avenue the next day, but he never said a word. My mother slapped the back of my head. Each one of her repeated assaults increased the hatred of her that would sustain me through the years to come. I fell asleep each night fantasizing about how I could harm Ada. Antipathy for my father was shrouded in fear.

My mother's rule was that condescending cliché that she repeated, "Children should be seen but not heard." She in fact did not want even to see us. She cooked one meal for herself and the boarders: pork chops, chips, and pie. Then she would feed the kids. We were usually fed some kind of stew full of onions that made me gag. A standoff would ensue for hours until bedtime. Ada left me in the kitchen, turned off the light and at bedtime sent me off with a cuff and wrapped the meal in waxed paper to return it to me the next evening. As I grew a little older, I managed to stay late at the hockey rink or in the streets so that I would miss these dinner rituals altogether, secretly filling up with bread and peanut butter and apples when I got home. I was never fed breakfast nor sent to school with a lunch. When it became clear at Davenport School that I was undernourished, I was taken into the nurse's room daily and fed a pint of milk and a piece of buttered white bread. The neighbours, particularly our Italian next-door neighbours, were appalled at how Canadians treated their kids. They sneaked me into their house (they were very afraid of my father) and fed me fresh, crusty Italian bread, sweet purple grapes and spaghetti drenched in tomato sauce. Annie Radford tried to supplement the clothes that Mrs. Devlin gave me. She bought me new shoes for the school year at Maher's on Dundas Street each September. I begged her to buy me running shoes, but when she did, I wore them out before winter, the laces broken and the soles flapping open at the toes.

Ada once told my sister Marian that she wished to God that she never had any children. With me at least, she wished that she had one less. She sarcastically mocked me for claiming that I knew things from the books that I read and ridiculed me for wanting to be with "his na na." Ada's favourite epithet for me was "fucking know-it-all." There were only two books in the house at Perth Avenue, the dictionary that my father claimed to have memorized during the war, and an old out-of-date single volume encyclopedia. I stared in wonder at the maps of Europe and the animals, trees, and heroes described in that encyclopedia. I took it from the kitchen and hid it under my bed so that I could read it at night. When foolish enough to recite some fact that I had learned in front of visitors I would be rewarded by Ada's specialty, as she called it the "back hander," knocking me sideways or ringing my ears. I hated myself that I could not retaliate as I might have done against bullies in the street. One night

I desperately fought back against my father when he roused me from bed to use me as a guinea pig, testing some professional wrestling move on me that he called the "Holger Neilson." He announced that by putting his arms under my armpits, and then pressing down firmly on the top of my head, that he could make me unconscious. More terrified of the stated goal than of him, I reared back with all my might and pushed him backwards into the stove, where he banged his head. His brother Don prevented him from killing me then, but Harry swore that he would get even by killing my cat Cuseo. I always wondered if he did. Once I found my father torturing that cat and made him stop with my screams. I found Cuseo dead in the alley not long after.

Every night I lay sleepless in the dark, fearing my father's footsteps on the stairs. Would he grab the newel post and turn onto the landing towards his bedroom, or would he burst into my room and turn me out of bed? It was always late when he arrived home. He drank at the Legion or in one of the few bars that still allowed him admission. He would take me down to the kitchen and make me open his dictionary to test him on the spelling and definition of words. I learned that it was dangerous to ask him a word that was too difficult or too easy. Either would incur his wrath. My mother would make him an onion and horseradish sandwich and sit there without speaking, not with pity for me but with boredom. One late night Harry roused me and told me to teach him chess, which I had learned by watching it played at school. He had either found or purchased a pocket, magnetic set, with a box that opened into a board. It did not go well. He reacted with particular frustration at the illogical moves I explained of the knight. "One up, two down; two down, one over, what the hell is that?" he bellowed at me. He had the same attitude about the unpredictability of spelling. "If the plural of mouse is mice, why isn't the plural of moose meese?" he demanded, blaming me somehow for the linguistic anomalies. Is there karma in this world? Or is it only blind chance that I later spent my career editing dictionaries and an encyclopedia?

On another night that haunted me for years, Harry roused me when the kitchen was full of people drinking and playing cards. He pushed me into the kitchen and told me to drop my pajama bottoms. When I finally did, he demanded that I tell him what my insignificant "pecker" was for. When I mumbled that it was to make babies he roared with derision. I just stood there blinded with tears, which infuriated me more for I had made a pact with myself that no matter what he did to me I would not cry. I did not know what I had done to become a target of these humiliations. Perhaps I was being punished for the bitter and violent fantasies that rose up like jellyfish from the depths of my mind.

Numerous times when Harry came home, drunk late at night, he ordered me out of the metal bunk bed and pulled me by the ear lobe into the bathroom. It was a place of torment for me because when my mother would put me in the tub, she would drag my head back by my hair and hold it under water to wash the "cooties" out of my hair. The terror I felt being water boarded like this instilled in me a lasting fear of putting my head under water to this day. Harry would inspect my feet with unnatural care and always declare them filthy. Dirty feet were a criminal offence with him. He forced me to run the hot water and scrub my feet over and over until they were burned clean to his satisfaction. "Hotter, hotter" he demanded as my feet turned crimson. As a result of these nightly attacks, or threats of intrusions, and my poor sister Marian banging her head against the wall, I got very little sleep. My teachers reported me as lazy, distracted, and unresponsive in class, except of course when I misbehaved, and then they punished me with the strap.

When on random Sundays at Norfolk, Annie would take me to St. Anne's Anglican church on Gladstone, the peaceful hum of the choir and the spacious dome enclosing us eased my mind. I was still a misfit, but I felt lucky, even then, that there was an alternate world in which, with luck, I might live forever.

CHAPTER 6

Streets, Laneways, and the Games We Played

"In my dreams of this city I am always lost."

– Margaret Atwood, Cat's Eye

AFTER SCHOOL or after dinner or midmornings on weekends, boys of all ages from the Junction neighbourhood spontaneously mustered in the cinder lanes to play games. Those were the sweetest times, in-between the miseries of school and home, when we moved to our own rhythms and made our own rules. We quickly chose leaders and teams and then we played. There was no supervision, organization, or instruction by adults, except when we annoyed them with exuberant noise, a stone through their window, or a ball in their yard. In those days there seemed to be so many boys of mixed ages and sizes loose on the streets that we always had enough numbers to form teams. There were known gathering spots, such as the Symington Lane—called by us the "cement lane" as it was one of very few that had been paved—the Connolly Street baseball diamond and natural ice rink, the nine or ten natural hockey cushions at Earlscourt Park, my own Perth back lane, and the Davenport School play yard. The boys could be complete strangers, but once the teams were chosen, they became brothers and we competed with all our will to win.

The first game I remember playing was "chase the ball" at Davenport school. At morning recess, a teacher would toss a soccer ball onto the field. A swarm of kids would chase the ball like bees after pollen, with the simple goal of kicking it as far as we could into the open field with the others in pursuit. Besides the joy of running and the thrill of being the one who managed a kick, by speed or by accident, the one who scored the most touches during recess claimed the pride of winning. I remember running nonstop among the often-aggressive older boys but only managed a few squibs of the ball into the turf. I fell asleep at night dreaming that I had kicked the ball so high in the air that it would soar over the fence.

In later grades I lost interest in this fruitless pursuit and spent my recess time playing against other boys with hockey cards, baseball cards, "Believe it Or Not," or "Bring 'Em Back Alive" cards. In "flipsies" one boy would flip a card to the ground. The second player would then flip his (always boys as I never played with girls) card and if it matched, head-to-head (the side with the player photo) or tail-to-tail (the side with the stats or story), he won both cards. If it did not match, he lost. "Closies" took more skill as we tossed the cards spinning horizontally against the brick wall on the side of the school. The closest to the wall would win them all. My friend Jimmy Devlin was so good at this game that he managed to assemble two entire 1951 NHL collections of hockey cards, one for himself and one for me. I spent hours Scotch taping the cards into an album by team and memorizing their stats. "Robert 'Ted' Lindsay—Detroit Red Wings, Left Wing, Goals 24, Assists 35, Min. in Penalty 110, Born Renfrew, Ontario." Max Bentley of the Toronto Maple Leafs (born in Delisle, Saskatchewan) was impressively "dipsey doodling" in the photo. Bill Barilko was frozen in mid-air, scoring that famous goal I had witnessed at Maple Leaf Gardens, squeezed on the bench beside Annie Radford.

Most boys carried a pocket full of glass marbles, small cat's eyes of all colours, sometimes solid colours, others with a flare in the centre, and a few big "aggies." A pickup game might occur anywhere you could find an opponent and a smooth piece of ground. Opponents began by drawing a circle boundary, about three feet across. It could be on the pavement, drawn with chalk, but we preferred dirt, where we could draw the "ring" with a stick. I practiced on my own for hours with my best shooter, a big aggie, which I called "the boulder." If we played "for keeps," we kept the marbles we knocked out of the ring, kneeling down and propelling the shooter with a flick of the thumb. If you hit the marble out of the ring, you kept it. If you missed, you lost. Mostly we seemed to play for a while and then leave with the same number of marbles we started with. It mattered who won but much more important were the communion with friends, the focus, the chatter, the disputes, the freedom, and the silences. We scattered after a game as quickly as we had gathered. I don't know where my modest marble collection started, but it aggregated nicely in its cloth bag over the years.

Our sports encounters began with brief quarrels about what game to play and who the two captains might be. Then a quick round of rock, paper, scissors would decide first pick. For the youngest or smallest kid, there was the shame of being picked last, or not at all. If a game was already in progress, a newcomer simply joined in on the shorthanded side. If a game became too one-sided, the captains would agree to make trades to even up. Games and rules passed on seamlessly from older kids to younger, from street to street and neighbourhood to neighbourhood. "No raising! No body checks!" We did not "learn" to compete. It was born in us.

The father of one of the boys who lived on Symington Avenue soldered plates of tin together to form a cowl on his boy's impressive go-cart. The rest of us cobbled together wheels and axles from abandoned baby carriages and attached them to boards of plywood. There was a rope for steering the front wheels and a slot in the back where a bigger boy could propel you with a broom stick. None of us was a match for that cowled speedster, especially on the downhill runs. The *Toronto Telegram* sponsored city-wide races on a prominent hill, but none of us competed. The same metal-working father also welded pipes to make two regulation-sized hockey nets. Strung with twine, those nets transformed our hockey scrums into true contests, as shooters could go high and "pick the corners." They put an end to arguments over whether the shot was "in" when the ball crossed between two stones or lumps of ice that would otherwise mark the goal. "Would've hit the post and bounced out! Would not've!" The games rattled back and forth no matter what the weather; a snowfall would make the game even more authentic. Teams formed and changed as boys came and went, as darkness warned that dinner was getting cold, or as sticks broke or a score became too lopsided.

When I was playing in the streets or alleys, I was hardly aware of time or place. I sensed that I was observing from another place, waiting or running, silent or shouting, focused on a ball or puck, running, deking, shooting—joyful on the street. In my earliest memories, I was the youngest boy, aged 6-9, called on by my older neighbour Jim Morrison (who later played for Father Bauer on Canada's Olympic team) to play goal, standing cold-footed between two blocks of ice until a flurry of action erupted in front of me. I swelled with pride when someone yelled "great save!" Boys always complimented the goalie, as few wanted to play net. As I got older, I moved out to play wing or forward (there was no distinction) in the fluid teamwork that was the pleasure of street ball hockey. I loved that game so much that I would always be the last to leave. When everyone else left, I would play against imaginary opponents, scoring at will and listening at the same time to the admiring commentary of Foster Hewitt running in my head. All the Leafs, Red Wings, and Canadiens played in my imaginary games: Gordie Howe, Maurice "Rocket" Richard, "Terrible" Ted Lindsay, Red Kelly, Jean Beliveau, "Boom Boom" Geoffrion, Doug Harvey. My Leaf mates with whom I exchanged imaginary passes and congratulatory nods were Ted "Teeder" Kennedy, Tod Sloan, Max Bentley, Fern Flaman, Harry Lumley, and others.

The happiest moments of my young life came on the Saturday nights when I was visiting Norfolk and Annie would take me to a live hockey game at Maple Leaf Gardens. It started when I was six or seven. The ticket takers knew her so well that she never failed to get me in free under the turnstile. She had a ticket in the first row of the last section, the "greys," and her neighbours moved politely along the bench to make room for me.

I would have arrived at Norfolk by streetcar Friday evening, responding to Ada's sarcastic "Go and see your Na Na!" On Saturday about 6 p.m. Annie and I would walk north on Brock Street, cross Dundas at the lights and catch the "Carlton" streetcar along College Street. I counted the stops from Dufferin, to Gladstone, Dovercourt, Grace, Euclid, Ossington, Bathurst, Spadina, and University Avenue at the Legislative Buildings. By the time we got to Bay Street, traffic thickened, parking-lot attendants beckoned, and crowds milled about in a pre-game anticipation. In those days, most of the men wore suits, hats, and overcoats to the Leaf games; women wore fur coats and fancy hats. We got off the streetcar at Bay Street under the imposing structure of Eaton's College Street and walked a block east to the Gardens at Church Street, past the fans jostling for position, hawking or buying tickets.

When we entered the Gardens near game time, we passed through the main lobby under the photos of the stars of bygone years: Frank Brimsek, Charlie Conacher, "Busher" Jackson, "King" Clancy, and Syl Apps. Annie often spoke of them because to her, always, the players of previous generations worked harder and thought less of themselves. We climbed the stairs (an escalator was built part way up some years later, but Annie refused to use it) and walked the narrow corridors, finally emerging at the very top row of the grey section. (Below were the greens, blues and, closest to the ice, the reds.) For years I could not lift my head when we reached the top aisle. I feared that great vaulted ceiling, the black void into which I imagined that they shot the clowns from cannons in the circus, where Foster Hewitt crawled out along a girder to his "gondola" to announce the games. Annie told me proudly that "tough-guy" American actor James Cagney froze on that girder and had to be rescued. Over centre ice a great blue clock with four faces hung precariously, keeping the time and the score. Above it was an ad for cigarettes, "Players Please." Every time I looked up at that clock the fear that it would fall caused an ache in the pit of my stomach; it appeared, swaying dangerously, in the void in my nightmares. At the south end of the Gardens, to our right, there was a balcony where a band would play, a real band, a pipe band on special occasions, not canned, not blaring with advertising shills and forced cheers, today's commands on the giant screens to *make noise!* I cannot understand how today paying for a ticket at an event offers no protection against a din of relentless advertising and gambling in a lottery. The excitement in the Gardens was generated by the drama of the game and by the joy or frustration of the fifteen-thousand fans. On special evenings, especially around Christmas, a classic tenor or soprano would step forward on the balcony and sing to us during the intermissions.

With the popcorn and program vendors, the standing-room-only crowd in the aisle beneath us, the feeling of being in the Gardens was intoxicating. When the game ended, I could not bear to leave. Life at home or in the school could not match the experience in the arena and my world would be empty until the next time Annie took me back. I felt an echo of the grandeur of the Gardens many years later when I entered under the vaults of Chartres Cathedral to the sound of a children's choir. When the games ended at the Gardens and we had cheered the "three stars," I usually managed to unearth a rolled-up, discarded game program, which I could read on the way home in the streetcar along College Street. Across the top on the front cover were the flags of the six NHL teams above a photo of a current Maple Leaf, such as Barry or Brian Cullen. Inside there might be a story on my favourite player Frank Mahovlich, "The Big 'M,'" and the lineups for the night with the numbers: #9 Gordie Howe 5 goals and 11 assists for Detroit, #11 Tod Sloan of Toronto 6 goals and 8 assists. I collected players' photographs by sending the labels from Beehive Golden Corn Syrup in exchange for 8 by10 glossy prints and pasted them carefully in an album.

It was there in Maple Leaf Gardens that I had a profound experience that I have never forgotten. I was seven years old when the game was played on April 21, 1951. The Leafs were playing the unspeakable Montreal Canadiens in the Stanley

KNOW IT ALL

Cup playoff finals. It was the fifth game and the Leafs led the series three games to one. All four games had been decided in overtime. From previous games I had taken a rambunctious player as my favourite and during this game tried to ask Annie his name over the crowd noise. She could not hear me. With a wetted finger I wrote his number on the wooden handrail, "5." I needed to know his name because at home I re-enacted every play using a yardstick and a rolled-up sock, with me making a save or pulling the trigger on a goal. Annie told me that his name was "Bill Barilko." Later that game he scored his famous overtime goal, taking a pass sent from Howie Meeker from behind the net and firing it past Montreal goalie Gerry McNeil—winning the Stanley Cup for Toronto. "You see I told you so!" I shouted to Annie. I have told the story for years but now that goal has become like the splinters of the true cross, witnesses proliferating with every new hockey book or documentary. Hero, saviour, Bill Barilko's name became magic, even in the Radford household, where they were more comfortable with the less flashy, and more Anglo Saxon, Ted Kennedy and Sid Smith.

Barilko's cult-like stature was sanctified when he disappeared in a plane crash the following summer, leaving just the memory of that goal and the magic of that number 5. It seemed, to a young boy, crushingly unfair that a hero could die like that, and that his body would be left lying in a hidden tangle of forest in northern Ontario. They did not find the plane wreck for eleven years, the exact amount of time it took for the Leafs to win the Stanley Cup again. His number—only the second one that the Leafs had retired—remains sacred to me today. I chose it for every uniform I wore, even Borje Salming's number 5 on his Swedish Olympic jersey.

Annie was a true fan, with her own favourites, usually the hard-working unsung players like defenceman "Hughie" Bolton. She loved the masters of the subtle "poke check" over the body slamming Barilko, Fern Flaman, and Leo Boivin. Then along came Tim Horton, whom she adored for his grit and determination, and perhaps for his rugged good looks. She rarely showed any negative emotion or anger at the games,

Streets, Laneways, and the Games We Played

Bill Barilko's famous Cup winning goal April 21, 1951. Barilko is still in mid-air, Maurice "Rocket" Richard (left) looks back helplessly. (Photo by Nat Turofsky.)

except when "Timmy" was not selected among the three stars at the end of a game. We listened together to Foster Hewitt's play by play when I slept over on Sunday nights, as the Leafs played in Detroit, Boston, New York, or Chicago. We shared an admiration for Ted "Teeder" Kennedy, the indomitable captain of the Leafs. Kennedy was the ideal Leaf of those days, without guile or flash—he once won the Hart Trophy as the league's "most valuable player" after scoring a mere nine goals. But he bowed magnificently before Princess Elizabeth when she visited the Gardens in 1951 and we all thrilled when that solo trumpet voice in the Gardens called out in the silence when the game was paused... "C'mon Teeeeder!"

In stark contrast for Annie were the flashy, deceitful, ostentatious Montreal Canadiens. In her rogue's gallery, Maurice Richard, that "louse," reigned supreme. He was French and Catholic! The journeyman Leaf thug Bill Eziniki was her valiant protagonist every time he dropped Richard with a body check

77

or goaded him into a fight. For me the Canadiens were less a detested hockey team than an alien force of nature, destroyer of my dreams. Although the Leafs won that cup in 1951 they soon sank to the bottom of the standings. I endured years of frustration when they could not even make the playoffs in a six-team league. Every trip to Toronto by the Canadiens ended in a rout. Annie persisted, believing that she could call upon some external power, yelling vehemently at the Frenchmen. She even travelled to Montreal where Leaf owner Conn Smythe got her a ticket so that she could hurl her galoshes at the "Rocket."

One evening after a game against the Canadiens, I stood nervously outside the Montreal dressing room holding a small autograph book and a pen. The players emerged in suits and ties and mostly rushed to the waiting bus, which took them to Union Station. Suddenly, a tall handsome man reached down and took the book and pen from my hand. He signed it "Jean Belliveau." He left his name in my book! He had the largest hands I have ever seen and smiled kindly on my awestruck face. He handed the book and pen to a teammate, who signed "Boom Boom Geoffrion." Annie Radford had warned me that these detestable Frenchmen would break my fingers if I approached them! Later I held out the book silently before my favourite Maple Leaf, Frank Mahovlich; he sullenly brushed me aside. The world was not as black and white as Annie portrayed.

I WAS ABOUT FOUR YEARS OLD when Don Radford took me skating for the first time. We went with borrowed skates to the ice rink in High Park. Don was ten or more years older than me, Annie's grandson by Grace. He was so quiet that he barely spoke a word during all the kind things that he did for me. There was a stigma in his life, as he had no visible father, and Grace had no apparent husband. Annie looked stern and disapproving whenever I raised the subject. Grace, for her part, seethed with angry resentment and hinted at ambitions thwarted and favouritism shown to her younger sister Jean and to her brother Jack, war hero and golden boy. She spoke as adults sometimes

Streets, Laneways, and the Games We Played

do to children as if they understood. For myself these puzzling conflicts only confirmed my assurance that the world was not made for me to understand and that I should avoid it, as Don seemed to do.

I learned to skate quickly. There was no one to teach me, to hold my hand, to encourage me or to comfort me when I fell. I did not expect it. I wonder at the over-attention parents, or in my case, grandparent, pay to the least setbacks of their children these days, helmeted and wrapped in the most expensive designer equipment. I simply hated falling on the ice and was determined to avoid it. Annie admired my pluck and took me to the skate exchange and bought me a pair of skates. I soon combined the skating with the stick skills I had practiced for hours in the kitchen at Norfolk and in the backyard at Perth Avenue, where I fashioned a small patch of ice with buckets of water as a launching pad for my shots. I re-enacted the Leaf games that Foster Hewitt called from the Gardens gondola—I imagined a cradle rocking high under the vaulted roof—and from around the rinks of the rest of the "original six."

Other times in the laneways, when there was no pick-up game, I joined an inner group that often included the Morelli brothers, Ross and Fred, Bobby "Sag" Solonius, Louie Justice and whoever else might volunteer to join us. Ross and Fred were dark-haired Italian boys, whose father owned a dry-cleaning outlet. Bobby's Finnish immigrant family arrived in Canada as refugees. He suffered from rickets and walked with a serious limp, like my father. The Scottish, Polish, and German kids never joined in our games—they played soccer—but they did roam the laneways with us, like bandits on the prowl, avoiding signs of adult life, barking insults at one another and any other kid we saw, throwing anything we could pick up, tossing knives into the rotting garage doors, scrounging for treasure in backyards or cars. We jostled among ourselves for position like wolves; sometimes one leading with ideas for mischief and other times another with bravado.

My first "best" friend Danny Strandhagan always commanded attention for he was the greatest daredevil among us, leaving no bridge or fire escape or billboard unclimbed. Sometimes I missed the organizing huddle, detained by my mother to wash the dishes with my sister Marian, or to run errands or being sent straight to bed as a punishment for "my mouth." I would hear my friends ask for me at the door and when told that I could not come out to play, they would summon me from the backyard and I would sneak out of the back-bedroom window, creep over the tar paper porch roof and climb down the rough-barked elm tree to join the gang.

We ran in bursts, lifted up like leaves in the wind, assaulting the evening like commandos. Sometimes we just fell into games of tag or hide and seek or "Nicky Nicky Nine Doors," a game with various colourful names, in which you knock on a door or ring a doorbell and then run like hell in all directions from an annoyed, angry, or perplexed householder. We got to know the grumpiest marks and of course bothered them the most. Those who stood on the porch and railed against delinquents brought the greatest fun and those who chased us with determination posed the greatest danger. One Perth Avenue neighbour anticipated the knock one night, fortunately not by me, and burst through the door, grabbed the boy and vehemently kicked his ass several times.

I first played the game we called "peggies" when a group of older boys set up the game in my backyard at Perth. I read now that it was a once-popular children's game in Yorkshire. The version I learned that day and played many times on my own required a longer and a shorter piece of dowel from a cut-down broom handle. The smaller piece, the "peggy," was placed, pointing upwards, at the front end of an oval hole dug into the ground. A player struck the peggy with the longer stick so that it would flip upward and then he would try to whack it in midair. A player had three attempts to hit the peggy and if he missed it the third time he was out, and it was the opponent's turn. The object in our version was to hit the peggy as far as you could. If the opponent caught it, you were out. If it landed, the defender could also get you out by tossing it back into the hole and under the larger stick, which was placed by the batter sideways across the opening.

Streets, Laneways, and the Games We Played

Along our traplines we collected loot like nomadic gatherers and would pack our pockets or paper bags with broken tools, wagon or baby carriage wheels from which we might assemble go-carts, dead flashlights, rusted garden implements, beer bottles, pop bottles, milk bottles, and bits of pipe, rubber, metal, or lumber from which we hoped to make some kind of weaponry. One or two of us had a knife. I had one given to me by my uncle Don Marsh one Christmas, which my mother confiscated but which I retrieved from the cabinet where she had hidden it. I spent hours practicing how to throw that knife and have it stick in a garage door or tree trunk. It was not for safety but for spite that Ada took it, for Uncle Don bought that gift for me after an argument I overheard about her never giving the pitiful boy "something" for Christmas. She never gave me a present for my birthday either, and I did not expect one. I never understood, of course, that my "birth" day was not a happy occasion for her.

We learned about weapons from watching cowboy movies and TV shows. One or two of the boys had BB guns and paid no attention to the stricture that they should never be fired in the vicinity of humans. The rest of us tried to fashion bows from plaster lathes and string and to sharpen arrows from branches or dowels. I learned from one inventive boy how to make a blowgun with a peashooter, into which I loaded small flowers fixed with needles lifted from my mother's sewing kit. The regular peashooter itself was ideal for everyday combat. It could easily be hidden, drawn, loaded and fired rapidly. The dried pea ammo was cheap and stung when it struck home. Short of pea projectiles, a boy could always chew up paper and roll it into a tight pellet. One neighbourhood boy loved to light firecrackers and fire them from his peashooter until one day in the rail yard he inhaled instead of blowing and had the ammo explode in his mouth. His teeth were black but intact. I carved model rifles and pistols with my penknife for war games but battles only ended in arguments over who got killed and who was only wounded by the mock firings. The only weapons we bore of real danger were the darts I borrowed from my father's collection and the slingshots that we made from a forked, Y-shaped branch, with strips of inner tube tied to a leather pouch as the launching mechanism. Small stones propelled by this device could break windows, but the deadliest projectiles we used were metal staples. The best boys could fire the slingshots from the hip, just like a gunslinger in the Wild West. We were proud of our arsenal and drew up elaborate fantasies of destruction and conquest of neighbouring lanes. But I was devastated one day when, in the laneway behind Symington Avenue, I struck and injured a bird with a staple. I never shared the pleasure many of the boys had in hurting animals.

Even without our diverse weapons, there were always stones. We knew better than to throw them at each other or at other kids, but there was rarely a target we ignored, from factory windows, signboards, lampposts, garage doors, boxcars and cats and pigeons. In winter, there were even fewer restrictions on throwing snowballs. We might spend hours forming and stacking them for a medieval war from one icy fortress to another. Snowballs gave much greater pleasure than stones, for when they hit, they burst into an icy shrapnel. The greatest kick was to burst out from a laneway between the stores on Davenport Road in a mob as a streetcar passed, plastering the side or back with icy grenades. Some of the boys took a greater risk and threw the snowballs at cars. That seemed more dangerous to me and I usually had run far from the scene by the time the car victim hit the brakes and began the chase.

Almost everything that I could pick up I managed to hurl into space, into backyards, at windows, walls, or fences. Snowballs, tennis balls, Indian rubber balls, miniature footballs, pieces of jagged ice, darts, lances, stones, pen knives, rolled-up newspapers, marbles. I simply did not care. My imagination took flight with the object as it landed in the catcher's mitt, the receivers' hands, the bullseye, the strike zone. At night before I fell asleep, I tossed a miniature football to the ceiling in a spiral, playing out entire football games in my imagination. My arm never got tired. And I never lost.

We knew the yards and garages that we could invade and the ones to avoid. The whole geography of our neighbourhood

Streets, Laneways, and the Games We Played

was shaped and determined by the rails. The railways spawned factories of all kinds throughout the Junction. Within walking distance from Perth Avenue were Canada Wire Mattress, Heintzman and Company piano factory, manufacturers of the Dodge Wood Split, the Pugsley Dingman Company's Comfort Soap works, and the Gurney Foundry, the stove maker, next to the United Church at the corner of Perth and Davenport. The sand stored in huge piles at the foundry was one of our favourite playgrounds as we climbed atop the protective metal roofs above them and leapt into the forgiving sand pits below. I often went to the pits on my own, having been sent out to play, and spent hours climbing and leaping with some jungle fantasy in my mind.

CHAPTER 7

Life in Toronto's Junction

"The streets and laneways of the Junction were a wild and open refuge from the dangers of home and the boredom of school."

JUST BEYOND the far eastern border zone of the Junction, at the defining corner of Lansdowne and Davenport, sits the 60-acre Canada Foundry site, with a now derelict but impressive powerhouse and a smoke stack that was once the second tallest structure in Canada. Along with railway tracks, bridge struts, and fire hydrants, the foundry also made the famous decorative dragons that adorn the Old City Hall. By the 1930s the Foundry was sold to Canadian General Electric and began manufacturing gigantic electrical transformers, which were shipped out on Junction rails on flatbed cars. What is left today of the whole brick complex has been converted to condominiums.

Canada Cycle and Motor (CCM) were the most famous manufacturers in the Junction area, thriving at a time when bicycle riding became popular. The company was the stuff that dreams were made of to our gang, as one or two of us managed to lift a baseball glove through an open window despite tight security. Ada's one job that I remember her holding was at the Canada Packers stock yard on Old Weston Road, which along with nearby Swift's created the foul stench of dead cattle and pigs that blew over our neighbourhood whenever the wind blew added immensely to the combative games, always attended by zealous families. At the north end at St. Clair Avenue was a baseball stadium, where competitive hardball was played. We crawled uncomfortably under the stands, dangling our legs over the beams, swinging our legs over the crosspieces, looking for dropped coins or bits of popcorn or gum. In the early days there was a natural ice cushion and a pond-like pleasure skating rink at the north end of Earlscourt but that was replaced by one of the first outdoor artificial ice rinks in the city. It featured a hockey cushion encircled by a wide pleasure rink. In the winter the park hill in the south by Caledonia was popular for tobogganing, despite the hill's abrupt decline into an iron fence.

Our gang's favourite route for rambling was north along the railway tracks and back alleys to Connolly Street, Rutland, Exeter (where my Uncle Reg and his family lived), Talbot and across St. Clair Avenue to Prospect Cemetery, where they buried dead soldiers, like my grandfather William Marsh, and Harry, one day. We hopped wooden fences, climbed roofs, crawled the alleyways between houses or factories and rummaged among the rusted chairs and tangled weeds until a dog would bark or a guard holler to get the fuck out or get our asses kicked. Always we boys were threatened with that "getting our asses kicked," which when it happened was an unpleasant sickening thud also resonating in the gut. In the hot summer air, the dirt and grit in the lanes parched and blew up in our faces and clogged the tread of our running shoes. In the winter we trod the same routes in the snow and slush with damp socks and frozen toes.

We scurried like rats when we needed to cross the open streets. Always the anticipation of a passing train added excitement and peril and we needed to be vigilant against the railway security guards. When they managed to grab us, we were lectured about the boys who had been killed by trains or who had lost limbs to the iron wheels, but those stories never deterred us. Once or twice, though, there were serious moments of panic when we were on the open rails and could not tell in the dark which tracks a locomotive was riding. Those looming giants hurtling relentlessly over the rails, spewing smoke with spiraling

KNOW IT ALL

power figured greatly in the menacing atmosphere through which we perceived our lives.

We rarely used our given names with each other, going by nicknames: Sag, Wop, Skeez, and my moniker Thief. I was also Marshy, Marshmallow, Swampy and other variations of my last name. I never heard the names Jim or Jimmy from my friends. One time my father heard a boy call me Marshy and he scolded him and told him that I had a name and that he had better use it. I thought it odd as almost everyone called him Moe. I fought hard to earn a better name and attacked anyone who called me Marshmallow for its soft, mushy connotations. At school I hated the name Jimmy. The threat of hearing that name was almost a bigger deterrent from teachers than the strap to me. But nothing humiliated me more than my middle name Harley, which I refused to acknowledge, even to the point of suffering detentions for denying it on school documents.

We boys acted brave, but we did a lot of running when there was danger, particularly from the junkyard dogs. I earned a reputation for being quick and sly and for a while supplied my family and friends with stolen goods. Some of these I lifted from the grocery store where I worked as a stock and delivery boy. Others were grabs through broken windows or dashes through open doors. Inside the candy store or Woolworth's or Kresge's, I stuffed items into my pockets or down my pants. I mastered the quick slip inside the windbreaker, which was useful for magazines and records. We coasted stolen tricycles down by Earlscourt Park and jumped off at the last moment to send them crashing into the curb.

Then I got caught. Ross Morelli took me to a record store on Queen Street and told me that the owner was an easy mark and he quickly skipped out with a number of records under his jacket. It seemed easy and with my heart pounding I tried the same maneuver. The angry owner spotted me and, in a rage, he grabbed my arm and dragged me to the phone to call the police. In terror I bit him on the arm and when he let go I fled into the street and ran and ran in dire panic until I collapsed and vomited, safe but stunned. I was caught stealing one last time after

Louie and I and some other boys broke the seals on a boxcar by the A&P bakery off Laughton Avenue. Stealing from that bakery was an almost nightly occupation of our hungry band. We crawled under the boxcars, avoiding the bleary eyes of the security guards and the headlamps of police patrols, and climbed stealthily up onto the concrete dock where the cardboard cartons were piled, cooling and awaiting storage on the boxcars. The braver boys crept from pile to pile and lifted the carton lids until they found the real prizes: jam doughnuts, chocolate cakes and cherry pies. I was never that patient and once I climbed onto the dock I grabbed at the first carton. It almost always turned out to be tasteless, doughy white bread. We hauled our loot across the soot lane into the Guerney foundry yard and crawled to safety among the piles of scrap metal and broken stoves into the hidden "forts" we had fashioned. We sat cross-legged and scooped up the warm pie fillings with our fingers or stuffed the doughnut's jam openings into our mouths. None of us was well fed at home and we always ate whatever food we stole. We worked together, some keeping watch, others providing diversions, and a vanguard making the lift. We always shared the booty. We were friends who trusted one another and lived for the experiences and the trouble we shared. We all had common enemies in our parents, police, neighbouring gangs, and teachers; we believed that the material world excluded us, except for what we could take.

But breaking the seals on those boxcars was, as we discovered, a more serious crime than the loss of a few baked goods at the bakery. We were a local nuisance, like flies at a picnic, and the guards were determined to catch us. There were numerous close calls on that A&P dock and around those boxcars. One night when I was eleven, a police car arrived suddenly, spewing dirt as it caromed in off Laughton Avenue. Warned by one of the boys, I flew off the dock where I was watching a boy break a seal with a metal rod, scurried under the boxcars and dashed across the lane into the Guerney scrap yard and up onto the roof of the foundry, jumping into the sandpits behind Davenport Church as I had done so often for fun. I dashed recklessly across

Davenport Road to my house on Perth Avenue, breathless with panic. I thought that I was safe, and I fell asleep in relief, but the next day a police cruiser picked me up as I walked to school along Davenport Road. A boy I hardly knew sitting in the back seat of the police car fingered me as one of the thieves—he had been caught in the roundup the night before. It was unbelievable to me, that I was tagged by a snitch, the worst crime in our order of things—worse than murder—but I didn't have the wit to deny my involvement. The boy also identified Louie Justice later that day at school. We were summoned by the police to court on Jarvis Street the next month and Louie, being older, was sentenced to a month in reform school. Strangely, that trip to juvenile court contains one of the few positive memories that I have of Ada. I feared that it was a great opportunity for her to abuse me. While she ridiculed me daily for anything that she perceived to be "smart ass" or "know it all" and wielded the "back of her hand" at my "mouth," she did not criticize me about that day in juvenile court.

I had to be absent from school for the court date. Ada was silent on the streetcar ride to and from the Jarvis Street courthouse, that same courthouse where I went to testify against my father some years later. I was asked to explain myself to the judge and inadvertently made him smile when I told him that I had no idea how the witness fingered me when I did not know him. He commented that I seemed to be a clever boy, perhaps too clever, and he imagined, incorrectly, that I was a good student. He blamed the older boys for corrupting me and dismissed me with a warning to stay out of trouble, an admonition I took to heart. Though at one time I was proud of my nickname Thief, I never stole a thing after that day.

That snitch, however, was unfinished business. After school, I spotted him shooting pucks in his street boots on the ice rink at Connolly Park, now called Wadsworth Park. I approached him rapidly from his side and kicked his feet out from under him. It was a nasty trick I had learned from having it done to me, jamming a boot into the side of the victim's foot and chopping him sidelong to the ice.

Life in Toronto's Junction

The boy fell hard, and I left him bawling, teary faced and grasping his arm. He showed up at school the next day with a cast on his arm, with his furious mother in the principal's office demanding that he tell the principal the name of his assailant. This time he kept quiet. I thought him lucky. Louie, my older, violent friend might have killed him. I was seldom strong enough or big enough—I almost always hung out with older kids— to fend off bullies, but having really tough friends helped with survival. When cornered alone, my tactic was always to escalate into a rage and strike out as hard as I could muster, screaming that my foe might beat me, but at a cost to himself. This deranged demeanor saved me a lot of actual fighting.

There was a kind of honour among thieving friends in the Junction but there were no rules for street fighting. Ross Morelli was the best fighter I knew. He had a brutal bravery that stood up to anyone. In a flash he would grab a handful of shirt or jacket, gain leverage, pull the clothes over the victim's head and then deliver a blow to the nose that brought blood and quick surrender. I had no success with punching. Both times I launched a blow to an opponent's head, once in a hockey fight and once at school, I broke my hand and ended up in a cast, so I tended to wrestle, push, grab and ambush.

Once I fought with a boy all the way home from school, punching, scratching, running away from and then charging one another block after block in turns. He hurt me and knocked me down several times so finally I grabbed him with all my might around his neck in a headlock which he could not escape and which I could not release. I failed to get a promise that if I let him go he would leave me alone, but no matter how hard I squeezed, he would not agree, even as a trick. Finally, his head simply eased out from my numbed arm, but we were both too exhausted to continue. It was never enough to be victorious; the defeated were always out for revenge. Once I soundly beat a boy in the St. Clair movie theatre and resumed my seat. He crept up behind me and smashed his fist into my eye, which soon swelled shut and turned purple. Harry's comment on seeing the black eye was that if he ever found out that the other boy did not have the same black eye, he himself would blacken my other eye. I was blind in that starburst eye for weeks.

Louie Justice was tough, not I felt as Ross was, from raw bravery, but rather from incipient madness. He once beat another kid with his fists for attacking me at a street hockey game. Usually, if Louis showed up to play the other kids ran off rather than play against him. He seemed to show his fury to everyone but me. He even had me come to his house to sleep in his bed overnight. He dropped out of school after his stint in the reform school. Some years later he acquired a gun and fired it into bedroom windows up and down Symington Street until the police arrived. He ended up in the same mental institution, 999 Queen, as Harry.

After John Hunter and I became best friends, we walked every day together to Davenport School. I crossed Davenport Road, walked through the United churchyard and met him in front of his house on Hibernia. We continued to school along Connolly. Though we walked together every day, I don't remember us doing anything together once we reached school. John never played sports, as I did, chasing the soccer ball around the schoolyard, racing, scrapping, skating, playing hockey on the rinks or in the streets, playing marbles, "closies" or "flipsies—the whole competitive maelstrom which was my world. We each had our own friends at school.

The girls at every age loved John, his black hair and dark eyes, and he had a pretty girlfriend by grade 8, long before I could even speak to a girl. Still, no matter what happened at school, we met afterward at the same spot and walked home together at the end of the day. I learned a lot more about the world from John than I did in school. He had boundless storytelling ability and held me captivated as he told me about the latest movie that he had seen with his mother or the latest book on dolphins or whales or science fiction that he read.

I was aware that girls lived in our neighbourhood and sat in our classrooms, but I never played with them. Girls had their own games and their own clubs, the Brownies and the Girl Guides. They seemed to me to have special powers. They could make me blush with a simple dismissive roll of their eyes or sly sarcastic crack. I kept a safe distance when I saw them in the streets skipping, singly or "Double Dutch," in which girls at each end of two long jump ropes spun them in opposite directions with one or more girls jumping simultaneously. I was spellbound by their skill and determination and particularly by the songs they sang.

> *Girl Guide, Girl Guide, dressed in blue,*
> *These are the motions you must do:*
> *Stand at attention, stand at ease,*
> *Bend your elbows, bend your knees.*
> *Salute to the captain, bow to the Queen,*
> *Never turn your back on the Union Jack!*

We boys never sang when we played. I used my sister's rope to jump skip, but soon ran out of breath and the once or twice I tried Double Dutch, I tripped. To me, girls seemed to belong to a different race of being. I vaguely sensed that I might like them to notice me, but I had no sense of attraction or even much curiosity in the early days—I had two sisters. Once in while I would grab one of their bicycles and circle furiously up and down the street, with them chasing me and beating on me with their fists playfully, and me hollering some kind of nonsense about it being an "emergency!" "Let me through!" But then they would run off, ignoring me and ridiculing me.

After we finished grade 6 at Davenport, a few of us were sent to Junior High at Perth Avenue School, an innovation in those days. John and I still walked together to school each day. Now he would wait for me across from my house on Perth Avenue, which neither he, nor any of my friends ever entered. We walked south down Symington, along a laneway parallel to Dupont, past the kosher butcher where they hung the chickens upside down and slit their throats, and down Perth Avenue to school. Those walks to school were a great joy to me, for I lived vicariously through the stories John told. He was pretty much my window on the outside world and my first source of information on how to make gunpowder, how to find the best jam doughnuts and most illuminating of all, how to imagine the mysteries of sex. He was a fount of information on how to fake illness to miss school. His methods never worked for me, as they required a sympathetic mother who might be concerned about the fake temperature (not too high as to cause suspicion) induced by gargling hot water. I was never allowed to miss school, except for the time the whole family was quarantined when my sister Sally and brother John contracted whooping cough. We had an embarrassing sign on the door "Quarantined!"

The streets and laneways of the Junction were a wild and open refuge from the dangers of home and the boredom of school. In all but the coldest weather I fled to freedom whenever I could, running, playing, stealing and living a life with the boys, building confidence, nerve and friendship. Once we formed a band, we were each other's support, free to vent the primal urges of boys, forgetting my mother's hands and my teachers' contempt. Most of the immigrant boys seemed to adapt, move on, pass school and become storekeepers or engineers. John and I managed to work part-time jobs and save enough money to go to university. We alternated semesters, one working and supporting the other in school. While I was at Wilfrid Laurier studying philosophy, John took engineering at crosstown Waterloo University but ended up following his love of animals to become a goat farmer. One of the boys from the neighbourhood joined a crime organization and it was rumoured that he became an "assassin." Another ended up committed to an asylum. I completely lost touch, as we do, with Danny Strandhagen and Jimmy Devlin, no matter how big a role they played in my early life.

CHAPTER 8

Huntsville, Muskoka

"I will show you fear in a handful of dust."

– T.S. Eliot, The Wasteland

Ada and Harry rarely planned outings: the churchgoing, attendance at school concerts, trips to Toronto Island, visits to the Riverdale Zoo, The Canadian National Exhibition or to a beach on Lake Simcoe that even the poorest families in our neighbourhood undertook. So, it was always a shock when my father would impulsively order us into the car and drive us north to Huntsville to visit Ada's reluctant family.

Well back into the mid-nineteenth century my mother's ancestors were born, lived or died in or around the wild, rocky woodland of Muskoka that forms an implacable arc of stone and water north of Toronto. None of these ancestors, back to great-great grandparents, were born in any of the satellite urban areas south of the Shield from Ottawa to Toronto. They were from, got married at, or died in Dorset, Bancroft, Port Carling, Peterborough, Bracebridge, Dwight, and Huntsville. Ada left her dad's subsistence farm outside Huntsville as a teenager, worked as a fruit picker in more prosperous farms to the south, and then as a domestic servant in Orillia. When she was nineteen, she moved south and worked as a waitress in Toronto.

These hurried expeditions north to Ada's family in Huntsville resembled refugee evacuations more than family outings. They would begin with four bleary-eyed kids pried out of bed when the world was dark. Ada, with a mixture of impatience, boredom and resentment, would marshal us into the car: myself, Marian and Sally in the back seat and John, the youngest, in front with her. I jostled my sisters for a window so that I could press my cheek against the cool glass and watch the lights fade in and out of view. My sisters would fall asleep. I never could.

On one of those trips, we stayed outside Huntsville at our grandfather Andrew Jenkins' house in a spot my mother called Beula and his obituary called The Locks. I only met him once or twice. Like grandfather William Marsh he had been a soldier in the First World War. Born in Mount Eagle Valley, Hastings County, Ontario, in 1882, he spent his whole life in Muskoka, working as a part-time farmer, road worker, and lumberman. He was the son of William Jenkins, born in Hastings County in 1839. Andrew often misspelled his own name as "Jinkins," which made his war records hard to find. William listed his "Race or Tribe" as Irish on the 1911 Census, though the name is primarily of Welsh origin. Andrew was the fourth of seven children. His mother Sarah Jane McDonald was born in 1848 in Renfrew County, Ontario. That placed a great grandmother named McDonald on both sides of my family. For some reason my mother told the story that grandfather Jenkins came to Canada as an Irish orphan, but that was not true.

My mother Ada Lillian Jenkins was born in Huntsville in 1924. Her mother, Rose Ann Tryon, was born in Dorset in 1885, the oldest of thirteen children. She died in 1938 after having eleven children, the last of which were Ada and her twin sister Alice. From her photograph my grandmother was a beautiful, slender woman with wide set melancholy eyes and neat blonde hair. I have traced my grandmother Tryon's ancestry back in Canada to the eighteenth century and the name ultimately to Dutch origin.

Grandfather Jenkins volunteered with the 109th (Victoria and Haliburton) Overseas Battalion on March 15, 1916, at age 34. The battalion trained in Lindsay until it reached a strength of

*My maternal grandmother Rose Ann Jenkins (nee Tryon)
after giving birth to eleven children.*

1,050 men, when it was activated. It sailed from Halifax July 23, 1916, on board the *S.S. Olympic* and was dispersed to reinforce other units. Andrew was in France a mere two months and six days when he was injured at Ypres/Passchendaele on October 4th by artillery shrapnel in his left hip and lower back. This was just weeks before the infamous battle of Passchendaele began on October 26, ordered by the bull-headed Field Marshal Sir Douglas Haig. Andrew was perhaps lucky being invalided out before the gruesome battle, in which some 500,000 men were killed or injured, 15,000 of them Canadians.

Grandfather Jenkins was the one person, with the exception of my brother John, for whom I ever saw my mother show or express affection. She proudly displayed his portrait, in his army uniform, in the place of honour on our living room wall, wearing his trench cap and battalion badge. Until some years later when I planted my oil-on-canvas imitations of John Constable or J.W. Turner landscapes on those walls, the only other picture was that of my father in his army uniform, driving some generals and a significant looking woman down a broad street in Ottawa.

Andrew Jenkins was a handsome, amiable man, 5'6" with blue eyes and a full moustache. He told me on our arrival at Huntsville that if I carried a pile of firewood, which had been delivered to the front of the house, and stacked it neatly in the back, he and my father would take me fishing at the lake the next day. It seemed the most romantic prospect of my young life and I spent the rest of the day hauling and piling the firewood at the back of the house. From inside the house I could hear "Aunt" Eunice, whose relationship to my grandfather I could not untangle, playing an organ, mournful tunes that she would repeatedly start and abruptly stop. I imagined myself out on that gleaming lake in a boat, the motor purring in the dewy morn and my father proud as I lifted a fidgeting fish out of the water. Later in life when I did have the opportunity to go fishing, with my Uncle Bob Jenkins at Long Point on Lake Erie, I hated everything about it—the boat, the smell, a bursting bladder, jamming worms on a hook, the hot sun and above all the boredom. Many things in life are happier as we imagine them to be than they turn out to be in reality.

I slept hard that dark country night. I was exhausted from hauling the hundreds of logs. My hands and arms were painfully scratched by bark. When I woke up Harry and my grandfather were gone. Ada gave me a look of amusement at my disappointment that dared reprisal if I questioned her. My betrayal was complete. I had not expected it of my grandfather after his promise. I ran down the driveway to the two-lane highway that crested not far away and then led down to the lift lock and oblong bay on Fairy Lake. I walked until I was worn-out, losing track of space; clearly, they had driven—why had I not heard the car start?

Finally, I spotted them in the distance in a motorboat, the two of them motionless, and no doubt silent, out on the lake. Any child can wonder what role he has been forced to play in an uncertain life; I had no idea of what possible connection I had

Huntsville, Muskoka

Grandfather Andrew Jenkins, age 34, in his Victoria and Haliburton Uniform.

to any of these people or to anyone in the world. In my obsessive avoidance of Ada's fierce hands and insistent sarcasm, I sensed the impossibility that I would ever have any real knowledge of her, of whether she hated just me, or the whole world. It was a recurrent, desperate feeling that made me long for Annie Radford. As for my father, he did not think of me at all. Duped and deceived, I crawled through a wire fence and lay down in a field of spiky grass, staring at the passing clouds.

The other times we went to Huntsville we stayed with Ada's older sister Grace, her husband Lorne Wright and their five children. They lived in a modest house at the north end of town, across a parking lot from a dairy. I always found my cousins on both sides of my family sympathetic—we shared a disaffection with the adult world. Aunt Grace and Uncle Lorne ridiculed we Marsh kids continuously for our city aversions to sun, wasps, outhouses, and mosquitoes. Water came to embody all my fears, the horror and humiliation of a naked cold public bath in the tin tub in the backyard. Most of all, for me, were the terrors of the lakes, the hundreds and thousands of waterways for which Muskoka is world famous. Aunt Grace ruled that children needed to learn to swim. She sent us by bus to a local beach on Fairy Lake. There an unsympathetic instructor dragged me into deeper water as though fear alone would instruct me. But every time I put my head underwater, I was overwhelmed by such fear that my eyes blurred with dizzy nausea and I thrashed uncontrollably. One performance of this resistance was enough to discourage anyone who tried to make me learn to swim over the years. At high school I lay awake the nights before swimming classes in a pale, cold sweat of helplessness. The cold shower before the swim class, naked and exposed, preceded the harsh blue echo of the pool. I would sit on the slick porcelain edge in the shallow end, next to the bulky Ed Markowitch, who was also afraid. Instructed to get into the water, I could not release my grip. The phys-ed instructor Mr. Lobb told me to get to the deep end and shouted at me until I jumped in and thrashed my way to the side of the pool.

One day, furious with me, Mr. Lobb grabbed my arm and hauled me like a hooked fish out of the pool, tearing the side of my leg on a metal grate that covered an underwater light. Though a coward in the water, I confronted him in his office afterwards, blood running down my leg. I told him that he would excuse me from swimming for the rest of the year or I would go straight to the school nurse and show her what he had done to me. This fear of water had clear origins, aside from Ada's waterboarding me in the tub and my father's scrubbing of my feet in scalding water. At Lake Wilcox, ashamed of his son's fear, my father dragged me into deep water and left me there to sink or swim. He was too drunk to retrieve me and after the fright and the panic and the stillness, I woke up on the beach with a stranger over me, pressing on my chest. It only made Harry angrier, that he had almost killed me.

Aunt Grace was strict, but she was resourceful and put big meals on the table. In her house, everyone ate the same food, unlike at our home where there were chops, chips and vegetables for the adults and onions and boiled potatoes for the kids. Aunt Grace insisted without exception that everyone eat a predetermined number of pieces of bread. Uncle Lorne was a wiry, powerful man. My most vivid memory of him was one night after dinner seeing him spring from his chair like a panther and catch a mouse on the fly, crushing the life out of it with his fist. He had no fear of Harry and his drunken aggression, as most other men had. I admired him for being the star dancer and caller at the country square dance hall just outside town.

IN HUNTSVILLE the older boys slept in an unfinished attic, which we reached by climbing a ladder. We shared a couple of old mattresses and blankets and I slept as best I could with the sound of mosquitoes amplified in my ears by the dark and silence of a country night. If by day I was a sissy and a scaredy-cat, at night I talked myself into the respect of my cousins. I cobbled together stories from fragments of movies, TV shows, books and inflations of my own imagination. I revealed a fantasy that had only recently sprung unbidden into my imagination of how I had saved a girl from an attack by thugs at a fairground. A girl as pretty as she would never have paid attention to me, I explained, but she saw that I was brave and when she told her mother of my bravery the two of them took me to bed and cuddled me. I scared myself revealing these stories, but they enraptured my cousins. I punished myself with guilt for having them. I did not then understand, any more than I do now, the origin or meaning of dreams or fantasy or if the shame associated with them is justified. Some bits of my stories were passed along to Aunt Grace who made it clear that she considered me a degenerate boy who had better clean up his language—and his mind. The reprimand only made my cousins more curious. They demanded more stories, but in more hushed tones. I extracted promises from them that they would not repeat them.

I made one frightening trip to Huntsville with Harry alone when I was nine years old. Ada decided that he was too drunk to drive, and she refused to get in the car or to allow the other kids to get in. Her concern did not extend to me, however, and she urged me to go with him. It was not the only time that Harry took me driving at night, me clinging to the dashboard or armrest as he swerved along the streetcar tracks. He was so silent and remote. He rarely spoke to me and so I never knew where we were going; sometimes it was to visit his brother Reg and sometimes grandfather Marsh. Sometimes it was just to a bar, where he drank, leaving me in the car. We were always unwelcome wherever we landed up.

Highway 400, which runs north from Toronto to Huntsville, was two lanes in those days. Harry drove it as hard as he had, I imagined, driven those armoured vehicles and Jeeps in Holland in the war. Much of the time he drove without a license, as he had been arrested for drunken driving more than once and had at least two recent accidents, once re-injuring his shattered leg. That night on the highway we hit the gravel shoulder and swerved more than once, dangerously passing other cars and pulling back at the last moment against the glare of oncoming vehicles. As we get older and precious time evaporates so swiftly, we forget how, for a scared child, perilous minutes never seem to end. The experience was made worse by the acrid smell of tobacco and the mouthfuls of liquor Harry swigged from the open bottle of rye. I had no sense then, as I do now, that Harry was a desperate man, full of pain and self-hatred; he was utterly incapable of expressing a relationship with me that might have brought him some ease and connection with his suffering world. Finally, he spoke as we neared a bend in the road, traveling through one of the towns the highway now bypasses—Barrie, Orillia, Gravenhurst, Bracebridge— and declared that he was just going to drive straight through the curve right through the picture window of a roadside house and "kill all the sons of bitches living there." He laughed as he jerked the car back to the road at the last minute. The only pleasure I am sure that he got from these cruelties was that he knew that they terrified me. I shut my eyes and held a death grip on the door handle.

We stopped at a roadside diner when we reached

Huntsville. Harry usually left me in the car when he stopped at taverns. Like a dog I sometimes had to wait for hours huddled in the back seat. This time he took me in. I must have looked a pathetic sight, for all eyes of the other customers seemed to follow me. The belligerence my father showed had no effect on the men sitting and eating their burgers, but it seemed to garner some sympathy for me, for when my father ordered coffee and a doughnut for himself and nothing for me the waiter brought me a glass of milk. My father glared at him and told him that he would not be paying for it. He tossed some coins on the table and we headed out to see Aunt Grace.

This time, in the middle of the night, with Uncle Lorne not home, my aunt refused to let us in. She shouted at him as he banged on the door that he was drunk and had to leave. Tired, inebriated and frustrated my father spread his coat on a pile of firewood in the yard that backed onto the adjacent dairy. He grabbed my arm and ordered me to lie down beside him. His grip released as he fell asleep, exhaling his pungent breath across my face. I crept over to the house, and knocked lightly. My cousin Bob opened a window and let me in. I could hear my father shouting my name, "Jimmy!" "Get the fuck out here!" I ignored him, joined one of my cousins in bed, and fell into a deep sleep. In the morning I went fearfully to the car, Harry staring straight ahead, leaning on the horn, but nothing was said, and we drove back towards Toronto. Why had we come here? I spent another few hours lying in the back seat while waiting for him to drink and pick a fight in a pub in Barrie.

Harry never stopped fighting when he was drunk. When he heard that our next-door neighbour Mr. Parks had cuffed me for retrieving my rubber ball from his yard, he reached over the verandah, grabbed him by the throat and lifted him off his feet. In a fistfight he knocked my Uncle Don through the second-floor banister and down the stairs, breaking his arm. He and his war buddy Buff Ransom were thrown out of and barred from almost every pub in the city until the Legion was the only place they could not be refused. They fought with air force and navy men, defending the army's pride and with any condescending "Brit" who crossed their paths. When they had no one else to fight, they fought each other.

When Harry was finally fired for drunkenness from his job at the Sunnybrook Hospital, he managed to lose all his severance pay that night after a brawl at the Legion. That terrible night he came home bruised, broke, and bleeding. He raised me from my bed and demanded that I tell him if I thought it was really his friend Buff Ransom who had stolen his money during that fight. It was the typical question, of which he was the master, which had only two wrong answers. If I suggested that it might have been Buff, he would rail at me for disloyalty. If I suggested not, then I was naïve and stupid. What did Ada think, watching this drama? She blamed Buff, but why was Harry asking me? It was like the movement of the knight in chess. I had no way to explain it to him that did not make him angrier. Now I wonder a little, as I could not then for fear, if he was somehow trying to reach out to me. His life was a ruin and he looked for answers from a scared young boy.

In my last trips to Huntsville the Wrights had moved outside the town, farther north on Highway 11. The house was cut into the woods and had an added terror for us city kids. The dreaded outhouse was at the far end of the property, down a path lined with kennels. My uncle Lorne had taken to boarding hunting hounds, which were all on chains that allowed them to reach the path. Now any trip to the foul-smelling outhouse was a trial, particularly for a boy like me with a vivid imagination. I was sure that snakes were coiled in the crap below the outhouse hole, waiting to strike at my testicles when I sat down, or that some fierce rodent would leap up and bite off my penis. Now to that fear was added the hounds who in the night would hear me creeping by to the outhouse and would lunge howling and snapping at my heels. I was so young, but I had already experienced the gateway to hell.

One summer my mother decided that I would go to Huntsville alone, for a summer holiday. It wasn't the first time I had gone off in summer. When I was eight or nine my father's sister, Aunt Jean, talked Ada into sending me to visit her in Hull,

Eel fisherman Uncle Charlie Laroque.

Quebec. She had married a handsome French-Canadian fisherman, Charlie Larocque, who had a house and dock on the Ottawa River. They had no children. I boarded the train at Union Station in Toronto and Aunt Jean picked me up at the station in downtown Ottawa. Despite growing up in the Junction, the very hub of the nation's railways, this was my first train ride. I loved that comforting world with its resolute motion and rhythmic clicking of the wheels. Nothing could stop us, I thought, and our route is certain, laid down in steel. Uncle Charlie was not pleased to see the city kid, and I was immediately bored and anxious. Charlie's specialty, he informed me with his thick French accent, was catching eels. I found their serpentine forms and slimy skin revolting. One day he insisted that I go eel hunting with him. The Ottawa River had flooded that year and the route was studded with half submerged trees and telephone poles. I gasped as Charlie netted the hideous black eels and dropped them squirming into the motorboat. I was so badly bitten that day by swarms of mosquitoes that Aunt Jean had to put me back on the train to Toronto the next day, covered with hives and swollen bites. My complaints convinced Uncle Charlie that I was the sissy that he said I was, and he bade me good riddance. Ada took me to a doctor in Toronto who considered hospitalizing me, but I recovered at home and the "vacation" in Hull was never mentioned again. Many years later, somehow, Charlie tracked me down in our house on Glebe Avenue, Ottawa. He was so taken with my partner Louise's beauty that he stalked her when I was out of town. One night she had to call our friend Manuel to evacuate her and our daughter Rebeccah safely to his place, with Charlie prowling outside our flat. Not long after, I got a phone call from the police that Charlie had died of a heart attack in the Hudson's Bay Company store on Wellington. My phone number was the only one that he had on his person.

Much of my summers in Huntsville were more like child labour camps than vacations, as Aunt Grace and Uncle Lorne put us to work picking blueberries. The best blueberries in the world are found growing wild among the mossy rocks near Gravenhurst. The small, sweet, wild berries lay clustered under bushes or across meadows and we hobbled around on hands and knees filling our canvas bags. Uncle Lorne with the aid of some kind of home-adapted metal device was able scoop them up at alarming rates, but we were never criticized for our smaller take. Vividly I remembered looking not so much for the blueberries as for wild raspberries, which I ate in whatever numbers I could find. I remember one of my cousins was stung in the bum by a bee while bent over picking berries. He leapt, two footed, high in the air, three times, like a hare. At the end of the hot day we were dunked naked into cold baths. Then we helped to clean the berries of stems and leaves. Aunt and Uncle would lay them on blankets and toss them into the air, the detritus blown away in the breeze. One of those summers, my cousins and I helped Great Uncle Rollie build his cabin on a remote lake deep in Algonquin Park. All the lumber, tools, hardware and supplies were loaded on a motorboat and ferried across the lake. The cabin was in a small cove, which offered me new country horrors in the form of voracious leeches and northern water snakes. But great uncle was sympathetic and not hard on me for being weak or lazy. He encouraged me to carry him 2 x 4s or bags of nails. He told me not to pull the leeches off but to wait for him to pour salt on them.

Near the end of summer cousin Bob and I got free and spent some time in downtown Huntsville. This was more like my domain and I persuaded him to hop the fence at the Kellogg estate and steal some ripe apples. We hung out at the locks at Fairy Lake and silently watched the yachts and ferries dock and go.

CHAPTER 9

School Days

*"Education is an admirable thing, but it is well
to remember from time to time
that nothing that is worth knowing can be taught."*

– Oscar Wilde

SOMEHOW, I graduated from Perth after grade 8. Despite the long record of failures and transgressions, my report card informed me that I would be sent to high school at Oakwood "Collegiate." Annie Radford gave me money so that I could join the other graduates in a celebratory trip across Lake Ontario on the cruise ship *Cayuga*. In the 1950s, numerous passenger ships were still carrying tourists across the great lake that formed the southern boundary of the city. We were taught in school that the Mississauga First Nations (called "Indians" in those days, and variously corrected now to Anishinaabe, Haudenosaunee, etc.) gathered in the area around the mouth of the Humber River. Governor John Graves Simcoe chose the harbour and its island barrier because he thought that it would be safe from American attack. He was wrong. In the War of 1812, an American fleet easily landed soldiers and burned down Fort York and much of the town. Despite the massive, ugly rail lines that completely cut the city of Toronto off from its natural treasure, the lake was always in the geographical background of our minds. We could reach it by a walking bridge over the Queensway towards

School Days

*Davenport, later Osler and then
Carleton School, now a police station.*

Sunnyside, or at the mouth of the Humber or downtown under the dismal tunnel by Union Station or by streetcar over the tracks on Bathurst to Lakeshore and Maple Leaf baseball stadium on the Eastern Gap, where the lakers passed. There was Canadian history there in the reconstructed fort, now far from the Lakeshore as the shoreline receded, and in the enclosed bay where the first Canadian international sports hero, Ned Hanlan, learned to row in the harbour. I learned most of the history of Toronto on my own in the libraries. We were rarely taught the history of our country, much less our city, in class. The exception was my favourite schoolbook, *Breastplate and Buckskin*, a lively story of the conquistadors and explorers that was presented to three generations of students, without a hint that these "heroes" destroyed an ancient culture for profit and religion. What did we know? You accept the heroes you are given. Radisson and Champlain seized my imagination.

Since 1907 the *Cayuga* was a part of the life of Toronto and, for many, a cruise across the lake made the summer complete. Leaning over the polished oak rail of that ship in 1954 gave me a feeling of speed and of wonder at the depths and origins of all that water and a sense of the timelessness around it and of the imposing "otherness" of the nation lying beyond us to the south. I do not remember the *Cayuga* arriving at Port Dalhousie or the crew attaching the hawser ropes to the bollards; only the return to Toronto with the massive Royal York Hotel looming over the skyline and Annie waiting for me at the dock. After carrying some 15 million passengers across the lake over the years, the *Cayuga* went to the scrapyard in 1960. By then, everyone was driving the Queen Elizabeth Highway to get to Queenston and Niagara Falls.

I still remember vividly when I was only six, the news of the inferno that destroyed the cruise ship *Noronic* on the docks at the foot of Bay Street shocked the entire city. The heat of that blaze was so intense, the newspapers reported, that it vaporized the water around the hull of the ship. The death toll was 118, with 104 identified as dead and fourteen more who were so incinerated beyond identification that they had to be declared beyond dead, as "missing." That word haunted me. Had their bodies simply evaporated? It was one of the few current events, along with the robbing spree of the notorious Boyd Gang, that I ever heard my mother discuss.

Once again for reasons unknown to me, except perhaps for my random good marks in social studies and English, the system chose John Hunter and me after grade 8 to attend high school at Oakwood Collegiate Institute. In those days a "collegiate," a word used it seems only in Canada after the early twentieth century, meant a secondary school of academic rather than vocational or technical focus.

When Oakwood was opened on St. Clair Avenue in 1911 it was still surrounded by farming fields and woods. By the time I arrived in 1956 the school was the heart of a thriving neighbourhood, surrounded by apartments, houses, restaurants, and shops. At that time the school enrolment of twelve hundred was about double what it is today. I suffered more than the usual forebodings that the outbreak of school invoked: nausea and a compulsion to run away. Fortunately, I had John for company.

S.S. Cayuga carried over 15 million passengers across the lake during its career, including the Prince of Wales, later King Edward VIII. I still recall the sight of the massive Royal York Hotel on the return voyage.

He reminded me that we were likely to encounter a bevy of pretty girls (who would be focussed on him of course).

The tall, gaunt, domineering principal of Oakwood, Vincent Tovell, lectured us from the podium of the first grade 9 assembly that much was expected of us at the collegiate and that little discord would be tolerated. I felt even more out of place than I was at Perth Avenue School and indeed I was little tolerated. Oakwood in those days was filled with well-to-do students from North Toronto and Forrest Hills and my shabby clothes, smart mouth and long hair made me an outcast and an easy target for the principal and teachers. "The problem for working-class children in a middle-class school environment," wrote Basil Bernstein, "is that they have little experience with the elaborated code, so when they get to school, they are instantly alienated from much that goes on there. They don't understand, literally, what teachers are talking about." I managed somehow to persevere. When my sister Sally was later sent to Oakwood, she withdrew after only a few months.

My homeroom teacher in grades 9 and 10 was the determined and feisty Miss Campbell, who taught us both literature and art. I clashed with her from the first day. She subjected me daily to lectures about my attitude and vehemently for my use of the double negative and other grammatical blunders. (I discovered too late for a rejoinder that her favourite poet William Wordsworth wrote some of his greatest poetry in the double negative.) She punished me by detaining me at the end of day so that I could not participate in hockey or football practice, so I had no chance of making either team—though I played pick-up with athletes from both sports. My appearance and smirk annoyed her as much as my attitude, which encouraged me to invent new behaviors to irritate her. I enjoyed contriving deviant meanings for the Shakespeare texts for which she demanded literal explanations. (She labouriously made us read the plays out loud word by word and line by line. Somehow my love of Shakespeare and his wisdom about life's greatest challenges—love, ambition, jealousy, melancholy, pride, etc.—survived this tiresome exegesis.) One day I really angered her. She demanded that I wipe a "sneer" off my face. When I claimed that I really did not have that kind of control over my facial muscles, she flew into my face, noticing that I had a pencil behind my ear. "Take that pencil off your ear!" she screamed at me. Then her rage exploded when she saw that I had a second pencil behind the other ear. "What is this!" she demanded. "My backup," I replied. The enduring smirk and the second pencil got me sent directly to the principal's office.

Principal Vincent Tovell had been a colonel in the Canadian army, and he tried several times to banish my shabby, inappropriate presence from the lofty halls of Oakwood. He was the custodian of the system's secret code. He had a small window installed in the doors of every classroom so that he could spy on student misbehavior. One day I was talking, or not paying attention, or performing some other transgression in Miss Campbell's class. A spying Tovell flung the door open, lurched

School Days

In high school, with the hopeless attempt at an Elvis Presley hairdo and the rebellious white t-shirt.

into the classroom and lifted me out of my seat by the scruff of my shirt. Miss Campbell shouted at him. "This is MY classroom! Put that boy down! You knock when you enter my classroom." Tovell released his grip and I slumped back into my seat. He left the room, closed the door, then knocked politely. Miss Campbell answered amiably, "Come in..." Tovell swung the door open and charged straight to me, grabbed me violently by the arm and carted me off to his office.

Though afraid of Tovell, I calculated that he was no more intimidating than my own father. He was known, literally, to haul boys into his office and cut their long hair. He hated my habit of wearing my shirt collars up and would grab me in the halls and forcefully jam them down my neck. I liked to wear a white tee shirt under my long-sleeved shirts. One day he ripped the outer shirts' buttons and ordered me to remove the tee. He had a particular loathing for blue jeans and specially for cuffs on jeans, which many of us wore to emulate Elvis Presley. He took scissors to my friend John's jean cuffs, but this brought an angry visit from John's mother Elsie. I had no one to protect me, but I warned him not to come near me with his scissors. He was particularly contemptuous of my peculiar hair style, long at the sides, like Elvis, swept back into a ducktail. I tried to comb the hair on top toward the centre and then forward. Annie hated this hairdo as much as Tovell and tried to forbid me to wear it. In truth it was a mess. My hair is so fine that the structure could only be sustained with globs of Brylcreem or Petroleum Jelly, which left my hair stiff, and my forehead dappled with pimples.

Tovell skidded his palm through my hair, shook his hand in disgust and then expelled me. Annie Radford was upset that I had been sent home, but she was intimidated by Tovell and was at a loss to find a way to get me back to school. I sat happily in my room at Norfolk, read books and listened to music, until four or five days into my sentence Tovell phoned and angrily ordered me to get back into his office. I was late for my appointment with him that day and was soaking wet from the rain. Tovell demanded that I go home and change my clothes.

I told him that I had no change of clothes and that I would just have to wear these until they dried.

This news completely unsettled him; he sat silent for the longest time. "Where is your father?" he asked. "In a mental institution," I replied. "He was badly injured in the war." The former army officer stared at me, shaken, leaned over his desk and wrote down the address of a clothing store on Yonge Street. He took $20 out of his wallet, gave it to me and told me to go to that store and buy some decent clothes. When I returned, Mr. Hobbes, the vice-principal, took me into his office. He told me that it was he who had insisted that Tovell bring me back, and that now I needed to behave. I could not stay completely out of trouble. I needed too much attention for that. I imagined that girls were entertained by my wit and defiance.

I EVENTUALLY WON OVER the ferocious Miss Campbell. I continued to take her art class over the next few years. I never had the talent of my friends for drawing; Phil, Jon, and Tony went on to the Ontario College of Art. However, on my own I had developed a deep interest in art history. I read the biographies of Rembrandt, da Vinci, Michelangelo, Vermeer, and other great artists from books I borrowed from the library. I spent hours under the vaulted ceiling of the Central Library on College Street, studying clipping files of reproductions of paintings and sculptures by the great artists. These files could be borrowed on my library card and taken home where I could study and copy them. My friend Tony shared this interest and we took long walks discussing what we had learned.

We walked through some of Toronto's exclusive neighbourhoods, peering through the windows and critiquing paintings on their walls. I talked enthusiastically about my admiration of the heroic works of Michelangelo and defended him against Tony's preference for the exquisite mysteries of Leonardo, whom I foolishly derided for wasting his talent on notebooks and technical schemes. It was never enough for me, though, to know only a few artists or only those from a certain era. I discovered the Impressionists through a book by John Rewald, which I read over and over, running out of renewals at one library and taking it out of another. The book provided a deep appreciation for the work and the personalities of the rebellious artists and was extensively illustrated. I can remember wandering through High Park dreaming of the elusive colours and the shimmering atmosphere of the great Monet and Pissarro landscapes. It led me to an even greater interest in Paul Cezanne, particularly after reading Roger Fry's persuasive book about the painter's "serene and stable art." Studying the lives of painters inspired a magical aura in my mind, that such ordinary men could create such beauty.

My independent studies made it easy for me to excel when Miss Campbell introduced the first high school art history course in Ontario, which she had been instrumental in designing. When it turned out that I achieved the highest mark in the province on the first provincial exam, she had to change her mind about me. She questioned and encouraged me. She helped correct my pronunciations of the names "Velazquez, "Van Rijn" and "Van Gogh." She shared her interpretation, knowingly I thought, of the mysterious smile of the *Mona Lisa*, a result she thought of Leonardo's anatomical studies. When I fell ill with thyroid disease and was in the Western Hospital for an operation, she visited me and brought me an illustrated biography of Michelangelo, which I still own. My English teacher Mrs. Wilson had also taken an interest in me. After reading an essay that I had written, based on my fantasies, she invited me to dinner at her house. She tried to persuade me that my salvation could be found in Christian Science (and gave me an embarrassing lecture on the evils of masturbation). She too came to visit me in the hospital and brought me a beautiful leather-bound book of the poems of John Keats, which I still read.

Despite these random, almost divine interventions on my behalf, five years of Oakwood high school still figure prominently in my nightmares, as re-enactments of alienation, humiliation, embarrassment, and desperation. In the

School Days

My friends Jon McKee (left), who arrived at Oakwood from Northern Ireland in grade 9 or 10, and John Hunter, whom I had known since childhood.

---

first year of high school, my home situation changed dramatically. I was spending the end of August at the Radfords' on Norfolk Street. My mother phoned to tell me that she had finally succeeded in having Harry committed to the asylum on Queen Street and that I should not bother to come back to Perth—I was only there at all because he had insisted on it. It was not the unequivocally happy development that I might have hoped for. Annie reluctantly accepted me, but Charlie was furious.

KNOW IT ALL

Annie's family was divided, with her daughter Jean in particular objecting to me moving in permanently with her parents. Whoever would blame them? I knew that I was an interloper. All I had ever dreamed of was to live with Annie, but now that my childhood was over it seemed an empty and ambiguous situation, no matter how caring she was to me. To my general insecurity and fear I now added guilt to the cocktail with which I had to endure adolescence. Sadly, I was completely unable to express gratitude for what Annie did for me, only anger and resentment, and she grew more and more frustrated with my presence. I was a sullen, unpleasant boy who saw mandatory gratitude as just another penance.

Two surviving report cards from grades 4 and 5 gave a precise characterization of a troublesome boy, who was in the teacher's words "restive" and "distracted." One teacher wrote that "Jimmy asks intelligent questions, but he is restless and inattentive. His desk is in turmoil!" Inside an edgy consciousness I felt shy, nervous and anxious, ashamed of the sexual fantasies I suppressed for fear that they were scripted on my face. I had a hair-trigger temper that I used to save myself from bullies, but which made life very difficult in other circumstances, particularly in classrooms. I had a number of mysterious ailments up to the age of 16, two of which Dr. Braiden (for whom Grace Radford worked) could not apply names to. I had an almost fatal fever for which Annie Radford brought a minister to try to get me to accept Jesus before it was too late. I was in a nauseous swoon and kept mumbling, "Leave me alone!"

When I broke my hand in one of many hot-tempered fights at school, Dr. Braiden put me in a cast and determined from further examination that I had to see a specialist. It was blind luck again from the Radford connection that he was friends with Dr. Sheppard, the outstanding endocrinologist in the city. The tipoff to Dr. Braiden that I had thyroid disease were my eyeballs, which were bulging out of their sockets. One of the disconcerting tests that I was subjected to for years after was for a nurse to screw a metal device against my eyeballs in order to measure the bulging. The determining blood test in those days was Protein-bound iodine (PBI), which measured the concentration of iodine-bound proteins circulating in the bloodstream. I was oddly proud when Dr. Sheppard told me that I had the highest PBI ever measured at the Western Hospital in Toronto. Strange accomplishment. At the age of 16, I had a standing heart rate of over 125 bpm, was eating nonstop but losing weight, had a pronounced tremor in my hands, was incredibly sensitive to heat but could play hockey in the winter without a sweater, had brittle hair and endemic sleeplessness. Most illuminating, the other primary symptoms were the very ones diagnosed by my teachers as failures of my character: nervousness, restlessness, anxiety and irritability, even perhaps the turmoil around my desk!

Unfortunately, the first treatment for hyperthyroidism, the drug Propylthiouracil, was worse than the disease, with side effects of vomiting, rash, and severe headaches. Despite my young age, Dr. Sheppard decided to order surgery to reduce the size of the thyroid. Otherwise, he determined that I would suffer permanent heart damage. I had to remain resting in the hospital for weeks to stabilize my metabolism before the operation. I enjoyed the attention of one of the pretty nurses, whom I taught to play chess on her breaks, but I was caught twice roaming the hospital with my friend Tony. I was warned that the thyroid surgery, necessary to save my life, would be cancelled if I were caught once more out of bed. Despite cutting out ninety percent of the gland, however, the remaining fragment was still producing enough hormone to keep me overactive. The intern who performed the surgery (in the days before Medicare, I was covered by some kind of welfare though not well enough for a proper surgeon) botched it as well by damaging the nerves to my vocal cords.

I was six months without a voice at all—difficult in a school year. I found out later in life that the nerve in my left voice box had been permanently severed. The remaining ten percent of the thyroid was so overactive that it had to be destroyed, this time by radiation. A nurse at the Western Hospital led me into a dark, shielded room. She pointed to a heavy lead container containing the dose of radioactive iodine; a bent straw protruded; reminiscent of Alice in Wonderland, she ordered me to "drink!" when she left the vault. It was the foulest tasting substance I have ever endured. After seeing a CBS television news story about the high incidence of throat cancer from this radiation treatment in the US, I worried about that drink. Dr. Sheppard reassured me that the dosages that he prescribed were far safer than those in the US. Once the thyroid was finally destroyed, I could undergo a more amenable treatment with a thyroid supplement to treat the now hypothyroidism (fatigue, irritability, depression) from which I now would suffer for the rest of my life.

It was not that I did not learn anything in my school years. Far from it. School authorities assumed that all students must learn botany, history, numerous maths, grammar, foreign languages, physics, chemistry, biology, drama, music, art, etc., etc. We even had innovative (for the 1950s) sex education, doled out by our phys-ed teacher Mr. Lobb. Self-aggrandizing, pompous (with endless lies about strangers he had heroically rescued from car crashes and other disasters), racist ("It may suit you to marry a Black person, but what if a Black baby popped up when one of your own children got pregnant!" which only encouraged us more to think him a fool), Mr. Lobb was utterly hopeless in offering any useful counsel to love struck, confused and sexually frustrated males. I composed a song we liked to sing "What to do on your wedding night/Call for Mr. Lobb" with several lewd verses. I chipped in some cash when some classmates arranged for a load of symbolic manure to be dumped on his front lawn. (In another triumphant protest at Oakwood, I joined a group of boys to arrive early one winter day and we stomped out the message "Fuck Tovell" in the snow. Tovell boomed out an order on the loudspeaker system for the grade 10 boys to put on their boots and stomp out the words.)

How any of the prescribed subjects related to the interests or aptitudes of a given student did not matter to the system. We were expected to digest what the school authorities dictated and to answer to them on exams. I had no interest in most of the subjects and almost never did homework, so I scored very poorly in most subjects. Teachers expelled me permanently for bad behavior from Latin and French, so I was never going to get accepted to a "good" university such as University of Toronto, Queen's, or Western, which had requirements for a second language.

CHAPTER 10

Turning the Pages

"In books I have traveled, not only to other worlds, but into my own. I learned who I was and who I wanted to be, what I might aspire to, and what I might dare to dream."

– Anna Quindlen, How Reading Changed My Life

ONCE I LEARNED TO READ, books were more real to me than anything in my life. I found in them a magical power to transport me out of my abusive family into other worlds. Books helped reveal who I might aspire to be and how I might cure my fractured mind. "Life happened," wrote Alberto Manguel (whom I was lucky to meet and share a meal with some twenty years ago), "because I turned the pages."

The astonishing thing to me about the collections of words and pictures in books was that they seemed to be free of adult control or interest. Any book on any shelf was available to anyone who could reach it. Books even had their own institutions: libraries. When I discovered libraries, my greatest thrill was simply to wander freely inside them, to browse, to sit at the heavy tables and most specially to take home whatever pleased me. A library card was a free license to the wider world. No one told us what books to read or when to read them. "The very existence of libraries," wrote T.S. Eliot, "affords the best evidence that we may yet have hope for the future of man." Our city of Toronto in the 1950s and 1960s was full of libraries, one in every neighbourhood it seemed, no matter how poor. By foot or by streetcar I could reach Wychwood Library (on Bathurst Street next door to my friend Tony's apartment), Annette Street Library (which now houses the Junction Archives), High Park Library (founded in 1916 with a grant from Carnegie, on Roncesvalles Avenue), and my favourite, Runnymede Library on Bloor Street West, designed by John Lyle, who also designed Union Station and the Royal Alexandra Theatre. The beauty of the Credit Valley rough stone on the Runnymede Library, its French gables and the impressive red doorway flanked with stone totems only accentuated the treasures inside. I felt that I was entering a mansion when I came through the doors and most of all that I was welcome. The librarians would smile approvingly of this lonely boy. He loved books.

The first book that I remember reading in English class at Oakwood Collegiate was *Prester John,* by John Buchan. I cannot imagine such an Imperialist adventure story being on curricula these days, but in 1958 Toronto was still in the twilight of "Empire." Buchan, 1st Baron Tweedsmuir, was after all a former Governor General of Canada. I found the book confusing and exotic and was swept up in its adventure, not so much through its hero David Crawfurd, whose "heroic" task was to grow into a man and become wealthy, but through the charismatic Zulu leader of the Black rebellion, John Laputa, who had taken the title of the legendary priest-king Prester John. Crawfurd's escape from impossible odds was thrilling, and not unlike that of Churchill's adventure in South Africa in his *My Early Life,* which we also read at Oakwood. Both were something rare: books that could excite a boy with ideas of adventure and bravery.

I developed an early love of Thomas Hardy at Oakwood. He was a pessimist; I suppose I found his fatalism romantic. In grade 10 we read *The Mayor of Casterbridge,* as a morality tale of how a man's bad choices affect his life. In a scene I still find shocking and mystifying, Michael Henchard arrives at a country fair, gets drunk and sells his unhappy wife and girls to one

Richard Newson. Later, on my own, I read *Jude the Obscure* and *Tess of the d'Urbervilles* with the same determined fatalism. My friend Lorna, hearing me praise these novels, joked that in real life I was more "Jude the Pooh" than Jude the Obscure.

In *The Bridge of San Luis Rey,* by novelist Thornton Wilder, I once again used that freedom that is given to us in books to form my own interpretation. Wilder wrote that in 1714, "the finest bridge in all Peru" collapsed and five people plunged to their deaths. While the point of the novel pressed on us by our English teacher was that the Franciscan missionary, Brother Juniper, tracks down the victims' individual stories to prove that their deaths are consistent with God's plan, to me, their power was that they were random misfortunes, like my own.

I did not quite know where to put George Bernard Shaw in the Pantheon of the great writers presented to us. Next to Shakespeare he seemed ordinary. I got mixed messages when we read *Arms and the Man*. Was it farce, ridiculing a romantic girl's ideals, or sympathetic to the harsher realities of war? It was a great eye opener for me when our school class attended the play on stage at the Crest Theatre on Mt. Pleasant Street. Did it make more sense, or did it just seem to be more serious when performed live?

The Grapes of Wrath, by John Steinbeck, was an unusual book to be read in high schools in the 1950s, having been symbolically burned in towns across the United States and banned in the communist Soviet Union as well. All of this added to our excitement and promised to open vistas onto the world that even D.H. Lawrence could not open. I found the book very frustrating to read as the Joad family is bullied and torn apart as they flee the dust bowl. The controversial ending, as Rose of Sharon Joad loses her daughter and offers her breast to a fellow Okie, seemed melodramatic and was lost on me. The best thing about reading *The Grapes of Wrath* was that it led me to read a far more philosophical and engaging book by Steinbeck, *East of Eden,* with its vivid depictions of the devastating consequences of the absence of love.

The educational establishment in Ontario in the 1950s still revered Shakespeare. At Oakwood we studied one play each year: *Twelfth Night, Romeo and Juliet, Antony and Cleopatra, Henry IV Part II, Richard III,* and *Julius Caesar* in my six years at high school. There was so much that I could not understand in the plots and words; yet so much that still penetrated: Malvolio's garters and humiliation, Juliet's reverie, Falstaff's wit, the hubris of the evil Richard seducing Lady Anne, the brilliant manipulation of Marc Anthony, the bravado of Hotspur (one of the first essays I remember writing was "Hotspur, Foil to Prince Hal"). We studied the "Golden Fleece" and "Prometheus" and other Greek myths, Milton's impenetrable "Paradise Lost" (with Miss Campbell hopelessly trying to discourage our fascination with Satan), "Autumn" and other magical poems by John Keats, Wordsworth's "The World is Too Much With Us," and a wide variety of other poetry, some of which we were expected to memorize. I still remember having to memorize, as many others have, before and after, Shelly's

> My name is Ozymandias, King of Kings;
> Look on my Works, ye Mighty, and despair!
> Nothing beside remains. Round the decay
> Of that colossal Wreck, boundless and bare
> The lone and level sands stretch far away.

I usually managed to cram a reading of the assigned texts into the last few nights before an exam and squeeze a pass on my report card.

In my private reading, it was curiosity, not curricula, that picked the books. I found them browsing by subject in the library (the helpful Dewey Decimal system), recommendations from friends and sometimes teachers and from booksellers. With a little enterprise I found a copy of *Lady Chatterley's Lover* in a used book shop on Yonge Street and passed it among the boys, who thrilled to its forbidden sexual content. "His heart melted suddenly, like a drop of fire, and he put out his hand and laid his fingers on her knee." We took turns reading out such descriptions to one another, breathlessly. Her knee!

I learned of the existence of Henry Roth's *Call it Sleep* from my friend Phil Balsam, who himself grew up in the Kensington neighbourhood of Toronto, notoriously hostile to Jews. In Phil's reading he also shared the redemptive love of a devoted mother central to that novel. Phil was always hostile to the idea that I, as a goy, could possibly understand anything about the sufferings of being a Jew. I in turn challenged him with the idea that he could never understand anything about me suffering from the absence of a loving mother. His mother adored him. She questioned me privately about his diet and wellbeing every time she saw me when I was sharing a house with him later on. (They came to Canada bravely as refugees who had escaped the Nazi invasion of Poland, Phil suffering from tuberculosis.) She was never happy about my reports that he ate nothing but TV dinners. In my reading of *Call it Sleep* I focused on the young child, David, who depends on his imagination alone to cope with a hostile world, beginning with his raging, alcoholic father. That I could understand.

I read *I Never Promised You a Rose Garden,* by Joanne Greenberg, at a time when I was convinced that I was mentally ill—I was in fact diagnosed as being "schizoid" by a psychiatrist at the Western Hospital. It was at a time when "madness" was being touted as a means of creativity and rebellion. I was already shaken by reading R.D. Laing's *The Divided Self: An Existential Study in Sanity and Madness* which seemed to describe me perfectly as being estranged from society, having to invent a false self to confront the world. (He was wrong, we now know, about the origins of schizophrenia.) In *Rose Garden* I identified with Deborah's anguish, which apparently started when she was five years old, with the traumas of a very painful operation and the birth of a baby sister. I felt that my distress began with my abduction from a loving home by my cruel, "real mother." The book was a brilliant depiction of what it means to be inside the mind of a mentally ill person who has lost contact with reality. The description of the dark inner world of Deborah's mind—the hallucinations, compelling fantasies and distress—haunted me for years. I clung to the idea that, like Deborah, my fantasy world was the only way to combat an evil and complex reality. It was why Nature provided me with an imagination.

My first introduction to philosophy was Will Durant's *The Story of Philosophy*. As a member of the Book of the Month Club I was the proud owner of Durant's 11-volume The Story of Civilization, which arrived with a free copy of his well-reviewed book on philosophy. (My membership in the Book of the Month Club was chaotic. I never remembered to return the "do not send" card on time and the unwanted books piled up along with the invoices. Resigning seemed impossible and I probably still owe them a fortune.) Durant's introduction to philosophy greatly appealed to me:

> So much of our lives is meaningless...We strive with the chaos about and within, but we should believe that there is something vital and significant in us. We want to understand....We are like Mitya in *The Brothers Karamazov*—one of those who don't want millions, but an answer to their questions.

(I struggled for years to read Dostoevsky's masterpiece.) Durant's book introduced me to Baruch Spinoza, "the noblest and most lovable of the great philosophers," more as a spiritual guide than as someone whom I truly understood. For me, Spinoza definitively refuted the myth of an interventionist God.

The book that influenced my personal life the most was Eric Fromm's *The Art of Loving*. I discovered it when I was eighteen. It was easy for me to sympathize with Fromm's declaration that the problem of human existence is one of separateness, that we are cut off, helpless, full of shame and fear. According to Fromm, love is the only true cure for our separateness. Fromm described how love was the most exhilarating and exciting experience in life, particularly for those who have been isolated without it.

The possibility of love became my strongest impetus for hope, though it led me to a lifetime of often-hopeless longing. I read and reread *The Art of Loving*, highlighting, underlining and annotating, trying to understand love as an "art," as care and respect. "Most people see the problem of love primarily as that of being loved, rather than that of loving, of one's capacity to love," Fromm wrote.

I encountered Paul Tillich's *The Courage to Be* later, when I was studying philosophy at university from a professor (also a priest) who had studied with Tillich. It was a time when, like many sad young men, I contemplated suicide. "The courage to be is the courage to accept oneself, in spite of being unacceptable," Tillich wrote. He gave what I thought was a brilliant interpretation of the anxiety I suffered, that it belonged to existence as such and not to personal neurosis. I accepted his dictum that if we could transform anxiety into fear, our courage could abolish it, but like so many ideas put forward to help us, I struggled to master it.

BY WRITING SOME supplementary exams on failed subjects, I managed to squeeze through grade 13 at Oakwood. (It was a challenge in those days—I ended up with thirteen full credits.) I had spent far more time reading books that interested me and agonizing about love and the girls who stalked my fantasies than I did studying chemistry, Latin, algebra, or trigonometry. Since my lack of a credit in a foreign language discounted me from most universities, I ended up at Waterloo Lutheran (now Wilfrid Laurier), where I managed to deepen my knowledge of Shakespeare, Marx, and Tillich. Mostly, though, I burned the days and nights pursuing Catherine. I met her at a party at her nearby apartment in the first term and was attracted to her feline presence and dark eyes. I had just played a vigorous game of touch football and had torn my pants. She had been watching me, and told me that, if I took the ripped pants off, she would mend them for me. I spent many hours lying with her and kissing her in the woods behind her apartment (to avoid her disapproving roommate Agnes) or in the back seat of my car. She had left behind a child with her parents in Arnprior. One of the verses I wrote to her, in which I tried to express her wild sexual energy, she submitted to the university poetry journal, *Chiaroscuro*. The editors published it with a comment that "No one knows who the elusive poet with the vivid imagination might be." My friend Jon was speechless when I brought Catherine to Toronto and introduced her to him (she vastly exceeded the guinea pig he had given to me as a girlfriend worthy of me). When I took her to see Gordon Lightfoot at the Riverboat Café in Yorkville, she left with the handsome folk singer. I later drove her back in silence to Waterloo and dropped out of university.

Most of what I learned about three of the treasured elements of my life, music, film, and art, took place outside school. "Without music, life would be a mistake," wrote Friedrich Nietzsche. All my early memories are infused with sound, awakening emotions, joy and sadness without explanation. Music penetrated the atmosphere of the hatred and anger of my parents and even engaged them outside their own disheartened lives. Early in my life at Perth, I sat mesmerized, as my father took a harmonica from its leather pouch, put it to his mouth and lost himself playing songs that he had learned while stationed in Germany after the war. He closed his eyes and cupped his hand over the instrument to create a wavering vibrato. One night at a drunken party, I learned the name of the beautiful song that he repeated, as his war buddies sang along in melancholic reverie, "Underneath the lamplight, by the barricks gate." It was "Lilli Marlene," and it opened a vast space inside me, of wonder and otherness, of nostalgia for times that I did not experience, but felt through my father's reverie. It was the only truly emotional connection, be it of loss and longing, which I ever felt with Harry, beyond fear. I would sit cross-legged on the kitchen floor until he finished, tapped the spit from the mouthpiece, and put it back in its pouch without acknowledging me. If it was an expression of the sadness and regret of his life, I somehow understood.

Ada had two escapes from her world of constant frustration and abuse. One was romance magazines (and chocolates) and the other was listening to the radio station from Nashville, Tennessee, the home of the Grand Ole Opry. From Nashville came an endless stream of broken-hearted country tunes, dominated by the particular genius of Hank Williams, doomed by luckless love to be alone, his voice cracked and worn. I assume that Ada learned this melancholy hillbilly music when she was square dancing as a girl in the dance halls of Muskoka. Her favourite song was Hank William's "Your Cheatin' Heart," as perhaps she suspected Harry's many sexual affairs during the war. In retrospect, I doubt that she cared what he did, and her melancholy tapped a deeper spring. I overheard talk between her and her women friends of another young man, from Huntsville, whom she should have married.

Country music was the music Grace Radford's son Don played on the car radio when we went driving past the homes of the young women who had broken his heart. When Ferlin Husky sang "Since you've gone/My heart, my lips, my soul inside/Know the reason why I cry," he sounded like a phantom floating above a celestial orchestra. Don loved that song and others, such as Don Gibson's "O Lonesome Me" and Patsy Cline's "Crazy." Ada's favourite singer was the smooth-voiced, handsome baritone Eddie Arnold. I loved his fake cowboy song "Cattle Call" and his haunting "I'll Hold You in My Heart/Till I Can Hold You in My Arms," which Ada played from a 33 rpm LP, with Eddie's handsome face on the cover.

The first music I remember hearing when staying with Annie at Norfolk were the hymns sung by the hidden choir at St. Anne's Anglican, filling the byzantine dome with solemn harmonies. I was certain that I could pick out Annie's familiar quavering alto. I could see on the faces of the congregation that the music expressed deep, if unexplainable, emotions. At Sunday school we sang "Jesus Loves Me/This I know." At public school we sang "Let the Sun Shine In." (Annie did not play music on the radio. She listened to the feisty political curmudgeon Gordon Sinclair, a loudmouth prejudiced precursor to Don Cherry, and to her favourite show "Helen Trent," that "because a woman is 35, or older, romance in life need not be over." That soap opera

*The Lumitone lamp radio, also called the "Rocket"
owing to its futuristic styling, was my segue
into the world of music.*

---

produced seven thousand episodes without Helen ever consummating a single affair. On special occasions Annie would put on one of the few recordings she owned, a 78 rpm disk of Handel's "Hallelujah Chorus," in which her daughter Grace had sung a part. It was thrilling. "And He shall reign for ever and ever. Hallelujah!"

It was when Annie put the radio that Charlie got as a retirement gift next to my bed on Norfolk that the wider world of music opened up for me. It was a strange, white plastic contraption, a Lumitone lamp radio, with a plastic station dial in its base. Spinning that dial, I first heard the exquisite andante of

Mozart's "Sinfonia Concertante." But then I heard Elvis. There was a station in Toronto, CHUM 1050, that in the mid-1950s brazenly began to broadcast only rock and roll; it revealed one startling revelation after another. The Everly Brothers, "All I have to do is Dream," Fats Domino, "I'm Walkin'," Little Richard "Good Golly Miss Molly," Gene Vincent, "Be Bop a Lula," Chuck Berry, "School Days," and Gerry Lee Lewis, "Whole Lotta Shakin' Goin' On." But then Elvis burst out of that lamp radio! "That's All Right Mama" and "Hound Dog." As Peter Guralnick wrote in his biography about the impact of Elvis, "The world was not prepared for Elvis Presley.... He hit like a Panamerican flash, and the reverberations still linger from the shock of his arrival." I combed my hair in a wave like Elvis, I wiggled my hips, singing "All Shook Up" at the top of my voice in gym class (and was sent straight to the principal's office). As soon as I could scratch some cash together, I started to buy Elvis's records on 45 rpm. My friend John helped me to find a beaten-up old phonograph in one of his uncle's garages. Of all Elvis's hit songs, the one I loved best was "Don't Be Cruel" (to a heart that's true). I sang it to myself constantly with his distinctive stutter. Rock and roll changed everything for that adolescent generation: our own music, hated by our parents (Annie Radford thought that Little Richard was, literally, the devil when she heard him wail "Keep 'a Knockin'" on the radio), its energy, and what we of course did not know, a conduit for the musical creativity of Black culture to seep into our white Perry Como/Pat Boone world. It was truly a companion to our sexual yearnings. Aside from his own sexual peculiarities, of which we were then unaware, the smirk and gyrating hips of Elvis were liberating expressions of our own confused yearnings.

In grades 7 and 8 at Perth Avenue Junior High, a dance was held each noon hour and on Friday evening. In the darkened auditorium, music became the atmosphere of the hidden world, the rising mist around the magic of boys and girls. I never mustered the confidence to ask a girl to dance. I stood in the shadows and listened to the music, mouthed the words and watched the moving bobby socks and pleated skirts. The school DJ played mostly ballads at these dances; among them the entrancing Platters "Tonight while our hearts are aglow/ Oh tell me the words that I'm longing to know." It was one thing to hide in my embarrassment and to suffer the pining of those words, and quite another to be forced to dance in our gym classes. All students were expected to participate in square dancing, which of course entailed putting your hand on a girl's back and holding her hand. The fire that this contact ignited in my blood was unbearable. My only escape was to volunteer to be the guy changing the records. Otherwise, the frustration of my shyness fueled my restlessness well into the night. I blushed so hard that I feared that it would burn the skin off my face and melt my ears down the side of my head. I suppose that this was the consequence of having developed such a powerful fantasy world that it lit up like dry tinder in contact with the flame of the "real" world: a waist, a hand, the exquisite closeness. I was certain that every girl could exactly read my mind with their inquisitorial eyes. The truth that they could not have cared less never occurred to me.

I am grateful, in retrospect, that in those days schools still introduced students to what it is now considered condescending to call "the arts." We were taken by bus to the Art Gallery of Ontario and to the Royal Ontario Museum. Guides introduced us to Renaissance painting, El Greco, Northwest Coast carving and Egyptian mummies. We attended a concert at Massey Hall and heard, of all things, Vaughan Williams' rarely played *Sinfonia Antarctica*, with its cool wind machine evoking the frigid trek of Scott to the South Pole. John and I left spellbound. We never forgot it. Our classes attended live theatre at Hart House and the Crest Theatre and once even travelled to Stratford by bus to see Shakespeare's *Antony and Cleopatra*. Yes, I loved, sang, and watched the girls dance to rock 'n roll, but we were at least exposed to the depth and wonders of much more complex music and arts that, with time and education, we could grow into and which would deepen our musical consciousness.

All music moved me. It seemed like the most unadulterated good thing in life. Only later did I become aware that different genres—rock, popular, jazz, country, and so on—were associated with different social classes, or at least in those days with different generations. I was thunderstruck when the dark-haired Norwegian teacher Miss Knudson, in grade 7, put on a record of the driving rhythms of the first movement of Beethoven's Fifth Symphony, my introduction to "classical" music. It was many years before I rediscovered that experience. I was obsessed with rock and roll. In mid-high school, my friend Tony and I discovered a shop on Yonge Street that sold cheap 45 rpm records that had been discarded from jukeboxes across the city. My collection grew, at five cents a record, and I spent many hours every day listening, memorizing, evaluating. I went to a lumber yard and brought home a collection of plywood and fasteners on the streetcar to construct a rickety stereo cabinet, which held my records, turntable, and speakers. (I stained it a streaky mahogany.) When I visited A&A Records and Sam the Record Man on Yonge Street, I was driven by curiosity to the large classical sections. At A&A the entire second floor was filled with bins of classical music, and jazz. In the days of vinyl LPs, the back covers were a goldmine of information about the works and the performers. I began to attend classical concerts on my own and saw pianist Rudolf Serkin and guitarist Andres Segovia at Eaton's Centre auditorium, violinist Henryk Szeryng and pianist Sviatoslav Richter at Massey Hall. Szeryng played the great Bach *Chaconne*. Moved to tears, I was shocked when he announced that he was not satisfied with his performance and repeated it. That *Chaconne* remains to this day captive in my consciousness for, as Johannes Brahms wrote of it:

> On one stave, for a small instrument, the man writes a whole world of the deepest thoughts and most powerful feelings. If I imagined that I could have created, even conceived the piece, I am quite certain that the excess of excitement and earth-shattering experience would have driven me out of my mind.

With Phil Balsam and Louise.
Phil is a brilliant musician, photographer and the composer of the Muppets TV series "Fraggle Rock."

When I was eighteen, I bought a classical guitar with Phil's guidance and took lessons at the Toronto Conservatory from a teacher, William Trotter, who told me after a few lessons that I would do a "nice job" but that I was obviously "not Segovia." Obviously. Later, I managed to see guitarists Julian Bream and Alexander Lagoya live at the National Arts Centre in Ottawa. When I moved to Ottawa, I took lessons from Dave Johnson, who was a good friend of the great Canadian jazz guitarist Lennie Breau. Dave brought him to Ottawa to give us a lesson in flamenco. In the 1970s Dave told me that one day all music would be recorded in computer code. I thought he was crazy.

KNOW IT ALL

WHEN I BEGAN MY CAREER IN PUBLISHING, I met yet another friend who had a lasting effect on my musical life. Al Hand was a fellow editor at Holt, Rinehart & Winston. He was under deadline fire from editor in chief Dave Harris, so I offered to help him with his projects, after work at his apartment on High Park Avenue. He, in turn, introduced me to his collection of classical music. He had very specific tastes, almost exclusively Brahms and Haydn, and very specific preferences as to who was qualified to conduct each: Klemperer for Brahms and Antal Dorati for Haydn. My devotion to Brahms to this day echoes the thrill I felt first hearing Al's recording of the first piano concerto (which I later heard live in Chicago with Georg Solti conducting). When I asked Al why it took Brahms so long to introduce the piano in the opening movement, he snapped at me "It's the way the man wrote it!" (I had a similar experience many years later after playing a Fernando Sor study for my classical guitar teacher at the Alberta Conservatory; he grabbed the guitar out of my hands and asked abruptly "Do you want to hear what the guy actually wrote!") Al moved into an attic apartment above the music lending library on Avenue Road. Visiting him there, I began to borrow albums from the library that introduced me, to Al's horror, to Gustav Mahler. By the time I got to Bruckner, I was lost to him.

I was never able to share my love of classical music with my other friends, or my partners, until I met Lesya, who introduced me to Bach. My friend Phil Balsam was an accomplished jazz and rock guitarist; he dismissed classical music as being "too predictable." Listening to a Beethoven symphony I was playing, he described the harmonic progressions that were a complete mystery to me. However, it was through Phil, John, Tony, and Jon that I was introduced to the wonders of painting. Three of them attended the Ontario College of Art after high school and all painted in their spare time. (John did not attend OCA but loved to paint. His large black canvas with the word FUCK! in the centre was improved when his Baptist mother insisted that he put a piece of masking tape over the word.) Jon McKee was a brilliant illustrator who published cartoons in the prestigious *Evergreen Review*. We five made frequent trips, crowded together in one car, to Buffalo, New York, where the Albright Knox Gallery displayed brilliant collections of contemporary art. There I learned to love the abstract field paintings of Rothko, Olitski, Frankenthaler, Klein, and others. But I had no interest in or understanding of the Pop Art that absorbed my friends. I had no sympathy for Warhol's blurring of the lines between popular culture and art. My favourite exhibit there was the Room of Mirrors, fashioned by Lucas Samaras. One person at a time was directed inside the glass cube, with brilliant mirrors on all six sides. The dizzying feeling caused by the endless reflections was overwhelming, as though you were standing suspended at the brink of a bottomless pit, as close to sensing infinite space as you can experience.

Whereas there were smatterings of literature, music, and painting in our formal education there was not even a mention of the twentieth-century's lone contribution to a new art form: film. Like every kid in the 1950s and 60s, I attended movie theatres regularly on Friday night or Saturday afternoon. Movies were cheap and often my friend Jimmy Devlin would pay my way. We watched whatever was shown, usually second-rate, dusty westerns, Abbott and Costello comedies, too puerile even for kids, Tarzan or Batman, all followed by hokey science fiction reruns of Flash Gordon, with his toy rocket and twitchy damsel in distress. My first inkling that there might be another world of film was when Annie Radford took me to see a rerun of *Gone with the Wind*. I knew it was more serious because we went by streetcar to the imposing University Theatre on Bloor Street near Bay (destroyed by developmental capitalism in the 1990s). The great theatre certainly added to the sense of gravitas, though I found the four hours of *Gone with the Wind* interminable. The only other movie Annie took me to was *A Man Called Peter* (1955), as part of her campaign to indoctrinate me into Christianity. All I could think about after two hours of boredom was the preacher's wife, played by the green-eyed beauty Jean Peters, my first screen crush.

I did not know where my friend Phil learned about film or why he wanted to share his knowledge with me. He taught me to judge it by its challenges to comfortable beliefs and for its craft. Some of the first films we watched together simply perplexed me, particularly Alain Resnais' *Last Year at Marienbad*, which Phil impatiently explained to me fused past and present into a story of two people who may, or may not, have met in the past. The first film that I remember piercing my imagination was Ingmar Bergman's *The Seventh Seal*, with its stunning imagery of Death playing chess with a Knight, ending with the image of Death leading his latest conquests in a macabre dance. Unlike school, or Annie Radford, or the church, Bergman questioned the meaning of life, of death and the search for God. "I want God to put out his hand, show his face, speak to me. I cry out to him in the dark but there is no one there," the Knight declares to Death. In Bergman festivals at the Towne Theatre on Yonge Street I sat breathless, alone, absorbing *Wild Strawberries, Through a Glass Darkly*, and *Persona*. Bergman's films had an almost unbearable intensity, and for a young man, a riveting, explicit eroticism and sexuality that I had never heard spoken outside D.H. Lawrence.

Phil also introduced me to the alien aesthetic of Japanese film. I first saw the films of Mizoguchi, Kurosawa, and Ozu with him or alone at the International Theatre. Some years ago, on a visit to Toronto, I relived this experience. I rode a streetcar to a surviving movie theatre at Bloor Street and Bathurst to watch Shohei Imamura's *Vengeance is Mine*, which astonished me. When the violent serial killer is captured, his father visits him in jail and tells him of his contempt for a son who killed strangers because he did not have the guts to kill the person he really hated—him. It reminded me so much of my father; of course, he was not a serial killer, but he did express his hatred of his abusive father with revenge on his own wife and children. As for Mizoguchi, in particular, it is only later in life from my film historian friend William Beard that I have come to understand his dark art, and to accept his genius in presenting the ephemeral nature of human suffering. I have watched over and over the great actress Kinuyo Tanaka express the tragic arc of the life of Oharu. In one heartbreaking scene we see her sitting anxiously at a gate. She rises and the camera tracks her despair as she moves, left to right. Mizoguchi transports us to her point of view so we can see what Oharu seeks. It is her son, now a grown man and the chieftain of the clan, whom she is forbidden to see. She manages only a glimpse, a magical summation of her entire life.

I LEFT WATERLOO LUTHERAN UNIVERSITY after two aimless years and attended random courses at the remote wasteland of York University before finishing a degree in history and art history, part time, as I was working at Carleton University in the 1970s and raising my daughter, Rebeccah. There, in evening, summer, and weekend courses, I was able to concentrate, participate in seminars, study, and write. I discovered that I could, with actual work, gain high marks in my papers, exams and final reports. My most enjoyable courses were in art history, which had an advantage of being taken with classes of almost exclusively young women. They were great company on our long, overnight bus rides to American Art Galleries in New York, Philadelphia, Boston, Washington, and Buffalo.

One summer, the art department at Carleton invited Carla Gottlieb, an American art historian and former friend of her fellow Romanian, the sculptor Constantin Brancusi, to deliver a course on modern art. It was the most inspiring educational experience of my life, as we spent three hours a day, five days a week for four weeks gazing at the flood of colours from hundreds of slides of paintings by Cezanne, Matisse, Braque, Kandinsky, Klee, Picasso, and others. Her descriptions of each slide began with a simple explanation of what the colour blotches or lines or suggestive shapes represented. "Vat do vee have here, vee have..." She never avoided the sexual inferences in many of the paintings, sometimes to the consternation of three nuns who had enrolled in the class. "Vee have here a voman's brrreast and zere vee have a guitar." We would meet and talk in the library, where she prepared her lessons. I managed to spend some time outside the classroom with her and at her invitation we visited our National Gallery, then on Elgin

Street, together. She stopped me in front of a painting by Paul-Emile Borduas and exclaimed, "Now you see, Canadians can paint. This man is worthy of a place in world art." Carla presented me with a signed copy of her wonderful book *Window in the Art of Matisse*. She awarded me an A+ for my essay on the magical paintings of Paul Klee. (I was told by a lofty history professor, with whom I used to play chess, that there was no such mark in his department.) I also wrote an essay on the American painter Barnett Newman, theorizing about how his Kabbalistic philosophy inspired the vast blocks of colour and dramatic "zips" in his paintings, which she proudly circulated through the department. Everyone should have the opportunity to have a new and perplexing subject presented by such a persuasive teacher. I was sad when I read her obituary in 2004.

I am certainly not alone in claiming that I acquired most of what I know and value outside school walls. My knowledge came from books and galleries, concert halls and movie theatres and above all from friendship. Yet any reflection on what we think we know reveals that it is fragmentary and full of doubt. In his thoughtful novel *Unnecessary Woman*, Rabih Alameddine writes on his character's behalf: "Giants of literature, philosophy, and the arts have influenced my life, but what have I done with this life? I remain a speck in a tumultuous universe that has little concern for me. I am no more than dust, a mote—dust to dust."

CHAPTER 11

It's a Fucking Miracle, James

The so-called unity of consciousness is an illusion...
we like to think that we are one but we are not.

– Carl Jung

As A YOUNG BOY, I looked through a persistent frown onto the outer world. Suspicion, fear, and defensiveness screened my perceptions. When I approached adults to speak or act it was only in anger or retreat. The humiliations that I felt from a father who dragged me out of bed in the middle of the night to ridicule me and to compulsively wash my feet, to torment me with unanswerable questions, to force me to drop my pants in front of strangers to explain what "my pecker" was for, and from a mother who mocked me for thinking that I had any right to be alive in her presence, left me scrambling for any sense of self-worth. I was so withdrawn and sleep deprived and had such constant physical pain that it was a marvel that I managed to move from grade to grade in school—decayed teeth, blistered feet, burns, bruises, frostbite, infected ears, anemia, black eyes, and one burning skin rash after another. My mother acknowledged none of these afflictions. Once I stepped on a nail that penetrated through my running shoe and deep into my foot. Ada ignored my whimpering that night until my father came and poured iodine on the wound and wrapped it in gauze; Ada watched scornfully and hectored me about being more careful where I stepped. I fell asleep that night with the uncanny presence of my father near me, like the guarding soldier he had been in his best life.

The adults around us did everything in their powers to make us afraid, not only of them, but of the world around us. The constant talk about ghosts made the hairs on my body rise to detect their eerie motion above and through me. There were endless explanations of the retribution that would descend on us from God, or school or the police, or gangs that seemed to roam ceaselessly, like pirate spirits, through the wrecks looking for you. Water would bring forth the stories of all the children who drowned, with staring eyes and weeds and slugs in their mouths. How often did I hear the apocryphal story about the British Grenadiers who fell through the ice in the pond in High Park and sank under the weight of their muskets and boots to leave their bones at the bottom for all eternity? Was this story repeated because, somehow, they deserved their fate?

Fire and gas threatened every home. Seeing a neighbour two doors down on Perth Avenue carried out on a stretcher, dead from gassing himself in his oven, added to the consternation that you could kill yourself as well as others with a kitchen appliance. For those of us in Toronto's Railway Junction there were descriptions of the gruesome losses of arms, legs, even heads cut off by a flying freight train so relentless that it could not, or would not, stop for any reason, least of all to save a careless trespasser. At school we stood in line, crept forward, bared our left arm and watched a nurse stab us with a needle to ward against disease, another mysterious unseen force that might destroy us. The same apparition in a crisp white hat would instruct the boys to drop their pants and place her fingers under the boys' testicles to test for hernias, pitilessly slapping any errant erection.

I was born with three hernias; during the Second World War I wore a device to contain them that, because there was no protective rubber available, made me cry incessantly and scarred my hips for life. All the terrible lurking diseases seemed to us to bear the names of monsters: diphtheria, tuberculosis, whooping cough, and most dreaded of all, polio—which would cripple you for life, or worse, entomb you in an iron lung.

When in grade 8 our music teacher, the pretty, young, black-haired Norwegian Miss Knutson, asked me a question, I could not respond except in a mumble with my chin down on my chest. I shook when she approached me smiling; she blew a tuner near my ear, saying, "Jimmy, sing the note you hear." I heard it in my mind, but I could not puff an audible sound. As a result I failed to qualify for further music instruction and never had the opportunity to learn an instrument or to sing in a choir. She assumed that I had no music in me. Yet I was profoundly influenced for life when she played us the first movement of Beethoven's *Symphony No. 5* on a vinyl disk in front of the class. I memorized lyrics and sang songs to myself constantly in my inner world and outside walking in the laneways or skating on the ice. When I was seventeen, I was singing Jim Reeves' "Put Your Sweet Lips a Little Closer to the Phone" in the classrooms as I worked alone as a part-time janitor, singing at the top of my lungs, at Wychwood School on Bathurst Street. A young teacher startled me and told me that I sang beautifully. Rashly, I asked her if she would go to a hockey game with me and I have somehow blocked the memory of her answer.

My shyness and fear abated when I played sports, evaporating in a raw competitiveness. I could play hockey well in pick-up games even against league players, but I had difficulty negotiating the process of persuading a coach to let me be part of a team. I served so many detentions that I could not attend after-school practices. When I did manage to join an organized team for school or church I was always being told by coaches and referees to "calm down." I could not distinguish between competitiveness and anger. In one game I played for Oakwood at the High Park rink, an opponent broke my nose with his stick. The coach could not stop the bleeding or prevent me from returning to play. Finally, as the blood dripped on the ice, the referee had to stop the game and tell the coach to drive me home. Ada did not take me to a doctor, as he asked her to, and my nose remains deviated to this day.

I erupted into a fiery blush whenever attention was directed to me at school. Girls naturally were repelled by such insecurity, not to mention the ragged, second-hand clothes that I wore. The more I longed for girls to pay attention to me, the more I was shunned. By the end of high school, I had cultivated a defensive coolness of fake indifference, but I was trapped in a fantasy world that drifted further and further away from reality and deeper and deeper into violence and revenge. The shame that I felt for these fantasies added a fresh level of despair in my dealings with the outside world. I was sure that the mask I had formed was transparent and that anyone who looked directly at me could see right through to those scenes played out in my imagination. I never shared this inner life with anyone; it was more palpable than any random connections in the outside world with actual girls, boys, or adults.

In late high school, after my thyroid operation, the empathetic endocrinologist Doctor Sheppard was also concerned about my state of mind and referred me to the psychiatric clinic. There, in a dark basement office of the Western Hospital, a young therapist diagnosed me as "schizoid." So, this is how the world would see me if I revealed my secret life? There was even a technical term for it. With my paternal grandmother's and my father's committals to "insane asylums" with schizophrenia, I feared that I was next. I never returned to that therapist; I worried that he might summon the faceless authorities to lock me up. I crawled deeper into my solitary prison. It was not that I had no interest in engaging in social relationships, as the diagnosis said, but more that I simply could not. It helped that I somehow became friends with Lorna Macewan, who arrived mid-term at Oakwood Collegiate from the private school Havergal. She quickly became the girlfriend of my Irish friend Jon McKee, so I got to know her casually at gatherings and walks. She was so kind that I felt comfortable with her to the point that McKee told me to "leave Lorna alone and get your own fucking girlfriend." He embarrassed me by buying me a guinea pig as my "first girlfriend." Lorna was heartbroken when Jon broke up with her and we spent time together every week, talking, driving, and, of course discussing Jon. She aspired to be a model—there are photographs of her in the Getty Archives. She was intelligent, charming and affectionate, and had beautiful hands. She wrote in a florid script with decorative capitals and hearts as dots over the "i's." Our favourite place to walk was in High Park. When we visited the park zoo, she would kiss the llamas' soft lips through the wire fence. I could not for the life of me understand why Jon rejected her. Abandoned by her journalist father, she was suspended in a fairy world and chided me gently for my pessimism and love at that time for Thomas Hardy. Lorna trained me gently to buy her appropriate gifts for Christmas or birthdays. Her presents to me were always books: Saint-Exupéry, Wordsworth, Gibran. I bought her a hand-cranked, wooden coffee grinder. I still own the copy of *Winnie the Pooh* Lorna gave to me, signed to "Jude the Pooh." I smiled every time I opened it later to read it to my daughter.

I did not fall in love with Lorna, despite her beauty, attention, and perhaps even love. By grade 13, I had focused my fantasies on a classmate, Connie Weeks, a tall, beautiful girl with golden hair, blue eyes, a curious smile, and slender legs. She was one of only a few girls in our class, so she was desired by every boy. She was also the cleverest student in the school. I simply could not muster the courage to speak to her. She sensed my interest, I am sure, as one day she descended on me in the hall and blurted, "You like poetry? Spice is nice, but liquor is quicker." I was frozen, wide-eyed and speechless. I despaired that she would disappear from my life at the end of the school year as she had won scholarships to several universities.

I don't remember how I managed to get Connie's phone number. Did I ask her? Did I ask her friend Leith? More likely I found it in the phone book. I rang it a dozen times, hanging up in a sweat before she could answer. I sat behind her in English class and shyly passed notes to her with fragments of verse, which she accepted without comment (a common theme in my life). Late in the year, the University of Toronto held a research project at Oakwood to determine the preconceptions that determined teachers' marks. A professor assigned a lengthy essay to

KNOW IT ALL

all the grade 13 students. When the essays were submitted, our names were coded and only revealed after a group of university professors read and marked them. We chose our own topics. I wrote about how curiosity about love was completely ignored by education in our schools. When our English teacher returned my paper, she threw it on my desk, muttering that some stupid professor had given me a 98, the highest mark in the school. Connie took note and turned around and looked straight at me quizzically. Some days later, my friend John was walking behind Connie in the school hall and heard her say to her friend Leith, "You know, Jim writes very well, and he is actually quite smart." Shortly afterward, she approached me and handed me a note. It read, simply, "When?"

Spurred on by John, who was always supportive of me in my distresses with girls, almost on the last day of school term, in desperation, I finally let the phone ring long enough until she answered. I said it was Jim. "Whatever took you so long!" she said with a sigh.

When I achieved the longed-for date to be with Connie, I was awkward and insecure. I ambitiously invited her to the O'Keefe Centre to see a performance by Harry Belafonte and Miriam Makeba, full of gay Caribbean costumes, Harry's rhythmic "Matilda," Calypso drums and Miriam's percussive clicks. I took a streetcar up Old Weston Road and gave her parents a framed oil painting—a murky copy of John Constable's *The Hay Wain*. On the car ride together down Old Weston Road, Connie presented me with a written list of topics that she thought I might like to discuss, from labour relations to the war in Vietnam. It was flattering, but I always seemed to know less than people thought I did. It was so hard for me to sit close to her and to respond to her earnestness. She was too beautiful for me to look her in the eye.

I invited Connie to take a walk with me through High Park one Saturday afternoon, down through the marshy paths I knew from walking with Lorna on the approach to Grenadier Pond. Around me floated the atmosphere of earlier times, in spring, when I wandered alone in the magical park, dreaming of the daubs the impressionist would make of the leaves and the sky. Connie broke the awkward silence by telling me firmly that I should stop trying to impress her and to simply be "myself." Despite receiving the best advice any girl ever gave me, I dissolved in embarrassment and never saw her again. I had no confidence that there was a "self" for me to show, much less that shy poet I had portrayed. She agreed in one last phone conversation that she would see me. When I arrived at her door, her mother told me sympathetically that Connie must have forgotten and had left with another boy. I looked through the doorway into the living room and saw the landscape painting that I had given Connie on our first date, hanging on the wall. The last I heard about her was that she had dropped out of University of Toronto after only her first term, despite her prestigious scholarship.

Recently, I chanced upon an obituary of Connie's beautiful friend Leith and it triggered memories of all those girls, their sparkle and energy, and their refusals to be fooled or impressed by me. I walked past the houses where they lived, the lanes where they walked and wondered endlessly about who they favoured and who they kissed. I changed my bus routes to Oakwood one year simply to chance upon an Italian girl in my class named Claudia, though when I did finally encounter her, I passed in silence. If only things had turned out differently, I imagined, if only I had courage or confidence or a stronger sense of a self, I might have said, "What bad timing; if only we had met years sooner or years later." Another pretty girl who I used to walk home along St. Clair from Oakwood next to a school where I worked every day as a janitor, invited me into her house and sweetly waited out my embarrassed silence. She put on a pop record called "Go Jimmy Go!" It is heartbreaking to remember the line she sang to me from that song: "You better start talking if you want me to be your girl." Another time I visited her after I had played tennis nearby on an extremely hot day. I sat on her piano bench and talked to her but when I got up to leave, my sweat had melted the varnish and the bottom of my shorts ripped off and stuck to the wood. We rarely met again that she did not burst into laughter. When I later went to university in Waterloo, I would stop by her place on a Sunday before the drive back down the 401. She always had prepared butter tarts and oatmeal cookies for me. In 1961 I took her in my car to the Mariposa Folk Festival near Orillia. We were supposedly going to spend the night together there in sleeping bags, which caused me intense anxiety. She left me when the evening concert began and partied with a group of drunken guys. When I found her the next morning she had been abandoned and was dishevelled and still drunk. I helped her to the car and drove her home in silence.

I DON'T REMEMBER how I found what turned out to be the greatest influence on my struggling mind: the psychiatrist Dr. Alexander Szatmari. It may have been a referral from the Western Hospital, where I had been declared "schizoid," or from my family doctor who had prescribed various mood depressing drugs for me. I do remember taking the St. Clair streetcar to his office in an old brick house at Parkwood Avenue. He was on the second floor with a large window behind his desk, overlooking St. Clair and the Spadina Reservoir. The most impressive thing about his office, aside from the stacks of patient files on his desk and his large, handsome, silver-topped head, was an exotic aquarium, filled with glittering tropical fish. Dr. Szatmari had graduated from Franz Joseph University of Kolozsvár, Hungary, in 1931. He later told me a story about escaping from the German soldiers when they invaded Hungary, and his heartbreak and guilt that he left behind the girl he loved as he climbed aboard a moving train. We talked about never lying to one another and so I believed him.

In the first, tense minutes sitting cross-armed before him, I struggled to find words. He asked me why I was seeking help and I listed symptoms and concerns: anxiety, fear, and anger among them. I told him that I could not abide authority figures, was in constant trouble at school and worst of all, I could not find love. When I told him the story of my "childhood," I recited it in a brave monotone. The first trauma when at age 3 the loving woman who had rescued me from the orphanage told me that I could not call her mommy anymore because my "real" mommy was coming to get me, the ritual scalding of my feet by my father, the sexual humiliations. Dr. Szatmari told me,

> Mental sickness can be used as an escape, and making a narrative of it is also a way to try to obtain love and attention.... Now I want you to repeat exactly what you told me, and this time I want you to speak it from your heart.

I had always prided myself that I never cried. This time, I spoke slowly, and I heard the echo of my own words; they unearthed sobs from deep within my chest. The long silence was shattered by a massive crash of thunder which blackened the lights. We sat across from one another in the dark, except for the eerie green glow of the aquarium. "It's a fucking miracle James," he said, "a miracle that brought you here."

Because he had a profound influence on my life, I recommended Dr. Szatmari to many of my troubled friends, but he never worked out for them. A friend of Rollo May and of Eric Berne, author of *Games People Play*, Szatmari detested patients whom he felt simply came to "display" their impressive mental illnesses. He quickly dismissed those who could not make an honest attempt to discard the advantages they gained by being ill. In our fourth or fifth session, when I was describing how my father, Harry, came home drunk in the middle of the night and raised me out of bed and made me wash my feet in scalding water, scrubbing them compulsively, he asked me my father's name. In shock he told me, by blind coincidence, that he was the psychiatrist who had signed the papers to commit my father to the 999 Queen Street mental hospital. He told me that Harry's brain fluid was saturated with alcohol and that he had diagnosed him with *dementia praecox*, another term for schizophrenia. Between the lightning bolt and the bizarre coincidence, a bond was formed between us, the first that I had ever been able to form with a man. I told him that I was awakened every night by a nightmare in which I was plummeting in a falling elevator. He paused and asked me what my father did for a living and I heard myself admit that he was an elevator operator. He insisted that I come twice a week and later put me in group therapy as well, something that I vehemently resisted. Most of the patients in the group resented me for being Dr. Szatmari's "pet."

Dr. Szatmari specialized in treating Jews who had survived concentration camps and non-English-speaking immigrants who suffered alienation. He likened my childhood traumas to the estrangement of those patients and the social rejection that they experienced. I have always believed that meeting Dr. Szatmari was a turning point in my mental life, but it is difficult to sort out just what happened. For me the memories of my mother's rejections, my father's violence and the poverty of our lives continued to erupt in fragments, as though the events were happening in the present. What component did they comprise of my mind and sense of self? When we began group therapy, we were asked to sum up our goal in one word and write it in chalk on the blackboard. I wrote the word "One," by which I suppose I meant the integration of my memories and dreams into a sense of an undivided present self. It was not well received by the other patients.

When I hear today that the vast majority of psychiatrists believe that talk therapy is useless, that they listen impassively to unhappy patients for ten minutes before writing a prescription, I wonder what happened to me. One of the powerful things I believed that Dr. Szatmari did for me was to sort out the anger and the hatred that I felt for my mother, who had snatched me from a woman who loved me and then punished me with her own sarcastic indifference. In group therapy, Szatmari paired me with an older woman whom he regarded as a destructive mother. I symbolically "killed" her by plunging a letter opener into a pillow in the centre of a circle our group had formed. A beautiful, troubled girl awkwardly poured out her love of Szatmari in front of us all. Despite his explanation of her behavior as "transference," I felt that there was a deeper connection in that girl's mind. When she never reappeared in our group, I asked about her and heard that she had killed herself. Group therapy distilled a lifetime's anguish among strangers into two-hour fragments, a perfect metaphor for our social lives.

My aggressive impulses directed at my mother, infantile in Szatmari's terminology, raged in nightly destructive fantasies, which in turn brought a fierce sense of guilt that embarrassed and humiliated me. Szatmari likened these imaginings to "the world destruction fantasy of a schizophrenic." To this day almost every night I dream of being lost in the ruins of a destroyed world, with burned-out buildings, ripped-up roads, haunted homes, sinking ships, blazing aircraft, the beautiful girls I longed for turning their backs on me, walking away. In every social situation I shook with the shame I felt in concealing these fantasies and dreams. They could never be revealed.

Dr. Szatmari finally let me go. "Endure your nightmares and tolerate your fantasies," he told me. I owed him a fortune in unpaid bills but he never asked for it. He told me that he was certain that someday I would accomplish something noteworthy, that he would read about me in the newspaper, and that most importantly, that soon I would fall in love. I believe that the actual relationship we developed, the respect we showed for each other, was the most transformative power of his therapy. He died in 1988 and never knew that I had fallen in love. Perhaps he read in the press that I had done something significant, as he had predicted that I would, in creating a national encyclopedia and receiving the Order of Canada. We had connected across the abyss, in a storm, and my life would never be the same.

CHAPTER 12

Unity in Diversity: A Centennial History for Canada

"Editors are very fallible people, all of them. Don't put too much trust in them."

– Max Perkins

I WORKED PART-TIME JOBS pretty much since I was ten years old, when I had my first paper route, delivering and collecting for the *Toronto Evening Telegram*. That was a lonely job, hauling 110 papers and distributing them over ten blocks. I never quite mastered the folding of the papers into thirds so that I could spin them onto a front porch without them flying open. On one delivery day, October 15, 1954, it was already raining heavily when I started my route. I persevered, head down, wind driving my hair, as the mounting downpour flooded the streets. Drenched and cold, I struggled home and was greeted at the front door by my Uncle Don who enquired: "Don't you know that there is a bloody hurricane out there?" It was named Hazel. It was the worst storm in Toronto's history. The cascading Humber River ripped entire homes from their foundations, sweeping them downstream, killing thirty people on a single street, Raymore Drive.

Much better were the summer stints as an electrician's "helper" at the Ontario Legislative Assembly buildings. Charlie Radford was the chief electrician there for years and got me a summer job with his successor. I learned to haul wires, hand tools to the tradesmen, run errands and each year to do more and more of the wiring and pipe bending. I got to wear a sexy (I thought) leather holster with dangling wire cutters and pliers. The Robertson, Phillips, and slot screwdrivers poked confidently from their sleeves. I answered the calls of pretty secretaries, whose floor plugs had gone dead or whose fluorescent lights were flickering. It was physical work, and I was proud of my biceps, inflated from holding heavy fixtures aloft. The "helper" (I was never an apprentice) was given the unpleasant jobs of crawling into the tightest spots or climbing the highest ladders. Some of the men I worked with were masters at extending the simplest jobs; they spent much of the workday playing euchre or drinking in the many hidden rooms or under the spectacular wooden vaults above the Legislative chamber. On one job the electrician sent me out under the roof of the western portico of the Legislative Building. I had to crawl like an inchworm, barely breathing, towards the faulty fixture. I confused the wires, felt a paralyzing jolt up my arm, and banged my head on the crossbeam. When I regained consciousness, all I could make out through the dizziness was the electrician yelling from the ground forty feet below: "What the hell are you doing?" I think of that dazed moment every time I pass that portico northward up University Avenue.

I spent the summer lunch hours and coffee breaks out in Queen's Park, reading Thomas Hardy and Will Durant. I got a reputation among the electricians as a bookworm. "Leave him alone," my defender Johnny, an ardent Shriner, would say, "He learns from books." Whenever I saw Johnny, he would look at me and whisper, "Whoooo...books..."

One summer, a senior bureaucrat in the Ontario government staff instructed the electrical department not to hire me as they had over the past few years. Instead, he put his son in my place—a spoiled, lazy boy, my friends later told me. I dropped off a resumé at a number of electrical companies and had a positive reply from the modestly named Adequate Electric, a small firm on north Yonge Street. I started the next day as the helper for a German immigrant electrician, Werner, who apparently could not keep a helper more than a few days. Werner worked me harder than anyone in my life. He was proud, he declared to me, of his trade and his work ethic. He bragged that he could wire a new house in half the time as lazy, complacent Canadian electricians.

We headed out at 8 a.m., broke briefly for coffee mid-morning and afternoon and took thirty minutes for lunch. He was compulsively well organized, so we never stopped: drilling holes in the crossbeams above our heads, yanking the wires through, installing plugs on our knees, dozens of light switches, and high-hanging chandeliers. I would tread breathlessly through these activities, fetching wires, electrical boxes, fixtures, screws, tools, and ladders. At day's end I particularly hated coiling and cleaning lengthy and filthy extension cords strewn across the site. When I returned home to Norfolk at the end of day that summer, I could barely lift a fork to eat dinner before falling into a deep sleep that left me wondering who I was when I awoke the next morning.

Werner's wife told him that his van was a mess and that he should fire me. But, he told me, he would not because he liked to talk to me. I was amazed about his life in the Wehrmacht and his capture and survival in a Russian prison camp. He claimed that he was never a Nazi but acknowledged that he never disavowed them. We argued vehemently about his anti-Semitism, especially when we took work in the garment factories down Spadina Avenue, where he declared that the hated Jews exploited immigrant workers so that they could afford their mansions in Forest Hill (where we also worked installing lights over expensive paintings).

I contested his warrior attitude about the superior German army by telling him of my father's regiment's victories in Holland. I found out at the end of the summer that, while I was paid a fixed wage each day, no matter how many hours I worked, Werner was making major bonuses from the speed with which we finished the work. He never shared any of that with me. I was so relieved to get my old leisurely job back the next summer at the Legislative Building.

My career in publishing began by pure chance. Grace Radford told the president of Holt, Rinehart & Winston, Mike Flood (he would send out furious memos if he heard staff drop the Winston—he started his career as a Bible and dictionary salesman with Winston) that I was smart and bookish and that I needed a summer job. Grace gave him weekly shots for his diabetes, and there was talk of marriage after his wife died. Mike interviewed me, asking mainly about Grace, gave me a job, led me to the second floor and presented me to the editor in chief, Dave Harris. I quickly learned that the two men hated one another, and Harris easily transferred that animosity to me. "You're here because that son of a bitch hired you," were his welcoming words to me, "so I guess that I have to find a place for you." He stuck me in a remote corner of his editorial domain in a two-storey building on a side street off the Queen Elizabeth Highway near Royal York Road. He dumped a pile of "galley" proofs of a new dictionary on my desk. "Proofread these," he commanded.

When I started in publishing in 1966, most of the editors I met were ex-teachers, either those who hated teaching, or had failed at it. The idea was that because they had been in the proximity of students, they must be able to edit textbooks. One or two were aspiring writers. Grace Radford got me a job by passing on my hazy claims about literary ambitions. My love of books started my career, if not my knowledge of books. At school I scored well on grammar, but I was a poor speller. I had read a lot of books but had no idea how they were created or edited. I had never seen galley or page proofs before. I had no inkling of what to do and when I approached the other editors for help, they pointed me in the direction of the esteemed lexicographer Thomas Paikaday. He explained that the company was producing a new dictionary and that he had decided to convert the pronunciation guides from whatever system he had begun with to the international phonetic system. Thomas was a kind, considerate man. I often saw him meditating cross-legged under his desk when I arrived to bother him with questions. Sometimes he would stay put and answer me from under his desk in a gentle voice. Day after day I sat writing phonetic codes, backward letters and shwas, in a strange herald of things to come. That's when I met Peter West, an ex-teacher, who was also working on the dictionary.

Peter and I became fast friends despite our difference in years—Dave Harris hated him as well. He was not a "failed teacher or aspiring writer," he told me, but a lover of language. He was born Cockney in London and joined the British Merchant Marine as a boy, travelling the world with a compendium of Shakespeare's plays, much of which he had committed to memory. His deep knowledge of words was self-taught, and we spent hours discussing meanings and reading poetry. He shared with me his poems to imaginary lovers. I read some of my own verse to him, during which he remained politely silent—a predictable occurrence in my writing life. When I did present some romantic verses to girls, they loved, it seemed, to revise and edit them, and particularly to correct the spelling. (I always put two "d's" in "shadow" my friend Lorna told me, without the praise I sought for my dark romantic vision.) I pestered Peter to stop smoking, which soon brought his health to a crisis with emphysema. He was most at ease when at the piano or organ, improvising and encouraging us to sing barroom classics at company parties or his home.

Peter saved me from humiliations and taught and corrected me without condescension. He never made me feel embarrassed when I asked him for help. He knew we shared similar class origins and reassured me that he had only learned the intricacies of English on his own when he was my age. We spent many hours at Holt, Rinehart & Winston reading from his bible, *Fowler's Modern English Usage*. Although I had stumbled into this avocation, I felt more and more that I had been born to it, for I never got bored when Peter and I read out Fowler's directives on the split infinitive, polysyllabic humour, popularised technicalities, or the choice between "all right'" and "alright." Fowler wrote that grammar is "a poor despised branch of learning." We disagreed and thought that it brought power and clarity, if only to our little cabal of gatekeepers.

What was better to know than "in modern English usage lay is transitive only, and makes laid; lie is intransitive only and makes lay, lain, and never laid"? I can still imagine Peter reading out loud, with dramatic emphasis, in his Cockney intonation, Fowler's example of rhythm in prose:

> And the king was much moved, and went up to the chamber over the gate, and wept: and as he went, thus he said, O my son Absalom, my son, my son Absalom! would God I had died for thee, O Absalom, my son, my son!" King James Bible.

We stared at each other in awe. We believed in the power of those secrets of grammar, as few do now.

I eventually managed to work myself into Dave Harris's better graces. He periodically fired staff; despite his martial exterior he always did it with a cruel cowardice. Peter West found out that he was fired when a letter was waiting for him at home when he returned from holidays. Social studies editor Tim came to work one day and was given a new seating plan—Dave loved to rearrange the seating to reflect his approval or displeasure with various editors—on which there was no desk for him. Tim went to Dave's office to point out the oversight and Dave told him coolly "It's because you won't need one." (The math editor Malcolm Lester was one of the few editors who left Holt on his own, in his case to form his own successful publishing company, Lester & Orpen Dennys.)

It was Dave's firing of one of the editors that transformed my editorial fate. Dave's pet project was a new history of Canada, written by Paul Cornell and three French-Canadian historians—Fernand Ouellet, Jean Hamelin, and Marcel Trudel—meant to be the company's contribution to the 1967 Centennial celebration. The four had worked out the plan at a Learned Society meeting. The manuscript editor was an ex-teacher who could not stop himself from knowing better, in this case better than the three eminent Quebec historians, on the proper way to write history ("more stories," he demanded in his letters, "more characters"). When he told Fernand Ouellet, who notoriously had had his book on Louis-Joseph Papineau censored by the Patriote's descendants, that his brand of economic history, and lack of interest in the narratives of the Rebellions and Responsible Government were boring, he was off Dave's seating plan.

Time was running short for the Centennial project and Dave decided that he needed a French editor to deal with the French authors. He hired Pierre and moved him from Ottawa to Toronto. Pierre said that he needed an English colleague to work with him and since the latest purge left us shorthanded, Dave asked me if I knew anything about Canadian history. "Yes," I exaggerated. "Did you take Canadian history?" "Yes," I said, hoping that the grade 7 textbook *Breastplate and Buckskin* qualified. Pierre and I became partners, French and English—biculturalism in action. We made my first airplane trip ever, to Ottawa; me terrified on the old rattling Viscount prop airplane. We stayed at the Château Laurier—real class, Pierre explained to me. He introduced me to the indulgence of the expense account. We ate in the Canadian Club restaurant; I drank Scotch for the first time. I could not believe that the company paid for this! We met Fernand Ouellet in an anteroom at the Château. We reassured him that he would get no lectures from us on how he should write history. It turned out that only I had taken the bother to read Ouellet's text (Pierre had not) and I was able to discuss it with Ouellet, with difficulty as his English was poor and my French non-existent.

The partnership with Pierre did not last long. One weekend, he borrowed the company's Polaroid camera, a novelty in those days. Dave Harris was the next to take it home and when he found some nude shots of Pierre's beautiful wife left in the camera case, he was out the door. I got full responsibility—I prevaricated about my inability to read French—for the project. "I'll manage" got me through. Dave's singular project was now in the hands of a long-haired, unilingual, inexperienced editor, with no time to spare. The finished book had to be presented to the premiers at the first First Ministers' Meeting, some few months away. I know it is glib management policy these days to say that if you are working long hours and taking documents home that you are visibly not up to the job. Mike Flood caught me in the office working late one night—I was there every night—and sent me home with a lecture to try working harder during the day to spare my evenings. But I had a lot of reading to do. I had the fractured manuscript and a dreadful translation cobbled together in broken English by a part-time translator from France—violating the principle of always translating into your own language.

Immediately, I detected a problem. The book was supposed to be about 600 printed pages long. I had a typographer help me with the math from the manuscript. We discovered that the section on New France, written by University of Ottawa historian Marcel Trudel, alone ran to 400 printed pages. I looked at the contract file. Trudel was clear—not a word of his text was to be cut. How did the previous editors miss this? I called Jean Hamelin who was based at Laval in Quebec City, and he told me that there was no use asking Trudel to cut. He had a fearsome reputation for being stubborn. I explained all this to Dave; he gave me one day to come up with a solution. I knew my nascent career hung in the balance. Next day, with nothing to lose, I suggested that we not touch a word of Trudel's text, which was forbidden, but that we publish it in a separate book. In exchange for this unexpected new publication, I asked Trudel to allow me to cut the New France text for the big book. He agreed only after I persuaded Dave Harris to publish an English edition of Trudel's *Atlas of New France* as well. The tenacious man's publications were growing by the day.

Day by day I ploughed through the English manuscript, a Funk and Wagnall's dictionary at my side, along with *Fowler's Modern English Usage*, and *Words Into Type*, Peter West's other handbook of rules and guidelines for editors. Each Friday I would take the edited text and drive to the University of Waterloo and go over the editorial changes with the lone English author Paul Cornell. I am sure that he despaired at my rawness, but he was as anxious to see the book finished as was Dave Harris. Most challenging, neither Paul nor I spoke or read French. (We barely managed to communicate in English, as the professor had a very unsettling habit of following your comment or question with a long, intense silence, leaving you unsure if he had not heard you or if you had just spoken nonsense.) I hauled out the original French manuscripts with a Harrap French-English dictionary and compared it word for word with the English translation, painstakingly correcting and rewriting every sentence. I reinstated Ouellet's cumbersome sentences and diffuse logic, learning along the way that he drew his inspiration from the French Annales School. I read patches of Fernand Braudel's *La Méditerranée* to understand what Ouellet meant by concepts such as *longue durée*, and I fortified myself for the inevitable rematch.

We met again in Ottawa, this time on my own in his office at Carleton University. The problem remained that Fernand was barely literate in English but thought himself quite a stylist in both languages. He revised the English text further to make it sound even more French, with odd usages and convoluted sentences. Stuck on the translation of *longue durée*, I suggested leaving it in French, since it was Annales School terminology: he considered this inspired. I never mentioned the lack of colourful characters nor the need to tell some good yarns about Louis-Joseph Papineau and his rebellious band or to give us an explanation of responsible government that was not just connected to the falling price of fur or the blight on the wheat crop. I persuaded Paul Cornell to include these interesting lacunae in his chapters. Years later, I read the great literary editor Max Perkins' dictum that "a book belongs to its author." I felt that dealing with the obstinate Ouellet, taciturn Cornell, and stubborn Trudel taught me this valuable lesson.

There was nothing that I could do about Jean Hamelin's treatment of Confederation either, which he dismissed in a few short sentences as unimportant and, to a Québécois, an unfortunate twist of history. He was far more approachable and affable than his co-authors but here was no use asking him to expand his text. After my visits to Cornell, the manuscript was returned to the typists who incorporated the endless scrawls. My focus day and night was on individual words and sentences, but I sensed more and more as I moved from chapter to chapter that an amazing book was emerging, a unique cooperative concoction that marked the celebration of 100 years of history by focusing on provinces and regions and leaving the Innis/Creighton St. Lawrence centrist narrative in the cold. Cornell and I went to Ottawa and scrounged hundreds of pictures from boxes in a back room of the National Archives, which was closed at the time for renovations.

The book had never had a title and it was assumed, as it always seems to be in publishing, that one would magically appear. I hired my friend Phil Balsam to design a cover, so it was critical that we get the four authors to agree. Cornell favoured "Canada: Unity and Diversity," but the French authors were lukewarm. I suggested "Canada: Unity in Diversity." Dave Harris hated it, but the authors, particularly Trudel, agreed that it was appropriate. Phil decided that the words were enough and arranged them suitably in the cover design. (This far predated the exact words being used as the motto of the Tokyo Olympics in 2021.)

Once the manuscript was typed and ready, I carried it in person to Ryerson Press, who were not only a venerable publishing company but typesetters and printers as well. The typesetters seemed to me to be all of advanced age (I was 24) and universally cranky. They were quick to respond sympathetically, however, when I showed interest in their craft. I recognized, finally, the origins of the term "galley proofs" in the long metal trays holding columns of lead type. I watched the operators sitting at keyboards striking letters rapidly one by one, each followed by a distinctive metallic clack, following the manuscript copies on their clipboards. This process set off a wild journey of letters in which their molds were filled with liquid lead and arranged into sentences. Everyone, I was told, who worked on and around the Monotype or Linotype machines had been burned or injured at one time or another. It will never be known how many typesetters suffered colic, emaciation, anemia, and worse from their exposure to lead. Most important to me were the side desks, where the experienced proofreaders spent their days under table lamps. They had endless questions and provided a failsafe for my nascent work that is rare in today's electronic world. Ryerson Press were very happy to have our business for this major text: they provided me with a free turkey, a box of chocolates, and a bottle of wine at Christmas.

Dave Harris was pleased with the progress on the book but not the result. He was a Conn Smythe, colonel-in-the-Army, Anglo-centric Canadian and he was appalled by the content when the pages arrived. I persuaded him that there was no chance of changing the approach and with time running out he decided to get Toronto author William Kilbourn, famous for a colourful narrative biography of William Lyon Mackenzie (*The Firebrand*), to write an introduction more fitting to the celebratory atmosphere of the Centennial. I had to chase Kilbourn around Toronto to get that introduction out of him, learning more about his personal life than I cared to know.

Kilbourn managed to raise Dave's ire once more, with his reference in his text to the new Canadian flag—a source of great pride to our editor in chief—as the "sad new running pink" (the faulty dye in the early flags ran in the rain, like the pink ink on the *Toronto Telegram*). Kilbourn's symbolism was either lost or obvious, not sure which. Phil Balsam designed the chapter and unit breaks, which he adorned with his own woodcuts, and we drove east to Upper Canada Village with his Hasselblad camera to take photographs.

When I began to get the corrected galley proofs, hand-delivered from Ryerson, I cut them into pages, sized, positioned, glued the photo prints in place, and wrote the captions and credits. Dave Harris was happy enough with my work that he let me take a carton of specially bound copies

Unity in Diversity *proved to be a very successful university text and a paradigm of what publishers were willing to try in those days to celebrate Canadian history. (Cover and woodcut by Phil Balsam.)*

to the inaugural First Ministers' Conference, hosted by Ontario Premier John Robarts. There was one copy for each of the premiers. I was frightened of elevators in those days and had rarely set foot in one, but I had to muster the courage to soar to the 56th floor of the new Toronto Dominion Bank. The kindly elevator operator calmed me and told me to close my eyes and to take a deep breath. He promised to get us there safely. The pit of my stomach lurched when we stopped at 56. Premier Robarts himself received the box of books and thanked me with a handshake. He did not recognize me from the time I worked as a teenager installing fluorescent lights in his office in the Legislative Building. The book soon after was published in French by the Montreal branch of Holt Rinehart. I hoped that Premier Robarts was pleased to present a copy of a history of Canada with three French authors to Premier of Quebec, Daniel Johnson.

I became a book sweatshop over the next few months, editing my assigned books during the day and helping with my friend's books in the evenings. When an author of a geographical "sample study" of the fishing industry dropped out, I suggested that I go to Lunenburg, Nova Scotia (I had never heard of it) in his place and write the book—it had been pre-sold to several boards of education. After I claimed blithely to Dave that, yes, I had written before, he let me go. It was the first time that I had been east of Ottawa, never mind near an ocean. I stayed in the Lunenburg Inn (a former sea captain's home) after a scenic drive in a rented car down the coast. I was spellbound by the ocean, which I had never seen, relentlessly surging onto the rocky coast, and laying a palette of subtle blues around the picturesque boathouses at Peggy's Cove and Blue Rocks. I ingratiated myself to the chef at the Inn by telling him that I was "an ignorant Upper Canadian" who had never eaten fresh fish.

Every day he called me down to the kitchen to show me the catch of the day. I was introduced to cod, halibut, scallops and on one special day, fresh Atlantic salmon, still twitching on the cutting board. I interviewed some old sea captains, one of whom told me nostalgically of how he used to run the "pretty nurses" up to the coast of Labrador. I interviewed the famous captain of the schooner *Bluenose*, Angus Walters, who humbly recounted some of his racing triumphs. (He died shortly after.) I also took hundreds of pictures with my Miranda SLR camera (which Phil had helped me to buy on Yonge Street), researched the history of the fishing industry and—fatefully—decided to go out to sea.

The young scientists at the High Liner fish processing plant were keen to help me to tell the story of Lunenburg and they persuaded me that I should take a trip into the North Atlantic on a fishing vessel. There was a genuine interest in my project to explain the fishing industry to school children in the rest of Canada. I nervously drove up to Halifax and got aboard a brand new "dragger" that was being delivered from the shipyard to the fleet at Lunenburg. I was a naval greenhorn

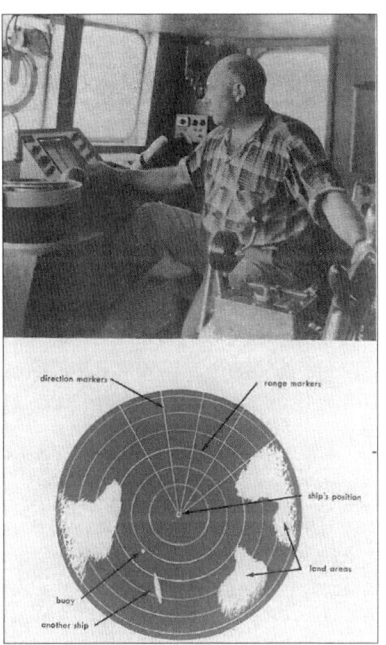

The cover of my first book, written in Lunenburg, Nova Scotia, published in 1968. To the right, the photo I took at sea of the vessel's captain and the new sonar used to locate fish.

if ever there was one. My seafaring experience amounted to a few nervous ferry crossings to Toronto Island and a brief excursion across Lake Ontario on the *Cayuga*. I was scared to death of water and the notoriously hostile North Atlantic swelled in my imagination. We slipped out of the dock and serenely passed Georges Island and the Halifax waterfront, then starboard past McNab Island—then headlong into the open sea. "Last time I took a landlubber out," the captain told me, "it was a cameraman from the NFB. He got so seasick that they had to send a helicopter to take him back before his stomach ruptured." My face was already a sickly green. There was no catch aboard, so the brand-new vessel was bouncing high and light in the water; the enthusiastic captain opened the throttle.

As we surged farther into the terrifying green swells, the water disgorged over the bridge. The captain saw my pale consternation and sympathetically distracted me by trying to show me how the sonar detected schools of fish. I took a photo, started vomiting and swooned near unconsciousness. The captain helped me into his private bathroom, where I crawled miserably into his shower, begging the ship "No. No. Don't go up... No. God. Please don't drop!" I must have been making a horrible racket as one of the crew fetched me, took me out on to the deck and propped me up in the spray against the mast. There my stomach calmed but my panic rose, as I could see a stark cliff of translucent water soar above the ship and as quickly drop completely from view. "Don't feel bad," the fisherman said to me, "I get sick ever' time come these past twenty years I go to sea." Somehow, I managed to take my camera out of its bag and snap a picture. Not often can we record our terrors, but I still have that photo of a wall of Atlantic water blocking the horizon. The gentle arms of Lunenburg Harbour were the most welcome of my young life.

The Fishermen of Lunenburg was published, along with a number of other volumes, in the school geography series that I edited, but it also was the centre of a serious dispute. My friend Peter West surfaced from his firing from Holt, Rinehart & Winston as editor in chief of Collier Macmillan, and he offered me a job. I was making $3,500 a year at Holt and Peter offered me $7,500. I dutifully went to Mike Harris and told him about the offer and asked him if he wanted to match it. He was furious and of course accused me of disloyalty. (I mentioned the fourteen or so editors who had been fired during my tenure, which only inflamed him). He offered me $4,000 and told me that if I did not accept it "I would never work in publishing again."

I LEFT AND STARTED WORKING with Peter at Collier Macmillan. A few months later, a fellow editor at Holt called me and told me that Dave Harris intended to remove my name from the book that I had written. I knew that there was nothing that I could do about recovering the text (they probably legally owned it anyway), but it occurred to me that the photographs I took, and which were essential to the book, might provide better leverage. I had never signed an employment contract or an agreement to write the book, never mind to take the photographs.

My friend used his key to get us into the building late one night and I removed the prints and negatives from my old filing cabinet and waited for the call, which predictably came in a few days from Dave. He threatened me with jail and repeated the threat about my bleak future in publishing. He demanded that I show up the next day with the pictures or to expect a call from the police. I waited him out and then got a call from Mike Flood. He asked to see me in his presidential office; I agreed. "What do you want?" he said. I said it was simple, that I wanted my name on the book that I had written. "Okay and how much money." "I don't want any money," I said, "I want credit for what I have done." "How did you know you weren't going to get credit?" he asked. To protect my friend I said, "Well you know Dave—what do you think?" He had his secretary draw up a letter promising me that my name would be on the book as its author. I retrieved the photos from the trunk of my car and handed them to him. My helpful friend, perhaps under suspicion, survived—for a month or two.

At Collier Macmillan I was quickly in conflict with the president, Vern. After my first paycheque, I calculated that I was not being paid $7,500 per annum, as promised, but $5,000. When the president told me that he had put me on a probationary salary for six months and that he would be firing me in any case if I did not get a hair cut, I walked out and went home. Peter West swore that he had no knowledge of this probation policy and knew of no one else who had been subjected to it. In a few days I was summoned back to the offices on Leslie Avenue. The president of the New York office was in town to deal with the crisis. During a meeting in which he questioned me about editorial matters and potential projects, he told the Canadian president that since I appeared to be the only person in the organization with any ideas, I was to be reinstated immediately at the agreed-upon full salary.

In the two years that I continued to work for Collier, I rarely saw Vern again, as he preferred his office at the company warehouse in Guelph.

After initiating a series of history textbooks using the same "enquiry" approach as the series I worked on in geography at Holt Rinehart, I made an agreement with Waterloo University through my association with the author of *Unity in Diversity*, Paul Cornell, in which graduate students would write educational texts on eras in Canadian history and use the published volumes as their master's theses. We had eight volumes published by the time I left, two of which I wrote, *The History of the Fur Trade in Canada*, and *Early Explorations of Canada*. Professor Palmer Patterson wrote a book on the First Nations, *The Canadian Indian: A History Since 1500*, which was the first textbook ever to tell a sympathetic and balanced history of what he called "the Original People." The book was a revelation to me, as well as to the students it was intended for and had a profound influence on me when planning The Canadian Encyclopedia. Patterson's insights were based on his viewing the First Nations, Métis, and Inuit as a "colonized people."

CHAPTER 13

Becoming Canadian

"I do love Canada, just because it isn't America and I have, I suppose, foolish dreams about Canada. I believe it could somehow avoid American mistakes, and it could really be that country that becomes a noble country, not a powerful country."

– Leonard Cohen

THE DUALITY OF MY LIFE, with my father on Perth and with Annie Radford on Norfolk, was reflected continuously on my developing self, as a student, an adolescent, in my religious or political beliefs, of my sense of being Torontonian and ultimately on my ideas of being Canadian. Harry had two medals for his service overseas, as I suppose every soldier did for participation, which I retrieved from his uniform when he lay in his casket. That maple leaf on his shoulder was proof that Canadian soldiers were different, but disrespected, that the sacrifice they made in saving "Blighty's ass" was not recognized. He and his army friends had particular scorn for the ex-British military who brought their snobbery to Canada as immigrants after the war. Harry and his fellow soldiers joined the Army for escape and adventure; they fought for their own survival, and for one another. That is what "Canadian" meant to them.

Annie Radford's Anglican Protestant upbringing, monarchist obsession, and longing for the "Old Country" (her father was born in England) were as perfect an expression of the old British Imperialism as I have ever encountered, even in history books. For Annie, talk of maple leaves and armies independent of Royal command was a kind of treason, despite her devotion to the Toronto Maple Leafs, because Canada existed purely for her as an expression of the monarchy and of the British Empire. The not being of her sentiment was of not being American. She was as anti-republican as a first-generation Loyalist. The very existence of the United States was an affront to the revered Queen herself. The supreme highlight of her life, along with the yearly Orange Day Parade, in which King Billy's white-as-snow, high-stepping horse relived the triumph of the English Protestants at the Battle of the Boyne—we knew it better than Quebec 1759 or Vimy Ridge or Normandy—was a Royal Visit. In one sublime moment her love of hockey and her admiration of the stalwart Ted "Teeder" Kennedy, honest hard-working captain of the Maple Leafs, came together, as Ted bowed and shook hands with the young Princess Elizabeth at Maple Leaf Gardens in 1951. Annie was in the crowd that night as she was at every Leaf home game; I was there too, squeezed in next to her on the bench in the Greys. A photograph of that famous event was displayed on Annie's wall, near the annual Maple Leaf hockey calendar, as a Catholic family might display an image of the Virgin Mary or the Pope.

Annie subscribed to *The Royal Family* magazine to follow the stories of the Queen and the Duke, and fretted about the wayward Princess Margaret, disapproving of her romance with the divorcé Peter Townsend. Her favourite read, next to the Bible, was a sentimental little publication called *The Scottish Friend*. All the calendars in the house, except for the annual Toronto Maple Leaf schedule, displaying home games in blue and away games in red, celebrated scenic Scottish glens and still, deep lakes—the romantic Old Country. Every five or six years she travelled alone, by passenger ship, to visit friends she had made in Scotland and Ireland. To Annie the most atrocious historical event of her life was not the World War, or the rise of Adolf Hitler or Joseph Stalin, or even the ascension of "that Catholic Frenchman" Louis St. Laurent to the office of prime minister, but the abject abdication of Edward and

Conn Smythe looks on proudly as "Teeder" Kennedy of the Maple Leafs bows to Princess Elizabeth, 1951, at a demonstration game of NHL hockey performed for her.

his inexplicable affair with that "floozy" American divorcée, Wallace Simpson. Edward was in her rogue's gallery, along with Rocket Richard, and she would not speak either name.

One of the rituals of Annie's historical narrative was her frequent pilgrimage by tour bus through the orchards of Niagara during peach season to Queenston Heights. I was six or seven when she first took me there and she persuaded me to overcome my fears both of heights and small spaces and climb the narrow circular staircase to the top of Brock's Monument. For a boy staring upwards it was impressive, its fluted column soaring triumphantly into the sky. At the summit is a five-metre stone-carved statue of Sir Isaac Brock, in a heroic pose, one arm holding a baton and the other resting on the hilt of his sword. When it was inaugurated on October 13, 1859, thousands of people from around the British colony gathered on the heights to admire the wonder of the age. (The only column, ancient or modern, that exceeds Brock's in height is Christopher Wren's monument to the Great Fire of London.) Even Nelson's column in London's Trafalgar Square is not as tall; a fact that impressed even Annie. The soaring Queenston column is a perplexing sight to American tourists, particularly as a vexatious reminder of a battle that they lost.

I stared intently down at my feet as I climbed the 235 stone steps (as I counted them recently) in a rising spiral, breathing deeply, hugging the rough concrete wall, fearful that the whole monument would collapse under me at any moment and bury us in rubble. At the top, I had to muster more courage and accept the lift of a stranger in order to peer through the slits in the small, open windows cut into the stone, from where I could see for miles down the magnificent Niagara Gorge. Could any other battlefield have such impressive geography? Could there be a more apt symbol of Canadian independence? Annie spoke with fervent pride about the hero Sir Isaac Brock, an Englishman after all, who died bravely on this site to repulse an American invasion during the War of 1812. We are not Americans thanks to him! (I did not know until told by Peter Gzowski in a radio interview that Brock's Canadian aide-de-camp, Lieutenant Colonel John Macdonell, is also interred there. Singer Stan Rogers wrote a song about Macdonell, lamenting, "Not one in ten thousand knows your name." No one at the site or in school knew it.)

From Queenston, Annie and I would re-board the tour bus on its way to Niagara Falls. She took my hand and led me to the precipice. We stared at the cascading water plunging relentlessly into the gorge, like a massive fluid freight train hurtling beneath our feet. The spray soaked our hair and shoulders. We walked to the green park lawn, bordered by showy flower beds, and ate a picnic lunch of bologna sandwiches, apple pie,

*Brock's monument, on the battlefield of Queenston Heights,
an enduring symbol of Canadian independence.
(Photo by James Marsh)*

and cheddar cheese that she had packed, the dim roar of the Falls constant in the distance. Annie boasted about how much grander "our" Canadian Horseshoe Falls were than that trickle on the Yankee side of the Niagara River. It was only a short walk along the edge of the gorge to the mesmerizing Niagara Whirlpool, where the torrent of water abruptly changes direction, spins counterclockwise and surges through the narrowest channel in the chasm—all of it in Canadian waters. Annie excitedly rode the swaying antique cable car across the gorge, high above the turbulent spectacle, but she could never persuade me to set foot in it. I waited impatiently until her carriage lurched back into the dock.

Annie and I went together on these trips. They expanded my geographic imagination, my sense of history and of wonder. While she failed to put that other saviour, Jesus, into my heart, she succeeded completely with "Teeder" Kennedy and Sir Isaac Brock.

Since Annie Radford was more a caring mother to me than Ada, it was naturally against her views that I rudely defined myself. I professed distaste for the monarchy (though I was spellbound by the broadcast on tiny flickering black-and-white televisions at school of Elizabeth's coronation June 1953. I fashioned plasticine models, with dried fruit for jewels, of her splendid scepter, orb, and crown). I adopted my father's view that the British "Empire" was a tired old nag that had been saved to stagger on by brave but unappreciated Canadian lads. Though Isaac Brock and James Wolfe were heroes to me, I rooted for the Iroquois in the conflicts depicted on television and in our textbooks. In our imaginary battles in the back lanes, I demanded the roles of Pontiac or Tecumseh, leaping out at unsuspecting friends with a handmade tomahawk and a pigeon feather taped to a bandana. These identifications were perhaps more natural for me, as I identified as an outsider.

I also sympathized with the French victims of the colonial wars and with the adventurous Nor'westers against the corporate, imperialistic Hudson's Bay Company. I felt a real empathy for *coureurs de bois* Etienne Brulé and Pierre Radisson, who were featured in a brief CBC television series in 1957-58, and for the golden age of exploration across the vast West, lead by La Verendrye, and into the Northwest Passage with Sir John Franklin. These stories of our history fit nicely into a sense of Canada as a northern frontier.

Unfortunately, one could not buy a Tecumseh or Radisson lunch box, so I had to settle for a raccoon-capped Daniel Boone. American media and its fabricated myths of the western frontier and the Alamo already dominated Canadian televisions and movie theatres. But still, there remained a sense that the lives of the Indigenous Peoples and the awkward relationship between English and French helped to patch together a different national identity than that assumed by Americans.

THE FIRST BIGGER IDEA I got about Canada was, predictably, from hockey. It was a great source of pride to me that most NHL players were Canadian in those days. I was well schooled by Annie in the values that owner Conn Smythe instilled in his Maple Leafs (named for that same military emblem). He enlisted hard-working, rugged players, ready to "fight them in the alleys as well as on the ice," the antithesis of the flashy fancy boys playing for the Montreal Canadiens. Over the dressing room door Smythe installed the motto "Defeat Does Not Rest Lightly. ... Each man is his own absolute law giver and dispenser of glory or gloom to himself, the maker of his life, his reward, his punishment." It was a stern Protestant lesson for any Toronto boy. (Unfortunately, there was no explanation for the fact that the fancy-boy Canadiens won most of the Stanley Cups.) There was no effort in English Canada in those days to promote a more inclusive national identity that might include the French, much less First Nations, Métis, and Inuit.

The idea of losing the Stanley Cup to some American city did not disturb me then, as it does now (a Stanley Cup parade in Raleigh, North Carolina, but not City Hall Toronto), but the idea that Canadians might lose to the Soviets was another matter. Even children's books in those days were full of the threat that the hammer and sickle posed over our necks. Maps of the world with the "communists" blocked in red replaced the equally exaggerated maps of the blood red of the former British Empire. The play-by-play radio reports of the "world championships" in the 1950s were spellbinding to me. But who were the Canadian heroes upholding the reputation of Canadian hockey, standing against the evil communists? I knew almost every player in the six-team NHL by heart, his records and his sweater number. But these amateur Canadian players from the Senior Hockey Leagues whom we sent to battle the Russians were either not good enough to make it in the big league or they had expired. Why were they sent to defend our Canadian honour? I worried. I wrote down their names and took to the back lane to encourage them against the grim-faced Bobrov and Sologubov. There was Bob Attersley and Harry Sinden of the Whitby Dunlops, who won the gold medal in 1958, and Bobby Kromm and goalie Seth Martin of the Trail Smoke Eaters, amateurs who won gold in the World Championship in 1961. These were the epitome of rugged Conn Smythe Canadians. I listened to those games on the radio, reveled in the few victories and hung my head when we lost, which sadly became more frequent.

Schools in Toronto in the 1950s still contained pronounced overtones of the British Empire. We sang "God Save the Queen" at every public and school function. The Union Jack or Red Ensign flew on every flagpole and half the teachers had English or Scots accents. The social studies homeroom had a large Mercator projection of the world, dominated by the red ink denoting the British Empire, with giant red blobs on Canada, India, and Australia. At school we were taught that Shakespeare, Hardy, Milton, Keats, and Shaw were the exclusive accomplishments of world literature. Every now and then a wrist-waving Royal would grace us with his or her presence to pretend that we belonged.

I think it was partly an inferiority complex that inspired me to look for some kind of Canadian identity from these mixed origins. My Italian neighbours reminded me relentlessly about how inferior we Canadians were in history, art, and religion to their homeland. Even our use of an "X" to denote Christmas was evidence to one of my Italian neighbours of our barbarism. My German friend Werner crushed me at chess; what else could be expected of a mere Canadian he declared? (I did not remind him of what happened to his country in the war, as he was two years older.) A Japanese girl in my class printed much more legibly than me (and also beat me at chess). To Annie's English war bride daughter-in-law Edna, no Canadian shoes or dresses or candy were good enough for her children. They must be ordered directly from England, which despite her reverence for the Old Country, offended Annie. I never saw pride in our place in the British Empire, only colonial subjugation.

My friend John, whose mother took him to many more American movies than I could see, took the view that, because of its technical prowess, the United States was superior to Britain, particularly in the things that really mattered, namely automobiles and military weapons. I went along with John in these judgments, though I harboured a secret admiration for Jaguars and Austin-Healeys and always thought that British aircraft (the wooden wonder de Havilland Mosquito and that bat-like delta-winged Vulcan bomber) were stylish. I hung models of both above my bed.

WITH MY OBSESSION with weapons, I had to be satisfied with admiring the Canadian versions of the Hawker Hurricane and North American Sabre until Malton-based Avro unveiled its quintessentially Canadian CF-100 "Canuck." It was our own jet fighter, not too fast or too flashy (like the Toronto Maple Leafs or the Whitby Dunlops), but sturdy and able to fly in cold weather. I loved that airplane and grew indignant at the American plastic model makers who ignored it. I wrote a letter of complaint to model-maker Revell and got a curt reply that "nobody was interested." (That is, if you are not American, you are nobody.) It is ironic that the man who first inspired in me a pride of Canada, John Diefenbaker, was the same one who proved to me what a little people we are, afraid to excel, when he cancelled the spectacular Canadian-designed Avro Arrow. I believed that the Arrow's cancellation was a betrayal of Canadian innovation and a cowardly retreat from taking our place in the world. It was a blow to whatever nascent nationalism I had developed. (I was encouraged in this outrage by a science teacher at Oakwood Collegiate who had lost his job at Avro. He gave me inside information and then an A on an essay that I wrote on the calamity.)

Annie turned up the radio when John Diefenbaker spoke, for he revered the Union Jack, hated that red maple leaf, and stood up to Americans. He toppled the hated continentalist (pro-American) Liberals and their rotating English and French prime ministers. My friend John was a big Dief fan too. When Dalton Camp engineered the review of the chief's leadership, John and I attended rallies across Toronto. We were there at the leadership conference at Maple Leaf Gardens in 1967, close enough to see the old warrior on the podium eyeballing the chastened Camp, his head down, we thought, in shame. Waggling his finger, Dief thundered his exclamations for "One Canada," "Canada First," denouncing the proponents of the Deux Nations policy that would build a "Berlin Wall" around Quebec.

Though he was the one who stirred my first feelings of nationalism—I cast my first vote for him—I could not forgive Diefenbaker for abandoning the Arrow. Imagine, that beautiful delta wing, that supreme expression of Canadian ingenuity, of independence, of power, crushed and obliterated by Diefenbaker and replaced by a hideous American missile—the useless Bomarc. "Fighters were obsolete" was the argument against building the Arrow and yet we turned around and bought the American built Starfighter, the flying coffin that killed some two hundred Canadian pilots. Still, I loved Dief's call for "One Canada," for his plea that, "Above all, let's be Canadians," and I had no idea that almost everyone inside and outside his party was mad at him. I only began to understand that nascent idea of a national identity based on British tropes was objectionable to French Canadians, not to mention the Indigenous Peoples who had lived on the continent for thousands of years.

In the early 1960s I was far too occupied with girls and awkward anxieties to give much thought to politics. We were taught almost no Canadian history in high school, though our military past was glorified on Remembrance Day, with earnest ceremonies and by the mandatory enrollment of the boys in cadets, in which we were instructed in the basic military drills with the long-obsolete Lee Enfield rifle. We boys dressed up in cadet uniforms and marched aimlessly around the gymnasium. I learned to turn right or left by squeezing the appropriate hand. There was a firing range and cadets shot rifles in a basement range

The Avro Arrow was the world's most advanced jet fighter. It flew at almost twice the speed of sound, without its more powerful Orenda engines. It was briefly a source of Canadian pride, shattered by its cancellation. (Canada Aviation and Space Museum).

at Oakwood Collegiate. (To my shock, on a visit to Oakwood Collegiate a few years ago, I was met at the front door by an armed guard who told me that there had been several actual shootings in the school.) I brought shame and ridicule on myself and my fellow cadets when I fainted and cracked open my head while on parade at the Fort York Armoury. Despite my fascination with the military, I hated cadets, and after that fainting episode I refused to take part. (I had an undiagnosed hyperthyroid condition.)

While authoritarian on most points of protest, the school seemed strangely ambivalent about my questionable pacifist insurrection. The guidance teacher, a former soldier who had lost a leg in the Second World War, tried to talk sense into me. With his false leg propped up on a stool under the desk, and the sole of his boot pressed against my thigh, he lectured me about how my unhealthy need for attention was tiring to both my teachers and my classmates. It was unmanly. I shamed myself on the parade ground. My marks were a disgrace, and he would have recommended that I be banished from the sacred collegiate halls to some lowly tech or commercial school, except for the inconvenience of my respectable IQ score, which indicated that I was only acting stupid. (In contrast to the lack of punishment for my pacifist objections, I was expelled for refusing to stand for "God Save the Queen," and was given numerous detentions for declining to read the Bible in front of the class.) My hatred grew for the insipid Red Ensign flag, with its shrunken Union Jack in the upper left corner, as a humiliating symbol of colonialism.

A Toronto high school in the 1950s provided a thorough grounding in what no doubt would now be condemned as a Euro-centric education. Our orchestra and band played Elgar and Beethoven. In art history we learned about Raphael, Michelangelo and da Vinci, even Rembrandt and Velasquez—not a mention of the Group of Seven much less the fine arts of China or Japan, or our Northwest Coast First Nations or Northern Inuit geniuses for that matter. More pervasive still was the literature. Somehow my interest in Shakespeare survived the deadly line-by-line, word-by-word reading and exegesis by lit teacher Miss Campbell. We read Dickens, Shaw, Milton, Wordsworth, and Keats. But in none of this schooling was there any sense of being Canadian. The closest that we got to a "Canadian" author was John Buchan (a Scot who was governor general of Canada in the early twentieth century), whose *Prester John* was to me the most thrilling book that I had ever read. A young Farley Mowat came to Oakwood and proved to us that a living Canadian could write a book. He read to us from *People of the Deer* and we were all very taken with his rugged self-importance. Now that was a Canadian, bearded and in mukluks, stomping the snowy vastness of Northern Canada, communicating with wild animals.

By the early 1960s the grip of Imperialist thinking was loosening, largely as a result of Britain's own failing prestige and the inundation of American media. Imagine that a modest Canadian, Lester B. Pearson, had to bail Britain out of the mess that they made at Suez, winning the prestigious Nobel Peace Prize in the process.

IT WAS WORKING IN MY FIRST JOB as an editor at Holt, Rinehart & Winston on the book *Canada: Unity in Diversity* in 1967 that formed a broader idea of Canada in my mind. I carried on my own course in Canadian history to try to make sense of the manuscript, reading Canadian historians Harold Innis, Donald Creighton, Mason Wade, J.M.S. Careless, William MacNut, Morris Zaslow, W.L. Morton, and Margaret Orsmby. None of those books, and the one that I was editing even less, dealt much in heroes, but there were forces of history, politics and geography, regional identities, religious, racial and linguistic conflicts and unresolved problems that seemed to me to define a more complex national entity. With three eminent French-Canadian authors (Marcel Trudel, Fernand Ouellet and Jean Hamelin) and one English (Paul Cornell), I could not avoid the idea at the heart of that book that there was an unresolved paradox in our history, one that made it all the more interesting to me, that we were incomplete, continually in an internal engagement between languages and cultures.

This idea of "limited identity" came from historian Ramsay Cook, who lamented the Canadian habit of deploring our lack of identity. "We should attempt to understand and explain the regional, ethnic and class identities that we do have," Cook wrote. "It might just be that it is in these limited identities that 'Canadianism' is found." Another historian, Maurice Careless, determined that it was diversity that largely differentiates Canada from the United States and that the whole may be greater than the sum of its diverse parts. This to me was a persuasive view of Canada that was to serve me well in later creating The Canadian Encyclopedia. I had a long conversation with Professor Careless when I was planning the encyclopedia. He told me that his delightful name derived from his Cavalier ancestors in the English Civil War.

My experience with editing the textbook *Unity in Diversity* and then with creating and writing a series of textbooks on Canadian history at Collier Macmillan furthered my education to the point that my next job was at the appropriately named Institute of Canadian Studies at Carleton University. The Institute was the only graduate interdisciplinary program in Canadian studies in Canada at that time. It also published a series of academic books on Canadian history and social sciences, called the Carleton Library Series. Not only was I researching and editing scholarly books and taking part in editorial meetings with board members from all the disciplines from anthropology to law, I was able to travel across Canada discussing potential projects with academics. I also managed to enroll in enough part-time courses in history and art history to finish a degree. Some of the Carleton Library board members were resentful of my long hair, lack of a PhD and of my role, insisted on by McClelland & Stewart, to try and choose manuscripts that might at least break even with their costs.

My sense of Canada was also deepened by the courses that I took when I was not editing manuscripts or raising our daughter. Canadian history departments in those days were dominated by a liberal (also Liberal) political narrative; advocates of what Herbert Butterfield called the "Whig interpretation of history," with its doctrine of history as political progress, in Canada's case, "from colony to nation." A few social and women's history outliers were on the fringes of the male senior historians, were looked down upon, and generally not tenured or promoted. I particularly liked the seminar that I took with John Taylor on Canadian social history and I still have a copy of the essay that I wrote on the use of propaganda in Canada during the First World War. Professor Taylor even circulated it among some of his colleagues. I became deeply affected by the conflicts in Canadian history, which I saw as being ignored or avoided, such as the treatment of Indigenous Peoples, the poor, and the working classes. I was always and continue to be, even living in Alberta, sympathetic to the linguistic and cultural aspirations of Quebec. Knowing Davidson Dunton, when he was the head of Canadian Studies (he had been co-chair of the Royal Commission on Bilingualism and Biculturalism), helped me to become a strong proponent of the view that our bicultural relationship with Quebec defined Canada and demanded a level of compromise and tolerance that were not accepted in the class-ridden society of Great Britain or the "melting pot" exceptionalism of the United States. I managed in my historical studies also to connect the fragments of an uncompleted degree in philosophy from Wilfrid Laurier University, to a course in philosophy of history. I never forgave the prof of this course who, to my delight, proposed that each of us develop our own grand philosophy of history, Arnold Toynbee-like. In an intense summer session, I feverishly delved into a long essay on "History as a Search for Meaning," based on a reading of Viktor Frankl's psychotherapy developed from his survival of a Nazi concentration camp. It was a longshot, but I was disappointed in the B+ I received. "How did the others do with this grandiose project you gave us?" I asked him. He replied, "Oh everyone else bailed." I had a measure of revenge, beating him at tennis later that day.

My sense of being Canadian germinated in the turmoil of ideologies of Toronto in the 1950s. The complex sense of becoming Canadian that I felt growing up suffered from the same split consciousness that I experienced in my family life. The slipping grip of British imperialism (and whatever insulation it provided from American influences), the growing dominance of American popular culture, and the influx of immigration from Germany and Italy, our two former enemies, contributed to change. In 1967 the Centennial celebrations were extremely effective, along with Expo '67 in Montreal, in raising popular awareness of the magnitude of the country and its diversity. Yet, when nationalist publisher Jack McClelland tried to persuade me to join the Committee for an Independent Canada ("we need young blood"), I felt sympathy but no enthusiasm for the obsession that group and those that followed had for the evils of "foreign ownership." Surely there were broader issues to engage the mind in a national community beyond business ownership? I thought of the Group of Seven, Farley Mowat, the burgeoning of Canadian literature with Margaret Laurence, Margaret Atwood, and all the poets in both languages.

Granted, when I worked for branch-plant publishing houses, I understood that they had little stake in giving a voice to Canadian literature, while filling the school curricula with books profitably "adapted" from American publications. Yet, when I started work in 1966 at Holt, Rinehart & Winston, that American-owned company seemed to operate independently under Canadian editor in chief Dave Harris. His Centennial Canadian history project, *Unity in Diversity*, was more ambitious than any undertaken by Canadian-owned or branch plant publishers for our 150th anniversary in 2017. At Collier Macmillan I developed a series of schoolbooks in Canadian history that was particularly supported by the president in New York, much more than the cautious, equivocal Canadian-born president.

I always thought Mel Hurtig's speeches and advocacy on issues of economic nationalism were persuasive, and was of course impressed by the overt nationalism of Jack McClelland, more a competitor than a colleague of Mel Hurtig, to the extent that his company used his government funding to sustain or even initiate the flowering of Canadian literature. But when I approached the challenge of creating an encyclopedia of the country I realized that its determining ideology was going to have to be deeper and wider, something perhaps that encased those limited identities described by Cook and others.

In my first week upon arriving at Carleton University as executive editor of the series of scholarly books co-published with M&S, I attended a party at Pauline Jewett's apartment. A former Liberal MP, Jewett rose to national prominence when she quit her Party on principle in 1970, opposing Pierre Trudeau's implementation of the *War Measures Act.* She was now director of the Institute of Canadian Studies. English Professor Robin Matthews collared me and shelled me with his rage over the American takeover of Canadian university faculties. He even identified to me the members of faculty at Carleton who were in the pay of the CIA. (This seeming paranoia was actually confirmed some years later.) He and James Steele wrote an influential book on the subject of the flood of Americans hired by universities a few years later, *The Struggle for Canadian Universities*. It was a challenging atmosphere.

In my ten years at the Institute of Canadian Studies, I met students from all over Canada who had enlisted to take a master's degree in Canadian Studies. The interdisciplinary seminar, which was mandatory for all the students, invited eminent guests, including David Lewis, Jack Pickersgill, Irving Layton, Réné Lévesque and others, to speak and to take part in discussions. Though I do not remember any coherent view of being Canadian emerging in the seminars—in fact it seemed to change from year to year—we always felt the excitement in the belief that the subject of Canada in all its complexity and multiplicity was important.

While Mel Hurtig was winning debates all over Canada in his opposition to free trade in the mid-1980s (even by the secret internal evaluations I saw of Prime Minister Brian Mulroney's observers at these debates), I chose to work with the federal communications minister Marcel Masse in his mission to exempt culture from the agreement. Masse, a former Quebec separatist, was the author of the Baie-Comeau policy under which fifty-one percent of the shares of a foreign-owned publishing subsidiary in Canada acquired by another foreign company had to be sold to a Canadian entity within two years. Masse and I got on very well. We had many discussions about his ultimate concern that Quebec had a better chance to survive against American influences if it were still a part of Canada (like the buffer against America that Britain had once provided for English Canada). I helped him and his adviser Patricia Finlay to write Cabinet documents and speeches on "cultural sovereignty" during his fight with Cabinet colleagues to protect Canadian culture from the terms of the Free Trade Agreement. He was a lone voice in the Conservative Cabinet.

In the end, unlike the more vociferous economic nationalists, we had some small success in influencing the Free Trade Agreement. Masse's efforts resulted in some cultural exemptions to free trade, such as our ability to fund our own film and publishing industries without countervails from the US, though just like the foreign investment legislation, it is ignored in the real world. The American negotiators (and their accomplices in the Mulroney Cabinet) infuriated me in their insistence that there was no such thing as Canadian culture, distinct from their own. On a cross-country tour I took with former Secretary of State Francis Fox, set up by Masse in 1987 to coordinate cultural policy between his Communications portfolio and the provinces, Hollywood lobbyist Jack Valenti and his staff followed us in a private jet interviewing the officials we had met, demanding to find out what had been discussed at our meetings. They were enraged when I persuaded journalist Robert Sheppard (a graduate of Canadian Studies) of the *Globe and Mail* to write a story about how we were trying to get ministries of education to buy textbooks only from Canadian-owned publishers. It succeeded in raising the ire of our opponents (and pleased Masse). American Ambassador to Canada Thomas Niles telephoned me directly and derided my naïveté about who really ran our cultural policy, how insignificant Masse was, and who his powerful friends were in Mulroney's Cabinet. Americans leave no stone unturned when their self-interest is at stake, historian Norman Hillmer taught me from his work on softwood lumber disputes, so I argued that neither should we. Nothing came from our little task force. Provincial officials proved even more indifferent about issues of culture than their federal counterparts. When Francis Fox took a deep breath and proposed a feature film fund to the officials in Newfoundland, they were enraged at such an idea at a time when the fishing industry was suffering (when isn't it?). When Francis wrote his report on the meeting he began, "The fish sticks were flying!" I went on to make our presentation alone to British Columbia, where indifferent officials interrupted my performance and told me that arrangements had been made to fly me to Los Angeles in a private jet so that officials in Hollywood could explain to me how important American film and television productions were to the BC economy. When it comes to cultural matters in Canada the word "provincial" applies in both its meanings. I reluctantly declined the trip.

The lost debate over free trade was the last gasp of that strain of economic nationalism that had been spearheaded by Walter Gordon in the 1950s and 1960s, through his attempts to reduce foreign ownership and his co-founding, with *Toronto Star* editor Peter C. Newman and economist Abe Rostein, of the Committee for an Independent Canada. Jack McClelland, Mel Hurtig and the editor of the influential newspaper *Le Devoir*, Claude Ryan became prominent CIC members, advocating greater Canadian control of Canada's own business, media and foreign policy.

The Committee had an influence on Canadian media into the mid-1970s. Mel Hurtig was perhaps its most persuasive leader, constantly called to be the spokesperson on television or the podium. Pierre Trudeau, the Liberal prime minister, was openly hostile to the nationalists' agenda because of his battles with the sovereigntist movement in Quebec. However, he adeptly exploited the movement to gain votes with the creation of the Crown corporation Petro-Canada, the Foreign Investment Review Agency, the Canada Development Corporation, and new rules for Canadian content in the media. Few of these initiatives survived, particularly when the federal Conservative Party took power.

Nation and nationalism have proved difficult to define anywhere, perhaps more so in Canada. When I arrived in Edmonton to plan The Canadian Encyclopedia, there was (and remains) little sympathy for my view that the dynamic of the French and English divide was at the heart of our history and thus our national identity. How could there be only one harmonious national community with our colonial conflict hanging over every national issue? This bicultural view did not however survive the rise of multiculturalism, of the increasing number of outspoken immigrant groups who were left out of this national portrait. Prime Minister Pierre Trudeau, ever the opportunist, embraced multiculturalism as the best way of "assuring the cultural freedom" of all Canadians, whatever that meant. We ensured in 1980 that there would be extensive coverage of every ethnic group our consultants could identify, almost twenty years in advance of the Encyclopedia of Canada's Peoples published by University of Toronto Press in 1999.

Others whose Canadian identity did not fit the peaceable, tolerant mythology of the nationalists were the Japanese, Chinese and South Asians, who suffered decades of racist intolerance and discrimination. Those in Western Canada who were irritated by the perceived favouritism of Quebec and indifference of Pierre Trudeau to their energy industries took solace in anger, alienation, and even separatism.

In 2021 it was revealed that the RCMP closely monitored the active economic nationalist movement, analyzing its pamphlets, gathering reports from snitches, and monitoring the Committee for manipulation by "radicals and Communists." In historian Stephen Azzi's description: "The RCMP intelligence unit appeared to be staffed by people with little knowledge, with scant research skills and with deep paranoia." It was a clear indication of how deeply embedded our politicians and bureaucrats are in global capitalism and how hostile they were to stirrings of independence, or in particular antipathy towards American capital.

These days, neither bureaucrats nor politicians show any enthusiasm to enforce the scraps of laws protecting Canadian culture that are still on the books, as the federally approved takeover of McClelland & Stewart by German-owned Random House in 2011 showed. Conservative Heritage Minister James Moore happily provided an exemption from long-established provisions of the *Investment Canada Act*, which specifically outlawed such takeovers. He granted the approval "on the basis of the commitments we made that demonstrated that this investment is likely to be of net benefit to Canada." There is no point in analysing the ideological basis of such a statement.

So what is our Canadian destiny? How are we to become that noble country inspired from time to time, as Leonard Cohen dreamed, by our not being American? Is it the best we can do to make the most of being forever unfinished, in process, driven not by some great nationalist dream, but by pragmatism and political compromise? Perhaps that is the only way we can survive the next, inevitable crisis facing our imagined community, as we are now with the catastrophic revelations of the deaths of children at Indian Residential Schools. Should nationalism, in the grander sense even be a goal? It is used to justify xenophobia and resentment all over the world, most recently in the "Make America Great Again" frenzy of our American neighbour. It is a cautionary tale, not just of the flaws of America, but of nationalism itself.

CHAPTER 14

The Place Where the Light Enters

*"The minute I heard my first love story,
I started looking for you, not knowing how blind that was.
Lovers don't finally meet somewhere. They're in each other all along."*

– Rumi

I FIRST MET LESYA at the publisher Holt, Rinehart & Winston in spring 1968. She was there working as a summer student, apprenticed to an editor from France, who was translating the full, extended French version of Marcel Trudel's text on the history of New France. I could hear the two of them arguing in English and French (he was clueless about Canadian history she declared) but otherwise I hardly noticed Lesya until she appeared at my desk one day, and struck me dumb with her thick black hair, dark eyes, and penetrating, skeptical stare. I remember how I lifted my head in shock at the sound of her voice, higher and thinner than I had expected. I was sure that she could hear the clamour of my heart. She knew, she told me, that I had met Marcel Trudel, the author of that text, and she demanded that I support her in her dispute with the handsome but, according to her, incompetent and arrogant editor. I did speak reluctantly to the cheerful Frenchman but all he wanted to talk about was how attracted he was to Lesya and how her prickly attitude excited him. She told me to walk her to the bus stop at the end of the day. I walked with her, but she refused to speak to me. She was annoyed and disappointed that I had not

190

helped her with her French antagonist. She turned her back and left me on the curb as she climbed into the bus on Royal York Road. "Take the next one," she instructed me.

I arranged a staff party for my friends at my girlfriend Liz's apartment and I timidly invited Lesya. To my great surprise, she came and brought along her imposing boyfriend, a tall, intense fellow Ukrainian named Roman. Both he and Elizabeth became distressed at the obvious attraction between their partners. Lesya and I discussed poetry and film with an increasing intimacy. What random chemistry afflicts the heart? What was it about this difficult woman that consumed my mind? I tried to act calm and indifferent to Roman's menace as he circled me with glazed eyes. I was thrilled that Lesya stood so close to me and ignored his tugs. The drama was not lost on Liz, who started to cry. As Lesya left, she whispered to me, "Elizabeth is a beautiful girl. She loves you very much." I had never fallen in love with Liz; I did not know why. She persisted, but I kept disappointing her in the gifts that were never a ring, and in the love making that never ended with a confession.

When I broke up with Liz shortly after the party, she did not feign surprise. She telephoned me, wrote to me, and sat naked under her raincoat on my front step. Lesya brusquely refused my invitations to meet. One day she phoned me and told me to pick her up as she had something that she wanted me to hear. In my apartment, we sat listening tensely to her favourite "original instrument" recording of Bach's Brandenburg Concertos, very new in those days, but she showed no interest in kissing me. We had a few other ambiguous encounters at work that were formless and awkward, with my interest sincere and hers reluctant and dismissive.

Lesya left Toronto at the end of August 1968 to attend Université de Montréal, where she enrolled to take a PhD in linguistics. She told me that she had no time for me. Her degree was going to be even more challenging because she was going to have to improve her French at the same time. I was sure that my feelings of emptiness and loss and rejection proved that I was "in love." My friends quickly tired of my complaints. What was the point of finally falling in love if this was the result? I was startled when Lesya phoned me from Montreal and invited me to visit her.

The car trip from Toronto was eventful. Near Kingston I sped absentmindedly through a police radar trap. I watched in the rearview mirror as the startled policeman ran back to his car. I pushed the accelerator to the floor, and squeezed the steering wheel as the speedometer swung over 120 mph. I hit the brakes near a little gravel turn-off and drove into the woods to avoid the roadblock that I was sure had been set up to catch me. I sat, heart pounding, in the car for two hours before creeping back out onto the dark highway, my heart in my throat as I drove under the speed limit all the way to the Quebec border. I told Lesya nothing of this—I knew that she would criticize me for it. I followed her directions to her apartment in a small brick building near the Université de Montréal.

Lesya acted agitated at my arrival at her apartment door and said that she had not expected me until the next morning. I reached to kiss her, but she pushed me away. It had been a month since I last saw her in Toronto. Despite all the subsequent days I spent conjuring her beauty in my desire, seeing her again dazed me. Her eyes were darker, more threatening, her black hair wilder, her movements impatient, feline. Whatever I imagined of her presence was only a shadow of her restless aura in person. She sat me down and told me about her break-up with Roman—I hated the sound of his name. The rejection had put him into a rage. He had quit university, started drinking and was hounding her.

I took my backpack from the car and we immediately left on a trip to the laundromat. Each time we left the apartment, Lesya handed me her keys, but every time we came to a door, she would snatch them back and open the door herself. We returned to her apartment and she made coffee. A man's shirt hung in her open closet and several burned candles lay on her desk. She told me more about Roman, how she hated him, feared him, tried to love him for her father's sake. She made her whole affair sound like a tragic nineteenth-century Russian novel, with their shared

Ukrainian heritage and parental intrusions providing the enigmatic context that she assumed I could never understand. "I don't know how to explain it" she said. She stared at me. I was there now; she lowered her head and sighed. She opened a book of poetry and read me Yevgeny Yevtushenko's "Colours," which she said had been on her mind since she first met me:

> When your face appeared
> over my crumpled life
> at first I understood only the poverty of what I have.

She paused and then turned to me, scrutinizing my face, my eyes. "You have changed so much, James. You were so hostile and angry and now you seem so at peace." She picked up another volume of poetry. She interrogated me. "What do you know of Dylan Thomas?" I surprised her. "One poem that sums me up," I replied. She found it in the index and read it to me:

> O make me a mask and a wall to shut from your spies
> Of the sharp, enameled eyes and the spectacled claws
> Rape and rebellion in the nurseries of my face.

My charismatic psychiatrist Dr. Alexander Szatmari had prescribed that poem for me.

Lesya put down the book and scrutinized my face again. She went to her desk and picked up a sheet of verse written by a male admirer. "What do you think?" I was jealous of the moment that he had handed it to her. I thought of my own, unread verse. She read and then defended it: "I don't care, I like it!" Then she changed her mind and said, "You're right, it's crap," (I had not said a word). Examining the look on my face, she said soothingly: "O you know..." On her desk was an open copy of the *I Ching* and on the floor beside her bed a worn copy of James Joyce's *Finnegan's Wake*, with which she said she read herself to sleep. Around 11:00 p.m. another man appeared at the door with a knapsack. Lesya opened the door, and he strode past her without invitation, squatted on the floor and threw long, contemptuous glances at me. We crossed swords briefly over his enthusiasm for Quebec separatism, but it was Lesya that he was interested in arguing with. I was astonished at his rudeness and aggression and the verbal jousting over politics and vaguer topics persisted. Was I just another one of her jousting antagonists? At last, Lesya told him firmly that I was staying with her that night and that he must leave. We would drive him to the YMCA. The fight was out of him by the time we reached my car. Had I won some kind of competition? Had she intended to keep him that night and replace him with me in the morning? Outside the YMCA he insisted loudly that she meet him for dinner the next night and she agreed. She did let him kiss her, his arm aggressively around her neck, but she did not keep the date. Lesya fumed on the drive back, calling him arrogant and presumptuous. I was relieved that she now focused her irritation on him but was disheartened that she had let him kiss her.

Lesya pulled the top mattress from her single bed, dragged it to the centre of the room and instructed me that we would sleep a safe distance apart. She stared at me again, suspiciously, as if I was about to utter some complex revelation that she feared. I took a shower and walked out naked; she undressed behind a closet door. With a heavy sigh of resignation, she dragged the mattress back across the floor past my nakedness and next to her bed. I lay down, with her above me. "What do you know... what do you know...tell me what you know," she purred down to me in a childlike voice. She leaned over me in the darkness and showered my face in the dazzling silk of her rich black hair. She whispered my name over and over, "James," swaying her head from side to side. As she chanted, she possessed me, stoked me, provoked me until I began to cry. Finally, I reached up to her, stroked her hair, and pulled her down onto my lips. "I am the one who is frightened," she said when I released her. "The way you kiss," she added in an accusatory tone. I felt again as I had that day I fled a schoolyard bully, that death's dark wings approached above me, the very moment that life swelled in my chest.

Next day we stepped out into the vibrant streets of Montreal, drank coffee and ate crêpes for lunch. She danced around me breathlessly like a colt, kissed me and praised me. She invented a game in which under no circumstance could we break the holding of each other's hands—bad luck to let fate intervene! We dodged the cars on Dorchester Street, hand in hand, her lynx coat trailing her hips, looking ahead. If I could have a photograph of any one thing in that past life, it would be of that crossing. "How do you know so much?" she kept asking me. The question puzzled me. She could not be referring to the bits and pieces of philosophy and poetry that I had cobbled together from books. Was she referring to her own thoughts that she read into my silence? Back at the apartment we ran out of words, and she decided that we should go out to a nightclub. I objected but she insisted; on the way, she told me of a rich French-Canadian suitor, whom we would meet. We sat in a noisy crowd with her friends, who entertained her in French, of which I then understood nothing. "Why don't you say something," she taunted. I felt desolate. I could not even drink. When we got back to the apartment, she was angry and told me that I was spoiled and selfish. I had not, to my own embarrassment, made any impression on her separatist friends and their lofty certitude. A dozen replies half formed in my mind, but I could not bring myself to say one thing.

I packed my few things determined to leave and to process my desolation in the long car ride back to Toronto. Abruptly Lesya changed again and said, "Stay, James. You feel so much, you respond so deeply." And then, "I am so afraid of you! It hurts me to be with you." "Some people call that love," I said. "No," she said, "I won't ... too bad that it will not, cannot, work with us, because I care for you so. We must just let it go." Despite her refusal, despite my failure to overcome her doubts or to be the person that she projected onto me, and despite the melancholy rising in me, I felt my senses sharpening and the meaning of my life unfolding. This is where my life began again, in conflicted love, in Yevtushenko's coloured world.

Then its particular light
on woods, on rivers, on the sea
became my beginning in the coloured world.

I told Lesya that our beginning and our end were both equally unknown to me. We did not kiss nor make love that night. I snuffed out the candles and scraped the melted wax off the floor with my nail as I tried to fall asleep. How much the image of the spent candle wax played in my mind in the empty months ahead. "I lit a thin green candle | To make you jealous of me."

What part of love lay in the embers after that first kiss? I marvelled at how much more difficult love was than I had imagined it to be; all those lonely nights I dreamed of being so close to a girl, to touch her hair, to hold her and to hear her tell me that she loved me. I dreamed that it was salvation, the happiness I craved since I was a boy. Now I lay awake in the thick darkness only inches away from this enigmatic woman, listening to the sporadic rush of night traffic on the street below, feeling alone with her shadow.

Next morning Lesya got up from the silence around the breakfast table and embraced me. She wrapped the shawl of her hair around me, shuttering the morning light. She pressed her beating heart against my ear. I bound my arms around her waist. She begged me to stay. "I feel that we have passed through, that I am at ease with you now," she whispered. I agreed to stay a while. That afternoon, we drove to Mont-Royal and walked in the chill air over fallen leaves. At the lookout she put her arm around me and said in a teacherly way, "You are smart, you know. Use your mind." A very long time later when I met her for the last time, I reminded her of what she said, and how important it was to me, and she admonished herself for her presumption.

Lesya told me about how her father was jealous of her when she was born but later grew to adore her, possessively. He did not want her to have feelings or thoughts private from him. She buried herself in books and learned to play with words—it was why she loved James Joyce, so beyond my understanding. What about Gerard Manley Hopkins, she said? She chanted his odd enunciations and sprung rhythms:

> Márgarét, áre you grieving
> Over Goldengrove unleaving?
> Leáves líke the things of man, you
> With your fresh thoughts care for, can you?

I told her of a time in high school, when my grade 11 literature teacher at Oakwood Collegiate read Hopkins with spit and passion, seeming to direct it entirely at me. I had memorized it and spoke it to her:

> The world is charged with the grandeur of God.
> It will flame out, like shining from shook foil;
> It gathers to a greatness, like the ooze of oil
> Crushed...

"Crushed!" This strange poetry connected us for the rest of our lives. By the time I was ready to go, the embraces were gentler and more comfortable. I did not say that I loved her again. I drove cautiously back to Toronto, my mind in a grip of confusion. That was late September. I went back to work at Holt; she to her classes at Université de Montreal.

Christmas 1969 was the last time that I saw Lesya—not counting a brief, sad reunion thirty years later. She came home for the holiday from Montreal. She told me that she would not, could not, see me, but nevertheless called me on Christmas Eve. "Hello." "Will you see me," I asked; as usual her evasions, then "Yes, no, oh, why don't you come and meet my parents?" "First I want to bring you here," I said. When I picked her up, she told me "I know, we will go to your place, but later...I want to take you somewhere first." Could we discover some kind of meaning together on Christmas Eve she asked? We drove to St. Vladimir's (now St. Volodymyr's) Ukrainian Orthodox Cathedral on Bathurst Street. It was crowded on that holy night, dark and festive. The worshipers and choir were indistinct in the candlelight flickering beneath the burnt umber arches. "Ritual is important in our lives," Lesya announced in her professorial way. "Are you moved?" she asked with a vexed edge. I said, "Yes, but it is not the invisible God that moves me, but the sonorous Vespers." "Yes, I believe that you are right," she said. "You do know." The beautiful male voices intoned through the candlelight; I would forever associate that dark sound with the inscrutable woman at my side. We left and bought a small Christmas tree from a street vendor. "To bring light into our darkness," she said. She told me about the Christmas tree's origins in the mythology of the Green God, Pan, and Gawain—how important it was to observe renewal and redemption. We set up the tree in my apartment. We lit some candles of our own and made love; she turned her head away and said, "James, I am so frightened." I lay awake beside her most of the night and took her home in the very early morning before the light. When we reached her door, I swept her back down the verandah into the side path. She yielded to my embrace. It endured so long that my arms faltered.

No matter how each encounter ended, the next time we met was awkward. "I don't want to see you, I can't," she would say. With persistence I could persuade her to see me one more time and once alone with her I could touch her and take us out of time and just lie with her, make love and listen together to Glenn Gould's *Goldberg Variations* or *Dvorak's Symphony No. 7*, which she said touched her Slavic soul. It was through this love that music penetrated me, bound up with hope and consolation and the new consciousness that she stirred. I played her the *andante* from Mozart's *Sinfonia Concertante in E-flat Major*, explaining that this was the first piece of classical music that deeply moved me, its sad dialogue between violin and viola tangled in an inconsolable sorrow—like us. Lesya lost patience, turned off the music and crawled over to me and whispered, "What's happening?" She chanted my name and said, "Your eyes, beautiful, kind, knowing eyes." I dared not let myself believe her; I focused on the music, to which at least I knew I might return.

One evening after Christmas I met Lesya's parents. Her mother was an elegant, aloof woman, the source of Lesya's dark beauty. A grand piano dominated the open space that stretched from kitchen to living room. There was talk of her brief concert career and of the William Kurelek paintings on the walls; he was a family friend. I knew instantly that they were not happy with me: the rootlessness, the reticence, the long hair, the disturbance I was to Lesya's education. Her father explained in a dismissive tone that he had chosen this open-design house so that there would be no closed doors (no secrets?). Lesya rescued me from the interrogation and indifference of her parents. We clasped hands and went downstairs into the recreation room. We played a record of Leonard Cohen that I had brought her:

I loved you in the morning
Your kisses sweet and warm
Your hair upon the pillow
Like a sleepy golden storm.

"I wish that I had written that about you," I said, thinking of our night together in Montreal. She responded, "Don't think that. Leonard Cohen is such a brat! I knew him, like he knew so many others, briefly." She brought me wine and ran her hands over my face like a blind person. As her beauty overtook me, it left me sadly aware of "the poverty of what I have," of all the days and years ahead that we would spend our lives apart. Now, here in her house and with her ghosts and determinations, I knew that it would not last. I knew that I could not follow her, and I said so. She told me that it made her care for me more (she would never say "love").

Another night that holiday week we visited her friend Ariadne in Swansea, who unnerved me with her direct questions. "He's lovely," she said slyly as though I were a tamed wild animal. Lesya seemed pleased with her friend's reaction. Ariadne told us that she had invited a well-known Hungarian filmmaker who had set up a projector to show us his new documentary film on Marc Chagall and another one he had directed, on Henry Moore. I was impressed by the films but could not keep my mind off Lesya, who just stared at me, not the films. Did she want me to sweep her away or just want me to disappear?

Back at my place we made love and apologized to each other for being such poor lovers. Those pleasures of a freer lovemaking that come with experience seemed insignificant compared to the profound intimacy of just feeling her warmth in my arms and tangling her hair in my fingers. As if in a trance, her eyes closed; she ran her fingers persistently over my face. How many times had I searched my own face in the mirror, spoken my own name, alienated from my own existence? Once, back in my teens, I stared for hours at a night sky through a back window along Quebec Avenue, and then into a mirror until my whole being dissolved in shards of light, in which I saw a terrified other self, staring back at me. Now it was Lesya.

One last evening I managed to buy standing room tickets at Massey Hall to take Lesya to hear the great Russian (partially Ukrainian I explained) pianist Sviatoslav Richter play Beethoven's "Emperor" Concerto with the Toronto Symphony. We stood in the dark balcony, shoulders pressed tightly in our winter jackets, my hand around her waist, breathing the music. I felt in my heartbeat the syncopation of the great first movement cadenza, Richter playing alone in the perfect silence. "When he played, he could liquefy your soul…his fingers supple and fluid smooth," wrote one critic. What an exquisite farewell.

The day after New Year's I took Lesya to Union Station to catch her train to Montreal. She would return to the Université de Montréal to complete that doctorate in linguistics. With some time to spare we sat in the station coffee shop. I accepted the silence up to now but finally when I wanted to speak, I could not. Lesya sensed these episodes of insecurity. She was cool and angry with me for upsetting her plans—did I not understand that her education was important to her? If I could not provide her with answers, now, then she could leave this shell behind. "What is it that you want?" she asked. "Don't you understand that we are a paradox...irresolvable opposites?" "Why," I asked her, "do you think that you can dismiss my love with such vehement disapprovals? What is it that you feel?"

Lesya shifted roles to the end, pestering me for answers to rhetorical questions that I could not provide, impatient for time to dissolve this distraction. On the platform she let me kiss her, her face firmly in my hands. The pneumatic brakes of the locomotive puffed an almost silent, steamy whisper. As she climbed into a passenger car, I could not stop myself from dreaming about all those things that might have happened. I turned away quickly so that I could not see where she sat; did she choose a seat from which she could see me, did she care that I might look back at her again and expose the fading colours in my eyes? We had so briefly discovered that we had been in one another but we were separate again. Did any part of me still lie within her? I walked back into the vaulted station and out onto bleak Wellington Street; I stood there, like one of those indistinct black daubs that imply people in impressionist paintings.

I waited days before I phoned her, long distance, lost in the stupor that melancholy brings. When finally, I gathered the courage to call her and to ask to see her again she said, "Oh yes, come please." And then she phoned back immediately to tell me no. "I care for you, I do, but I cannot see you." This time she was not near, so I could not let her read her own ambivalence in my eyes, could not take her in my arms and persuade her to let me love her. I determined not to chase her as other men had. She was lost forever.

I bored my friends with lovelorn self-pity, for months and months—I thought that I would die of grief—but the recurring dream I had during the long nights held a sharper edge. In it, I stand in the hall at Perth Avenue, my childhood house. Lesya comes to the door—her presence obscure and questioning. I ask her to stay but she takes only one step into the hall, which is smothered in darkness; the wind surges from the street and tangles her hair and rain streams under our feet—it is sweat on my forehead and shoulders when I wake. She looks anxiously back at Roman, waiting angrily in a car. She is wrapped in lynx fur drawn up around her neck and I am ashamed that she has come to my door in charity, like the Salvation Army or the earnest church volunteers with baskets of food who knocked at Christmas. Roman calls to her impatiently. I strip off my shirt and stumble towards her into the rain. "This is doing you no good," she tells me, and urges me to go back inside.

Being in love, I had been sure, would save and redeem me— Eric Fromm and Dr Szatmari had promised me—but loving Lesya inflicted on me all the pain of that condition the poets and singers describe the world over. The habit of longing for love that had afflicted me in childhood was a virus, for which there was no cure.

The last time that I had that dream, I sent a letter to Lesya. I never understood the world the way she thought I did, I told her. I tried to explain how she had lit me, like God into Adam's finger across the Sistine ceiling. The letter ended with regret, possibly recriminations. I immediately hoped that she did not read it.

Some thirty years later Lesya wrote me a very tender letter. She had been sitting in her piano room in her Westmount home one random day, she said, and saw a picture of me looking up at her in an article about The Canadian Encyclopedia in the *Montreal Gazette*. She had cancer, she explained to me, and may be dying and she wanted me to know how important I had been in her life. Could I come to her? I flew to Montreal. She picked me up at the Ritz Carlton Hotel. I hardly recognized her. Her splendid black hair was gone, burned off in the chemotherapy, replaced by an awkward wig.

She wanted to show me her favourite places: the university where she taught, the park on the river where she walked, the coffeehouse bookstore where she loved to spend time alone. She parked out front and insisted that I go into that bookstore and sit down by myself, which I did briefly. Did she think of me when she sat there alone? We drove to her house in Westmount, sat on the floor and talked. She told me sternly that she had seen me wandering through the Pompidou Centre in Paris in 1986. It had been fate. Why had I not greeted her? It had saddened her. I had no memory of her presence there. "The day that I got married," she said, "a mutual friend told me, 'you are marrying the wrong man, you are in love with Jim.'" What to think of all those longing nights I spent despairing of my loss? I did not ask her if she got the letter I sent, telling her of the dream that I had of her abandoning me, but I recited part of the poem that I had written for her:

> You say it is my eyes
> That touch the dark places
> You say that you play Bach very well
> Though I have never heard you

In her house in leafy Westmount, Lesya's beautiful daughter slipped into the room to say hello. She motioned Lesya into the next room and asked her if she was in love with that guy. "I always have been," she told me that she answered.

CHAPTER 15

On to Ottawa

"Luck is a matter of preparation meeting opportunity."

– Seneca, 75 AD

IN SPRING 1970 Anna Porter (then Szigethy), who had been my predecessor at Collier Macmillan and was now editor in chief at McClelland & Stewart, asked me to go to lunch with her and the legendary publisher Jack McClelland at the Inn on the Park to discuss an editorial job. I saw in his body language and avoidance of actually looking at me, that Jack did not like me. Nevertheless, trusting Anna, he supported her decision to offer me a job to move to Ottawa to become the executive editor of the Carleton Library Series, a collection of scholarly books on Canadian history and social science. It sounded like a remarkable opportunity, but I had no clue of what was involved or why Anna had recommended me. I remembered that she had talked to me at length about the cleverness and knowledge of another man who had worked at M&S, who had unfortunately left M&S to join the National Gallery in Ottawa. I knew that I was her second choice. The only thing I remember Jack saying to me was that I would be given a $5,000 expense account and that I should spend it all, "but not one penny more." I would have to move to Ottawa where I would be in the unique position of being co-employed by M&S and the Institute of Canadian Studies at Carleton. Many years later, I gave a speech to group of aspiring editors in Edmonton about my publishing career. At the end, one aggravated participant asked me, "Why were you so lucky?" How was he supposed to get a job, when I had used up all the good fortune? I admitted that I did not know and that I was probably the wrong person to be giving this talk. In my defence, I might have quoted Seneca, if I had known him then, that "Luck is a matter of preparation meeting opportunity." It also mattered, as it always does, to have connections: first Grace Radford and now Anna Szigethy.

I had only been to Ottawa once before and knew very little about it. I drove there for an interview with the Carleton editorial board, which had to approve me as well as Anna and Jack. I parked my Volvo P1800 behind the library and found Patterson Hall, where I had met Fernand Ouellet a few years before while editing his chapters in *Unity in Diversity*. I was greeted by Professor Rob McDougall, a Canadian icon who had founded the Institute of Canadian Studies, and with Jack McClelland, who had created the Carleton Library Series. Rob sensed my apprehension and kindly told me not to worry, that I would do fine in the interview; we walked out over the university quad and talked. He was a gentle man, perhaps amused by Jack's choice. I resigned from Collier Macmillan with regret, since I knew that I had disappointed my friend and mentor Peter West, and I prepared for the greatest move of my life up until then.

The Carleton Library Series was a companion to the better-known New Canadian Library, the latter focusing on Canadian literature and the former on Canadian history and the social sciences. Both sought to resurrect important books, provide them with scholarly introductions, and make them available to the public, and in particular to university students, in affordable paperbacks. The CLS board consisted of professors representing political science, history, sociology, anthropology, economics, geography, and law. It was the board's role to bring forth projects in their disciplines, including new collections as well as reprints. The executive editor was to research new

205

projects, edit the manuscripts, and deliver them to production at M&S. Among the important volumes in the series so far were *Lord Durham's Report, The Confederation Debates, Laurier: A Study in Canadian Politics, The Rowell-Sirois Report* and *The Jesuit Relations*.

My long hair and casual dress were impediments, clearly, to some board members, as was my lack of a PhD. One participant questioned the "quality of my mind," a man whom I later learned had blamed his own failure at his PhD board on an imaginary theft of his work from another student. I recounted numerous Canadian books that I had edited and three that I had written. My editing of the impressive history of Canada, *Unity in Diversity*, and my dealings with the challenging historian Fernand Ouellet suggested that I could work with academic board members and authors. When the discouraging interview paused for coffee, Mike Whittington, who was the political science editor and much the youngest member of the board, told me to pay no attention to my detractors; he would support me. I passed a secret board vote, not unanimous I was sure, and set out to find a place to live, still feeling that I was patching together an uncertain career, and life.

With some guidance from Rob McDougall about neighbourhoods, I roamed the Glebe and found a ground-floor apartment in an old house on First Avenue near Bank Street. On my first day in the apartment, a beautiful woman in sandals and long brown hair approached me outside the front door and said, "Hi, my name is Joan. Are we going to be lovers or friends?" "Friends?" I replied timidly. "Okay," she replied, pointing to my sports car parked out front, "as long as you are not some bourgeois conformist!"

I had been living with Sue Gibbs in my two-room apartment in Phil Balsam's house, on Winona Street in Toronto. We had met at Collier Macmillan and had managed to get along despite her impressive father's severe disapproval. She joined me in Ottawa and we set up a life on the first floor of that old house, with Joan on the third floor. On the second floor were an architecture student Gary and his wife Laurie, who would study Russian at Carleton and become a successful translator. We quickly became acquainted with the chain of friends around them. General editor of the Carleton Series David Farr welcomed and entertained us in his beautiful home on Sussex Drive. I was amazed when he invited me into his gorgeous office with wall to wall walnut bookcases filled with neatly arranged books. He put on a red smoking jacket and offered me a cigar, which I declined, and a sherry, which I accepted. We felt like we had stumbled into a set for *Brideshead Revisited.*

Gary Bean, my second floor neighbour, was a young man of biting wit. His problem with studying architecture was that he detested the corporate world. He was far more interested in becoming a rock guitarist. He had a tall, gawky Robert Plant look about him. When he graduated, he avoided joining the conventional firms and began building an original house (the bedrooms were tiny as they were only for sleeping) in the countryside near Aylmer, Quebec. Gary was skeptical of my bourgeois values (I owned a car and was not living on student loans) and my love of both fine art and classical music. One day he brought his guitar to my apartment and a bass guitar that he had borrowed. He handed me the bass and taught me three cords. "Just alternate them in some kind of rhythm," he told me and then he proceeded to bend languorous riffs at top volume from his amplifier. Seeing me dabbling in front of my easel, he told me, "Your problem is that you want to paint, but have no idea of what to paint!" He handed me a bunch of oil paints that he was no longer using.

One day Gary and Laurie asked Sue and me to visit the house he was building on the Quebec side of the Ottawa River. After we arrived, we drove together to a convenience store/gasoline station outside Aylmer. As I turned into one of the grocery aisles, I stopped in my tracks as I saw a beautiful young woman staring at me. I did not know her, so I turned away and backtracked into the next aisle. She reappeared; her eyes still fixed on me. In an instant she swept down the aisle and into my face, wrapped her arms tightly around my neck, and kissed me firmly on the mouth. Her two friends approached, told her to let go and gently unwrapped her arms. Our lips parted and they escorted her to the parking lot.

There is more random chance in life than we admit. Did this girl rediscover me, remember me from some past incident? Did she recognize her longing in my look? Was she simply disturbed? Gary, Laurie and Sue looked at me standing there, in confusion. I wanted to speak, but not to my friends, whose skeptical disapprovals suppressed and trivialized my experience. Gary's comment, with scorn, that "I suppose that you think that you are something special?" shocked me. I was not ashamed that I had experienced a connection, however brief. Ironically, I now felt even more alone, alienated from my friends and Sue, turned deeply inward to the darkness the stranger touched, and away from the world that belittled me. Perhaps she had found in my arms some solace for her own loneliness. I fruitlessly searched for a sign of her in the parking lot.

IN 1971, IN MY TENURE AT CARLETON, I used the expense account that Jack had warned me about to take a trip across the universities in Western Canada, to meet scholars who might identify important books that should be reprinted, as well as new projects. I heard over and over from the professors that Toronto publishers had never spoken to them, and that they ignored the history and politics of the West. I gained valuable information about who researched or wrote about what subjects—invaluable in my future endeavour with the encyclopedia. I was introduced in particular to a range of western topics, such as co-operatism, political protest, social credit, socialism, alienation, that I was later able to translate into ideas for books and for my own future history of Canada. After landing at the airport in Winnipeg, I abruptly cancelled my flight to Regina. I had been so traumatized by my flight from Ottawa that I doubted that I could ever get on an airplane again. I shook, sweated, and my heart pounded so hard that I thought I would have a heart attack. The experience of flying was my fear of elevators writ large. I took the train to Regina, then to Saskatoon, Calgary, and Edmonton. In

Saskatoon I met the respected political scientist Norman Ward, who, acknowledging my interest in painting, invited me to his home to show me his wonderful art collection, which included a painting by Alex Colville. Years later I invited Norman to join the Advisory Board on the encyclopedia.

In Edmonton, student protests over fees and demands for representation in University governance were in full force. I had to arrange many of my meetings with professors in the HUB Mall or the Student Union building, as some of the main buildings were occupied. A fellow editor at Collier Macmillan learned I would be visiting Edmonton and she gave me the name of a friend who, she told me, reminded her of me. She had unmistakable, unmatched eyes, one blue and one brown. Once I noticed this, I found it hard not to stare impolitely at her, and she acknowledged my curiosity with a tolerant smile. We went to dinner and discussed our lives, full of sadness, challenges and questions about God, science, philosophy and evil. Her religious views, coherent and passionate, challenged my declarations of atheism and the primacy of science. She told me that I had to read her most revered author Pierre Teilhard de Chardin, who, from the questions I was raising, she said would be a revelation to me. I remember her telling me his insight that "animals know, but man knows that he knows." She said that Teilhard would answer my questions about science by explaining how evolution itself was a progression towards God. She was insistent that, despite my denials, I still had faith, a strange echo of Annie Radford? She guided me across the University of Alberta's jumbled campus and showed me where she was studying biology in preparation for medicine. She gave me potted histories of the construction of each building and the financial scandals associated with each. The next night, she invited me to a concert by the Edmonton Symphony at the Jubilee Auditorium, built in 1955 to celebrate the 50th anniversary of Alberta. (It would be to celebrate the 75th anniversary that the encyclopedia would be funded.) I was suffering at the time from an irritating skin disease that had eluded numerous doctors, for which she proposed a diagnosis that I have forgotten. It was later proven to be dermatitis herpetiformis, a variation of celiac disease. Some years later she visited Ottawa, then a physician, and telephoned me. We met but our connection was broken; I got to see her remarkable eyes one last time. She confirmed my diagnosis.

I took a taxi to catch a train from Edmonton to Vancouver but on that very day CN declared a rail strike. I managed to board a bus at midnight. Between the darkness, fog and mud-covered windows of the bus, the legendary Rocky Mountains were obscured. I reflected on the history and social science professors who welcomed me from Manitoba to Alberta. They were united in their critique of Ontario-based publishing, which almost entirely ignored them. I collected lists of new manuscripts and PhD theses on fascinating topics such as social protest, agrarian movements, prairie settlement, Indigenous history, battles with eastern banks and railways, even the strangeness of Social Credit. Many of these topics became original volumes or books of readings in the Carleton Library Series. I was proud of one of my discoveries on this trip, Ian MacPherson, whose *Each for All: A History of the Co-operative Movement in English Canada* became one of the most significant contributions to the Series.

Vancouver was a challenge for me, as I was ignorant of how distant the two universities were. The taxi fares depleted my cash. The Holiday Inn called me to the desk and told me that my credit card had been refused. The accountant at M&S bailed me out. Astonishingly, my next-door neighbour at the hotel was Ravi Shankar. I knew it was him by his practicing at night as I was practising my own rudimentary classical guitar pieces, and I managed to locate and attend his concert. Also at the hotel was the rock group Lighthouse, whom I met and talked to at breakfast. They told me about their upcoming concert, which I also attended. I enjoyed our Canadian band, but the revelation at that concert was the final performance, the relentless and dazzling albino blues guitarist Johnny Winter.

On the bus ride to Vancouver, after my reflections on my heterochromia companion, I decided to phone Sue and tell her that we should break up. She interrupted my intentions with an abrupt announcement that she was pregnant. I was amazed, shocked, and perplexed. I swiftly realized that I really wanted to be a father, though it had never been discussed. On November 5, 1971, I succeeded in persuading Dr. Howe to allow me to be the first father permitted to witness a birth in the Ottawa Civic Hospital. Several nurses tried to bar my entry, but Dr. Howe told them to get me a mask and gown and to bring me into the delivery room. He lifted the blue baby up into the air, cut the umbilical cord and hung her by her ankles upside-down. She was howling as he cleaned the mucus out of her nose and mouth. A nurse tightly wrapped her now-pink body in a blanket, which immediately calmed her, and then she handed her to me—the most heart-stopping moment of my life. In my frozen brain I remember thinking, "It's not just a baby, it's a girl!" Poor Sue, without her glasses, missed much of this until the nurse passed the girl, whom we called Rebeccah, to her.

MY LIFE IN OTTAWA, at Carleton, with my friends, editing the manuscripts, studying history and art history, was an advanced course in Canadian studies and life. The ten or so books we produced each year fell below the general numerical standards of M&S editors. I knew that they blamed me for the low return and for the commercial failures of most of the titles. But I was at the mercy of a glacial board and of the lengthy and scholarly nature of the books. I loved living in Ottawa, with my tenth-floor office in the Arts Tower overlooking the canal, the rapids of the Rideau River on the other side of campus raging in spring, the bike rides with Rebeccah in tow along the canal to the university daycare or downtown to ByWard Market or to Major's Hill Park.

There was an excitement of being exposed to national politics all through the day. I was still an outsider, neither academic staff at Carleton nor full-time editor at McClelland & Stewart, but it suited me. Every year a whole new class of thirty young students arrived from all over Canada to take their interdisciplinary master's degrees. In every new group I made lasting friends, with whom I could attend movies, talk, party, argue, play chess, attend music, date, or visit the art gallery. I attended the weekly interdisciplinary seminar and engaged with many of the guest speakers. I picked Irving Layton up at the airport and he asked me about what he should say to the class. I told him that he should tell these "ignorant social scientists" something that they have never heard before, that poetry revealed the deepest secrets of life and love. He performed that imperiously, in his resounding voice, reading scraps from one of his books, shifting his eyes towards me approvingly. "Got them, eh?"

My fear that I was a fraud in this academic world faded as I dealt daily with the lofty professors, whose own flaws emerged as they tried to perform editorial duties. Historian David Farr's tenure as general editor passed and his replacement Michael Gnarowski and I became good friends as well as editorial partners, dealing with the difficult board. Being hired from Sir George Williams University in Montreal, he too was an outsider and we shared skepticism of some of the more stubborn board members. Michael had a devotion similar to Rob McDougall's to Canadian literature and books, as he managed his own small press, which published important poetry over the years. I slowly made friends with a number of other professors, by playing squash with some and others by playing chess. One historian, Stan Mealing, a cool, quiet character who had few publications but a sharp wit and skeptical gaze, became a regular chess opponent in his corner office in Patterson Hall. We played almost every Friday afternoon in his office, to the same result. He would study his openings during the week and take long, thoughtful, silent pauses between moves, constantly pawing at his chin. If I gained an advantage, he inevitably shook his head and simply moved all the pieces back to their starting positions and insisted that we start again. The most fun we had was replaying the games of the Fisher-Spassky match in Iceland in 1972. I would collect the results printed in the *Globe and Mail* in the morning and rush over to his office, one of us playing Spassky and the other Fisher. We played squash a few times, but he declared that I was "too damned fast!" and refused to play me again. When Stan wrote an introduction for me for one of the Carleton

Library volumes, I discovered another one of his eccentricities. His extremely tiny written script was almost invisible without a magnifying glass. It was not a coincidence, I think, that historian Norman Hillmer became my lifetime friend out of all the people I met in the faculties. He too was an outsider, employed by National Defence but lecturing at Carleton. Since Carleton got him cheap, it took many years before they finally hired him full time. He was a great support to me during the trying times ahead, despite his having to forgive my condescending ridicule of his taste in television shows.

In my office in Canadian Studies, next to the director's door, I was often the first person approached by new students scrounging for inside information about the best profs and courses. Each year I met new friends who played a role in my life long after they achieved their degrees, meeting them in educational situations, or on national boards, or on film and web projects. One of those friends brought his wife Louise from Vancouver. It was the second time I fell in love at first glance. It was a wintry day, in the foyer of the Arts Tower at Carleton. I was fortunately holding a very cute baby, Rebeccah, and Louise swept in from the cold to admire her. I would not soon, or ever, forget that enquiring face. Her blue eyes, shining beneath a snowy fur cap, struck me like a vision of Lara sweeping in from the Russian steppe into the arms of Zhivago. "Hear my soul speak," wrote the bard in *The Tempest*, "of the very instant that I saw you, did my heart fly at your service." We have been life partners ever since.

In 1979 I gave a presentation on my upcoming list of books in the Carleton series to the full sales and editorial staff of McClelland & Stewart. It was universal in the publishing world that the sales reps were skeptical and bored by editors trying to sell them on their esoteric projects. If an editor could not make a persuasive point in about three minutes, their minds would stray into dismissive boredom. With my insecurities still close to the surface, I was a nervous speaker; as presentations progressed around the table and it came closer and closer to my turn to speak, my temperature rose, sweat moistened my shirt, and my ears began to burn. Why it happened, I do not know,

KNOW IT ALL

Louise Edwards was raised in Kitimat, BC, moved to Montreal, then Simon Fraser University before fate or blind luck brought her to Carleton University. (Photo by Phil Balsam.)

but somehow, I began to speak; I proved to myself that no matter how apprehensive I felt, that I could still talk. My confidence grew and when I was done, people around the table clapped and murmured their approval. Even Jack McClelland turned his skeptical gaze on me with mild consent. After the meeting, the college and secondary school sales managers came to me and said that they had been looking desperately for an author for a new "social" history of Canada and that I was clearly that person. Jack McClelland and the managing editor Linda McKnight were doubtful. Linda asked me why we should publish yet another history textbook of Canada when there were already so many. I told her that it would be because ours would be different and

Our daughter Rebeccah in Toronto with Annie Radford, who was thrilled to embrace her as she had once, perhaps, held me.

because it would be "better." She agreed that I should write a proposal. On the principle that it was to be a "social" history, we managed to persuade the Canadian Labour Congress to pay $50,000 to help with production. As social history, our text would be on the cutting edge, telling the stories of those who were left out of our historical narrative, notably women, workers, and "Original People," as the terms First Nations or Indigenous were not yet current.

Since the project was clearly too much for me to write alone, I invited Dan Francis, whom I had met when he was a student at Canadian Studies, to co-author the book. We did fill the text with descriptions of everyday life on the farms, in the factories and lumber camps or at sea, and of the experiences, challenges, and roles of women. We included the interpretations of historians and archaeologists, as well as numerous original documents, questions, and projects. We designed dozens of historical maps and researched many hundreds of archival photographs in the National Archives in Ottawa. When the two volumes of New Beginnings appeared in 1981 it had excellent reviews, but it never sold well, partly because the system was not ready for it and partly because M&S did not have a secondary school sales staff. Writing that book greatly deepened my understanding of Canadian history. The book's imminent publication was an important part of my resumé when I applied for the job as editor of The Canadian Encyclopedia. The books also launched Dan on an eminent career as an historical writer, for which he was later awarded the Governor General's Award for History.

With its commercial difficulties, the importance and reputation of the Carleton Library Series had to rest on more ephemeral grounds. In its initiative in the editing, reprinting, and dissemination of significant books important to the history and social sciences of Canada, it was of inestimable value to Canadian students. For the first time important primary source documents became widely available, in an affordable paperback format. For decades, Canadian university students, and students studying Canada abroad, have bought these volumes. The series was not only another tribute to the vast contributions of Jack McClelland to Canadian publishing, it was the scholarly initiative most associated with Carleton University.

Two volumes of the Carleton Library Series still stand out in my memory. In 1974, Wallace Clement, a young member of the Carleton Department of Sociology, brought us a manuscript based on his PhD dissertation, analyzing inequality in Canadian society. It was not the usual reprint, and Wallace and I spent many hours together clarifying and polishing it. We worked into the night at the Guild Inn in order to clean up the galleys and get it to press. I had to pick up Louise at the airport and Wally came with me so that our discussion would not be interrupted. A decade had passed since his mentor John Porter had published his renowned book, *The Vertical Mosaic*, the first analysis of power and inequality in Canada, which received acclaim both at home and abroad. Clement's book described how the capitalist economic elite of Canada concentrated its base of power and confined avenues of access into its inner circles. The book turned out to be brilliantly reviewed and to become the equivalent of a bestseller in the series. Though little recognized in our own company, it was the most important book published by M&S that year.

A second memorable publication was a return to my old *bête noir*, historian Fernand Ouellet. My own edited translations of his chapters in *Unity in Diversity* were often cited as the clearest example of his important interpretation of nineteenth-century Quebec history. His major work *Histoire économique et sociale du Québec, 1760-1850* was published in 1966 and the Carleton Library Series had commissioned a problematic translation that was delivered to the history editor. The board was keen to see the translation into print, as was I. At every meeting, for years, the board member responsible for the manuscript reported that the translation was not ready, despite his own dedicated and thankless work deep into many nights trying to fix it. He repeated how he had to deal with the intricacies and subtleties of Ouellet's prose and the complexities of his ideas.

After years of these tales, our general editor Michael Gnarowski finally wrote to the editor and demanded that he deliver the manuscript. I was sent to his office to collect it. The huge typescript was left for me on a counter in the general office. When I got back to my office, I scanned page after page and eventually the entire manuscript. There was not a single editorial mark anywhere, in pencil, pen or marker, not even, it seemed, a fingerprint. The board never asked for nor got an explanation of what had happened from that inexplicable board member. I began editing the huge manuscript, once again working daily with Ouellet, dictionaries at our sides, to clarify the awkward translation and we got the book published.

Despite its many achievements, The Carleton Library Series' focus on previously published works made it difficult to represent any re-evaluation of Canadian society. After multiple volumes on Lord Durham, Confederation, Laurier, Champlain, Senate Reform, Transportation, Money and Banking, the very first volume that came forward on Indigenous issues was a manuscript "Canadian Indians and the Law," brought forward by anthropology editor Derek G. Smith.

As I neared my tenth year with The Carleton Series, I began to talk to my friend and colleague Michael Gnarowski, who was the series' general editor, about me moving on. M&S abandoned the series to Macmillan for a few years before Michael developed plans for it to become an independent university press. The books were wonderful and educational and the contacts with authors valuable, but there was little challenge for me. I applied for the position of head of the book publishing program of the Canada Council. After a long and engaging interview, the committee told me that I was the most qualified candidate, with a thorough knowledge of publishing, but they could not give me the job because I did not speak French. I discussed a position with McGill Queens Press but before a decision was made, the goddess Tyche appeared with her wheel.

CHAPTER 16

A Gift to Canada

"The purpose of an encyclopedia is to bring together the knowledge scattered over the surface of the earth to expose the general system to those with whom we live, and transmit them to those who come after us."

– Denis Diderot

MEL HURTIG wrote in his memoir that he first had the idea for a new encyclopedia of Canada while sitting alone in a school library, waiting to talk to a group of students, growing despondent at the lack of Canadian reference works he saw on the shelves. A former bookseller in Edmonton, Hurtig had embarked on an ambitious publishing program in the 1970s. Through his energetic involvement with the Committee for an Independent Canada he had become a well-known spokesman on television, radio, and public meetings for nationalist causes. He spoke persuasively in his distinctive baritone voice of how much better off Canadians would be if they, and not American capital, controlled their lives. Hurtig was a publisher like no other and commanded attention in the media and among nationalistic Canadians far beyond the scope of his modest publishing company.

Although he was known through the Canadian media for his nationalist issues, Mel was proud of his Alberta, particularly his Edmonton, identity. (I was encouraged to hate the Flames and Stampeders, cowboy hats, and to bypass Calgary at all costs on my way to Banff.) Coming from Ottawa, I was aware of the fractious disputes between Albertans and the federal government over petroleum, tempered by the books I had uncovered in my exploratory trip across the West in the 1970s describing intricate social, agrarian, and Aboriginal issues that were a part of its history. Mel was himself an outspoken critic of his Conservative provincial government and was abused in conservative and anti-Semitic circles. Most of the people Mel introduced to me, such as political scientist Larry Pratt, were also hostile to the province's oil policies, but no one seemed sympathetic to my bicultural view of the Canadian identity. I soon learned that Canadian politics were far more varied and divisive than in the East, which condescended to the spectre of Western alienation. Much later, in the early 2000s, I must have earned my Western chops, as I was selected by a distinguished panel of historians to write the unit on the Lougheed years and those constitutional disputes for the official history of the province, *Alberta Formed Alberta Transformed.*

For some thirty years Mel spoke out for Canada in a way that no one does now. He was one of those rare people who had such unbounded confidence in himself that he started things: a bookstore, a publishing company, several nationalist organisations, and a political party. Mel was a great enthusiast. When he persuaded me to move to Edmonton to edit The Canadian Encyclopedia, he told me that it was the greatest city on Earth. I am still here.

Mel was the driving force behind the encyclopedia project, but his story of its origins is not correct. The location of that school library in his story varied according to where in Canada he happened to be speaking. Ivon Owen, former head of Oxford University Press and founder of the literary periodical *Tamarack Review*, and freelance editor-writer Morris Wolfe had approached Hurtig with the original proposal for a new encyclopedia in conversations and an exchange of letters in 1975. Grolier's *Encyclopedia Canadiana*, published in 1958 but based largely on a reference work published by Macmillan in the 1930s, was by then badly out-of-date, not only in obvious

A Gift to Canada

Mel Hurtig speaks during the launch of his National Party in Calgary, February 2, 1993. (Canadian Press/Dave Buston.)

things, such as statistics, but in how it represented the country. In a critical review, Owen had panned *Canadiana* on its publication as a regrettable missed opportunity. Hurtig was excited about the proposal, both from his political inclinations and for the survival of his struggling publishing company. He sent the proposal to the Canada Council in 1976 for financial support.

The proposal outlined by Wolfe and Owen was for a single volume of about a million words, based on the model of the single-volume *Columbia Encyclopedia*. Scheduled to appear in 1981, it was predicted to cost $1.3 million to produce and was expected to sell for $35. Hurtig asked the Canada Council for $750,000 and committed to raising the deficit of $455,500 "from other sources." In his submission Mel included letters of support from literary journalist William French, international literary theorist Northrop Frye, journalist-editor Robert Fulford ("Now where's the book? I'm impatient to have it on my desk..."), novelist Hugh Hood, broadcaster Knowlton Nash, poet Miriam

221

Waddington, politician David Lewis, and others. Except for a hazy budget for editors and writers, there was no indication in the documentation as to how Owen, Wolfe, and Hurtig planned to carry out making this encyclopedia. The Council expressed interest, but following its bilingual mandate, insisted that Hurtig would have to set up duplicate French and English editorial staffs and offices so he could publish a French edition simultaneously with the English. Unfortunately for Mel, the Council was not willing to pay for these added expenses and the project faltered.

Fate intervened two years later as Alberta's 75th anniversary (in 1980) neared. Hurtig approached the Alberta government with the idea that it fund the national encyclopedia as Alberta's "gift to Canada," as part of the province's celebration. The Conservative Alberta government had allocated $75 million for celebratory projects and festivals—some frivolous, such as Edmonton's High Level Bridge "waterfall" (now defunct). Funding a national reference work was a novel idea and caught the attention of Premier Peter Lougheed, who despite his conflicts with the federal Liberal government over energy policy, considered himself no less a Canadian nationalist than Hurtig. He no doubt thought that such a project would counter his image in the rest of Canada as "the blue-eyed sheik." On November 15, 1979, the legislature announced that the Alberta government would underwrite Hurtig for the encyclopedia's development costs with $3.4 million for research and development and would donate a further $600,000 to pay for delivery of a free copy to every school and library in the country. It was all done on condition that no other (particularly federal) funding be accepted—it was to remain an Alberta initiative. Hurtig spent the next few years raising the money for printing and marketing from reluctant banks as his publishing company was in debt. This level of investment was ambitious even with the provincial money. It would be a publishing endeavour unprecedented in Canadian publishing history. The awkward issue of producing a "national" encyclopedia without a French-language edition was put aside with a promise by Hurtig that once the English version

A Gift to Canada

was published, the rights would be "donated free" to a Quebec publisher. Ironically, it was this failure to promise a bilingual encyclopedia that enabled me to become the editor in chief, since I did not at that time speak French. Sometime before his proposal to Lougheed, Hurtig dropped Owen and Wolfe from the plans. Owen never spoke to Mel again, but Morris Wolfe was to be of enormous help to me and to the project.

The excitement around Hurtig Publishers must have been palpable. This project not only dwarfed this small Edmonton publisher, it was greater than any single commercial enterprise in Canadian publishing history. Hurtig hired a general manager, Frank McGuire, who set up offices on the second floor of an old brick house (Ring House 4) on the campus of the University of Alberta in early spring 1980. McGuire had been director of "communications production" for the provincial government. Former university president Harry Gunning was appointed to head an advisory board. Above all, Mel needed an editor in chief, by his account the most important decision he would ever have to make. He held a nation-wide search through his extensive connections in the media and with a national advertisement in the *Globe and Mail*. When I finally saw the ad years later in the Hurtig files (now in the Alberta Provincial Archives) it read in large letters "Editor in chief $35,000 starting salary." It declared that Hurtig Publishers in Edmonton is "planning an absolutely first-class comprehensive reference book covering all things Canadian." The main qualifications for the position were that the candidate must be "a full [sic] experienced, highly respected editor" and be "a generalist with a lengthy background of working in Canadian topics, and have excellent academic and other connections across Canada." The ad promised that this was "a once-in-a-lifetime opportunity" for "the very best person."

I read later in the Hurtig files that more than three hundred applicants each believed that he or she was the very best person. In my letter, I focused on my editorial experience and on my self-image as a generalist and waited to hear from Mel. I was encouraged by my friends and family, but I had serious doubts about my prospects, particularly about my lack of knowledge of

French in a national endeavour. I also had reservations about my ability to be chief of anything, as I had no managerial experience. I eventually received a note from Mel telling me he was headed to Ottawa and that we should meet. His letter to me had been lost in the Carleton University mail system for two weeks and I received it only two days before he arrived. He was in Ottawa to be interviewed on the radio. After a hasty phone call, we arranged to meet afterward at the restaurant that was in those days located in the basement of the Château Laurier.

I recognized Mel from hearing him speak at publishing gatherings, where he would spring vigorously onto the stage and in his edgy voice, broken by a persistent clearing of his throat, deliver pungent critiques of the domination of American companies of our businesses, particularly of our publishing houses. I had heard much the same from Jack McClelland, who had tried to engage me in the activities of the nationalist organization, the Committee for an Independent Canada (CIC). (Jack and I had met for dinner in that very restaurant before a meeting of the CIC. I had nervously said that it was an old-fashioned place and he corrected me that it was a splendid and very Canadian place. I never mastered the correct tone dealing with Jack.) I failed to muster the same passion for economic nationalism as Jack or the committee, or Mel for that matter, but I fervently supported the principle that Canadian authors should have access to Canadian readers. I listened to the interview on the car radio. Mel was having a terrible time apologizing for his persistent cough.

Brunch with Mel at the Château Laurier was much like the many breakfasts, lunches and dinners we shared over the next ten years. I thought that I was there to impress him, but he proceeded ardently to tell me in great detail about his own accomplishments, narratives of his bookselling days in his locally famous Edmonton bookstore, and his initiatives in establishing a publishing business in the West. He recounted anecdotes of his customers, of his authors, of his golf game, and his victories over hapless opponents in debates. Mel's charm and earnestness always tempered his self-importance. We were down to

A Gift to Canada

our last coffee refill before he finally asked me about my background in publishing. I had tried to prepare myself with answers to obvious questions and planned to appear confident and calm. I told him that there was probably very little that I did not know about publishing, since I was a student of everything that I got involved in, from typesetting and printing to proofreading and editing, to dealing with authors, all the way to having written several books myself. I explained that over ten years at the Institute of Canadian Studies at Carleton University, I had been involved in seminars and courses and in editing a hundred scholarly books on Canada. Almost with a sense of naïveté he asked me if I was a generalist. I was prepared for that question and responded that I was in Isaiah Berlin's term a "fox," having a little knowledge about a lot of things, from literature, classical music, sport and art, to social science, philosophy, biography, and history. Above all, I told him that the driving force, almost the redeeming force, in my mental life from the time I was a boy was curiosity and my love of books. How much of our lives is determined by these encounters in which each person tries to evaluate the other, guessing, interpreting and either trusting or evading our instincts? Mel persuaded me that he was a self-confident, accomplished, ambitious man, but what did he think of me? As long as I knew him, he never said.

In preparation for that first meeting, I had tried to find out everything I could about planning and producing an encyclopedia. Any glance at an impressive set of volumes of Britannica, World Book, or other great reference works suggested that it was a daunting task, but very little was written about how to go about it. I had had a passing acquaintance with encyclopedias in my youth. The only two books in our house when I was growing up on Perth Avenue in Toronto were a dictionary and (ironically) an old one-volume encyclopedia, whose maps and photographs of exotic places fascinated me. I would spend hours with a clump of plasticine trying to model the wild animals and famous buildings I saw in that book. I recalled that one-volume encyclopedia on the kitchen shelf when I was living on Perth Avenue—its fascinating maps, photographs and entries on exotic animals.

225

At Oakwood Collegiate in Toronto, an English teacher thought she was punishing me by making me copy out pages of the Encyclopedia Britannica, something I enjoyed rather more than the punishment of redrawing multiple copies of the innards of a frog meted out by my biology teacher (he was furious when he saw that I had done the twenty-five drawings he demanded in miniature and had fitted them onto a single page). As a teenager I applied to sell encyclopedias door-to-door but I failed the recruitment. These passing encounters with the great books fired my curiosity but gave no clue as to how they were made.

On excellent advice from historian David Farr at Carleton University, I had also requested the papers of John Robbins, an acquaintance of his who had been the editor of Grolier's *Canadiana* in the 1950s. An archivist retrieved the boxes from back rooms in the National Library. From his papers, letters, and memos I learned very little about how Robbins organized his encyclopedia (it was patterned on and Canadianized from Grolier's world encyclopedia, with much of its contents taken from the 1935 Macmillan Encyclopedia of Canada) but I noted his frustration with the editorial interference of Grolier's head office in New York. *Canadiana* was in most ways a branch-plant publication based on the American view that, with a few tweaks, Canada was not much different than the United States. Though he was a loyal employee and a thorough editor, Robbins was not happy with his lack of authority. I determined that any new endeavour should be entirely made in Canada and that its editor in chief must have complete editorial control. On this point Mel entirely agreed.

After an intensive and persistent search, an encouraging librarian at the National Library eventually unearthed two useful articles in an obscure library science publication about the creation of the Columbia one-volume encyclopedia. It provided rare and excellent background on principles, processes, and methodologies. Since Columbia was Mel's original model, he was impressed. A quick reading of the book *Caught in a Web of Words*, the story of the great lexicographer James Murray and the making of the *Oxford English Dictionary*, elevated my ambitions and livened the conversation with him, though he was taken aback when I told him that Murray had only reached the letter C when he died. Mel would have long been bankrupted by then, he told me. I was a complete unknown to Mel, the editor of an important but specialized series of scholarly Canadian books, and the author of several textbooks on Canadian history, but including research and production costs, this was going to be an eight-million-dollar project (half of it Mel's), and an enormous gamble for any publisher to put in such inexperienced hands. I did not have a graduate degree, much less a PhD like many of the other candidates, but I had pretty much spent my whole life learning, reading, and studying. As a boy in the Junction area of Toronto I managed to spend almost as much time in the local libraries as I did making trouble in the back alleys.

I asked Mel many times over the years why he chose to hire me out of three hundred applicants, but he never told me. He left no hints of what he thought of me in the files. He told everyone that his whole future depended on getting the right person for this most important job. But as in so many other instances, Mel made tough decisions only with the advice of others. He told me as we left the hotel that I was a leading candidate and that I should write him a "strong" letter "in less than two pages," telling him why I should be successful and to gather some references. I fretted over the wording of that letter, dreaming that I might write something that would have an impact on him, as Leonardo's letter had on Ludovico Sforza. In a positive way, I was not a specialist, wedded to a particular discipline as academics are, though my preference was towards history and art. I had broad experience dealing with academics as authors and I knew their strengths (knowledge) and weaknesses (schedules and clear language). I had never missed a deadline and had written four books, including a co-authored two-volume social history, *Canada: New Beginnings*. Through publisher Jack McClelland and founder of the Institute for Canadian Studies Rob McDougall, I had been intimately exposed to a heady Canadian nationalism.

Mel telephoned me after he received my letter and arranged for me to go to Toronto to be interviewed by Morris Wolfe, the Toronto-based journalist, editor, and teacher at the Ontario College of Art, who had co-written the original plan for an encyclopedia. I met Morris in the famous rooftop bar at the Park Plaza Hotel at the intersection of Bloor and University in Toronto. It was a favourite drinking spot for Canadian literati over the years, from Morley Callaghan to Mordecai Richler, June Callwood, Peter Gzowski, and Margaret Atwood. Morris introduced me to the almost-as-famous bartender Joe Gomes, who had been working there since the 1950s. On Gomes' recommendation I ordered a single malt Scotch on ice. I remember that evening not so much as an interview but as a long, enjoyable conversation with Morris about our common interests in the arts and literature. We were able to discuss the original proposal for an encyclopedia and also my own research in the National Library. By coincidence, at the same time, I was reading Jackson Bate's biography of lexicographer and polymath Samuel Johnson, who had become an inspiration to me. Morris would not tell me why he and Ivon Owen had been sidelined in the project, but he did warn me that I would need to be very wary of the ambitious general manager Frank McGuire, whom Mel had already hired without any input from an editor in chief.

I asked historian David Farr, current general editor of the Carleton Library Series Michael Gnarowski, historian Norman Hillmer, former head of the Royal Commission on Bilingualism and Biculturalism Davidson Dunton, geographer David Knight, and executive editor at Macmillan Virgil Duff, to write letters of reference for me. Norman phoned and read me his beautiful letter; an act of friendship that he declared with confidence would get me the job. Mel and Frank had already interviewed Virgil Duff for the position. Virgil told me that he was very hesitant to work with McGuire and was disturbed by the haphazard way the interviews were conducted. He was at the same time offered a job as executive editor of University of Toronto Press and was relieved to go there instead. I only saw the letters written for me later when I went through the files in the archives. David Farr's letter was touching in its details and its elegant prose. Mel phoned Norman and asked him bluntly, "Can he do it?" "Yes, he can," Norm replied. Michael Gnarowski called me professional and his friend. Dunton and Duff, and in telephone interviews my colleagues at McClelland & Stewart raised concerns about my lack of management experience—a fair judgment that seriously concerned me as well. I told Mel that of course I had chosen references that might praise me but if he wanted to hear the "other side," he should speak to Jack McClelland. He said that he would not, but he did. In the file, he wrote in large script with his typical red felt pen, a quote from Jack that "I'd rather not say anything." These reports damaged me by aggrandizing McGuire's role as an organizer and manager in the organization, but I would prove them wrong.

I never saw Morris Wolfe's notes to Mel about our interview at the Park Plaza, but they cannot have been negative because Morris called me later in the week to tell me that Mel wanted me to fly, with my partner Louise, to Edmonton. If the trip was a test to see how I could manage, it was a good thing that no one but Louise saw me on the airplane. I was terrified of flying and had refused to set foot on a plane for the past five years. My heart was racing; I was in a desperate, pale-faced sweat. I honestly thought that my most serious deficiency in applying for the job would be my inability to get on that airplane, a fate far too close to the nightmares of falling down an elevator shaft that I had most nights.

Mel had promised to pick us up at the airport and to give us a tour of Edmonton, but he never showed up. We took a taxi to a downtown hotel. I tried to get instructions from Mel about hotel arrangements and meetings, but he never replied. On a very cold evening I walked down bleak, windblown 101 Street to buy Louise some cold medicine. Mel phoned and told me to meet him for breakfast at the Four Seasons Hotel the next day. I asked him to bring me all the files and contracts related to the project so far. He arrived with a large box. Over breakfast he told me that the "rap" on me was my lack of organizational ability. I answered that I had the ability to plan and to work with intelligent people. I recounted in detail how I had "organised" the centennial project *Unity in Diversity* and how I had planned and with co-author Dan Francis had written a complete two-volume social history of Canada for high schools— to this day the only textbook of its kind. I had successfully organised and published a geography series at Holt, Rinehart & Winston and a Canadian history series at Collier Macmillan. I might have a messy desk I told him, but I had a very organized mind. I then outlined to him clearly and in detail exactly how I would organize and produce the encyclopedia.

Mel sent me to a government office in downtown Edmonton that afternoon to be interviewed by Frank McGuire. If McGuire was not exactly a government watchdog planted on the project, as numerous people warned me, as a condition for Mel to get money from the Conservative government, he was extremely tight with the conservative government bureaucracy. Premier Peter Lougheed was supportive of the project, but Mel was hated and distrusted by many in the Conservative Caucus for his liberal and nationalistic views. Conservatives were more disturbed by Mel than they were of the almost complete American control of the Alberta oil industry.

McGuire made me sit and wait for ages in the anteroom, before finally asking his secretary to escort me to him. He sat imperiously behind a huge desk in his office and began my interview with a long speech about his own competence, his experience as a printer, his organisational and with special emphasis his management skills. After patiently listening, I told him that was all very interesting, but did he want to know how I, as the potential editor in chief, would actually go about making an encyclopedia, as opposed to managing one? I explained how I would choose and organize staff, consultants, writers, editors, subjects, articles, and illustrations. Fidgeting in his chair, he informed me officiously that yes, I might be on the right track. It's what we call a "systems approach," he said. It gravely concerned me about how Frank and I were going to work out our roles in the haze of his management clichés and the muddled lines of authority Morris Wolfe had warned me about, and I anxiously discussed it with Morris over the telephone that evening. He suggested that I needed to read McGuire's contract carefully before getting in any deeper. I wondered if Morris had been involved in this process and had pulled out when he met McGuire, as Virgil Duff had done.

I have no idea what was said between Mel and Frank about my interview. The criticisms of my organizational abilities and Frank's bragging about his own skills were a toxic potion that almost derailed the whole project over the next few years. Mel phoned me at the hotel and asked Louise and me to meet him for dinner at the Royal Mayfair Golf Club. The cab driver had no idea where the club was; he actually had to drive over a median to get us there when we called out that we had spotted the club sign. It seemed a bad omen, as Mel was incredulous that anyone in the city did not know where his famous golf club was located. Was this a confirmation of my disorganized mind? Everyone, including his friends, journalist Bill Thorsell and broadcaster Don Newman, and his partner, former Miss Canada and then-broadcaster Barbara Kelly, were already seated. The conversation never touched on our reason for being there. Thorsell was particularly polite and engaged Louise in talking about Edmonton neighbourhoods. Mel was at the far end of the table and we hardly exchanged a word.

The documents that Mel loaned me—to his credit it was the whole dossier—caused me great concern. I was shocked to read McGuire's contract, in which Mel paid him a much higher salary than he was offering to the editor in chief. McGuire was to receive a pension, a car, a percentage of the profits, and most troubling, a percentage of any amount of the $4 million budget he could prevent the staff from spending. None of these perks were offered to the editor in chief—by Mel's admission the most important person in the project. How important had the government made it that Mel hire Frank? At a dinner the next night with Frank and his wife, Louise and me, the atmosphere was tense. We were all tired and had little in common to talk about. I told Frank that he and I needed to meet again; this time in my hotel room. I spoke to Mel before the meeting,

231

telling him that I was very concerned that Frank had negotiated a deal that left little room for the person who actually had to create the encyclopedia. They both seem to have had the idea that I would be sitting in the library with a few editors quietly writing the encyclopedia, dutifully delivering it to Frank, who in his bureaucratic mind set would have been completely incapable of knowing what to do. I explained that a true encyclopedia, one that would make Mel proud and would fulfill Peter Lougheed's ambition of being a great gift to the nation, would require the involvement of a huge community of scholars from every part of Canada, assembled by an editorial staff under my guidance. Mel paused and then told me that he was "finally impressed" with me; for the first time he saw that I really might be the right candidate. I guessed that we had been dancing in the dark up till then.

In our meeting next morning in my hotel room, I told McGuire that he had negotiated a sweet deal that benefitted him and left little opportunity for the editor in chief. To his credit, Frank leaned back on his chair, put up his feet and said, "Go for it"! He said that he would be delighted if I could negotiate the same deal for myself and that his salary was partly based on the idea that he would be working for Hurtig Publishers "setting up computer systems." A stocky, competitive Scot who had been hardened on the soccer pitch, Frank shone when engaged or confronted. He was surprised when he saw that I was the same, toughened on the streets of Toronto's Junction.

Still confused by the whole process, with no real feedback or encouragement, I phoned Hurtig from the airport. "Are you thinking of hiring me?" I asked him bluntly. He paused and said "yes" with emphasis on "I think the three of us can make the encyclopedia together." I told him that I would not ask for more money, a pension, a car, or other perks given to McGuire, but I insisted that I would also receive a bonus equal to Frank's if the encyclopedia was a success. I told him that I wanted a job description of the editor in chief's role included in my contract, and that I would write it myself and send it to him. I sent that letter on April 2, 1980, and Mel sent me the formal offer in early May. He accepted my condition that the editor in chief, alone, would be "100% responsible for the principles and content of the encyclopedia"—and that included Frank and himself. My bonus would depend, in his words, on the encyclopedia receiving "excellent" reviews.

CHAPTER 17

To Shine a Light on Canada

"What grace may be added to commonplace matters by the power of order and connection."

– Horace, Ars Poetica

AFTER I RESIGNED from my position at the Institute for Canadian Studies, the Carleton Library Board held a farewell party for Louise and me at the Centre Club at the University of Ottawa. We had made many friends in Ottawa over the years. In the middle of dinner, Professor Syd Wise whispered in my ear, "You just got the best job in Canada."

I flew to Edmonton on my own in June 1980 and Louise and our daughter Rebeccah followed a month later. It was a difficult time for us. Edmonton's housing market was booming while the market for our house in Ottawa was depressed. A frenetic real estate agent ran me all over town trying to find me a house that would remind me of Ontario, but red brick is rare in Edmonton and the oak trees she was sure I would fall in love with were barely six feet tall. I finally settled on a new condominium building one block from the university, which suited us well for the next ten years.

General Manager Frank McGuire had the idea that the entire staff could operate out of two small rooms in Ring House 4 on the western corner the University of Alberta. The editors, he decided, would be spending all their time in the library. He had already hired me a secretary, who confided that he had ordered her to spy on me. I told him he had to negotiate with the University for another office in Athabasca Hall, where at least the senior editors could set up desks, and another in Cameron Library, where the researchers could park their coats and books. Neither of us foresaw the small army of staff that would eventually be needed.

In the midst of moving my family from Ottawa, arranging financing for our new place in Edmonton, finding a school for Rebeccah, and helping Louise find a job, I tried to grasp at least some order in the chaos around me. I felt lucky that neither Mel Hurtig nor Frank McGuire had preconceived ideas about the task ahead. Aside from reading whatever I could find about the history of encyclopedias, I resolved to ask the few experts who had succeeded. I arranged to visit the staffs of Britannica and World Book in Chicago, and those at Columbia and McGraw-Hill in New York. The editors and technical advisors all gave generously of their time and saved me from numerous pitfalls. The editor of Britannica was particularly welcoming. We spent a lovely afternoon at the Yacht Club on Lake Michigan talking about our project, which seemed of great interest to him. He was surprised that I knew about conductor Georg Solti and the Chicago Symphony. (Later that night I stood in a long line hoping for a ticket for a concert with Andras Schiff playing Brahms' *Piano Concerto No. 1*. Suddenly, a man swept through the front doors, seemingly straight to me, and offered to sell me a ticket. An ailing Schiff had cancelled at the last minute and a brilliant young Polish pianist replaced him. I was spellbound as Solti briskly sprang off his feet as he conducted, landing always on the beat.) The editors of the great encyclopedias approved of my plan and introduced me to staff members who advised me on many crucial details: how articles and contributors were organized, how they dealt with schedules and word counts, how they had articles read and edited, how authors were picked and paid, and so much more.

From my experience dealing with the indecision, delays, and politics of a board of academics at Carleton University, I knew that, to produce the encyclopedia in five years and to make it coherent, I had to keep total editorial control. I appointed several prominent academics from across Canada to an advisory board, which gave the project important early prestige. Davidson Dunton was of enormous help at our first meeting, held at the president's residence at the University of Alberta, when Professor Pierre Maranda, an internationally renowned anthropologist, insisted that no one encyclopedia could represent the whole country. We must produce two completely different encyclopedias, he declared, one for English Canada and one for Quebec. Fortunately, Dunton, a co-chair of the influential Royal Commission that had defined Canada as bicultural and bilingual, persuaded the board to defeat the motion. Interestingly, British Columbia, Saskatchewan, Manitoba, and Newfoundland later produced their own encyclopedias, but not Quebec. I never called another board meeting, though I met with and spoke to the board members in person whenever possible.

Like McGuire, the head of the advisory board, Harry Gunning, a former president of the University of Alberta, thought that he was in charge and that I reported to him. He summoned me to his office to discuss some early article lists I had sent him. When he asked me why we would be wasting words on the likes of Métis leader Gabriel Dumont, I told him I would come back when he had more time to study the lists. Having recruited the book *Cuthbert Grant of Grantown*, by Margaret Arnett MacLeod, for the Carleton Library Series, which described the Métis fight against encroachment of their lands and rights, I was determined that Grant, Dumont, and Louis Riel were as important to our history as any explorer or politician. We never discussed the article lists again. Mel Hurtig always supported me in these disputes, convinced when I told him that these interferences would seriously delay the encyclopedia. The rest of the board was indispensable, including Miranda, in helping to persuade scholars from all over the country to write or consult. Our association with the University of Alberta was invaluable, not only in providing office space and easy access to academics and resources, but

Our first offices were in Ring House 4 on the University of Alberta campus. We soon spilled out, as our staff grew, into Cameron Library and eventually into two larger houses on the opposite end of campus.

also in establishing our credibility beyond Hurtig Publishers. In return for their help, Hurtig agreed to make a large donation, which he honoured, to the University of Alberta Library.

Several days spent studying the files of the *Dictionary of Canadian Biography* (DCB) in Toronto and receiving sage advice from its English-language editor, Frances Halpenny, guided me in how best to deal with academic authors and tight deadlines. The 1970s–80s were a golden age for Canadian reference works. The *Dictionary of Canadian Biography* (now over 8,000 entries), the *Historical Atlas of Canada*, and the *Encyclopedia of Music in Canada* were all in development. Unlike The Canadian Encyclopedia, however, they all had university or government affiliations and generous funding from the Canada Council, which enabled them to survive long delays that would cripple a small commercial publisher like Hurtig. Harold Kallman, who shared the editorial control of the Encyclopedia of Music in Canada (EMC) with two other chief editors, advised me urgently not to divide editorial control. He was based at the National Archives in Ottawa, Robert Winter was in Toronto, and

Gilles Potvin in Montreal, tripling the movement of articles. I greatly admired Kallman and was later able to repay his help by digitizing EMC, putting it online, updating much of its content, and integrating it with the search engine of The Canadian Encyclopedia.

As much as I was buried in the everyday practicalities of correspondence, the hiring and training of staff, finding thousands of authors, and organizing schedules, I was still starry eyed that we shared a destiny with the great reference works of the ages. Denis Diderot's first stirrings of l' Encyclopédie saw how rewarding, as well as useful, it would be to present in one work the new knowledge and discovery of the great age of French science and letters—the epoch of Descartes, Racine, and Bossuet. What an opportunity he saw for the enemies of prejudice, ignorance, and superstition to create a weapon of enlightenment. Whatever current skepticism can be levelled at such authority; few would question the success of l' Encyclopédie in achieving its goals. The Canadian Encyclopedia would give us a similar opportunity to shine a light on Canada.

But how to find the best staff to fill the critical roles? There were few experienced editors in Edmonton, where the book publishing industry was slight at that time. I did hire two senior editors locally: Adriana Davies, who had just returned from England, where she had worked on a major reference project, for the Sciences; and Diana Selsor, a creative professional photographer who had been widely exhibited, for the Arts. After extensive interviews in Toronto, I hired two more, notably James Ogilvy, who brought valuable experience (and a perfectionist knowledge of grammar and usage) from the *Dictionary of Canadian Biography*. At one of our first editorial meetings, I responded to a question that I had not decided yet. I had a rude shock when the inquirer said in an elevated tone, "You mean when we decide!" The restlessness around the table was worrisome. Within three years, I had replaced two of the senior editors with more experienced professionals, Mary McDougall Maude and Rosemary Shipton. McGuire opposed hiring these two women because I did not ask them to move from Toronto

With Patricia Finlay in her office at the encyclopedia, possibly in our ongoing discussion about how social science is a "science."

to Edmonton (they could not), but their qualifications were far more important to me than daily face-to-face contact. The Toronto-based senior editors turned out to be in the forefront of the home-office revolution and their success provided a model for us in the future. The troublesome area of the Social Sciences saw several changes in senior editor until Patricia Finlay, who had written me a persuasive letter of interest in the encyclopedia, arrived from Ottawa to see it through. Without these changes, the encyclopedia would never have succeeded in reaching its goals or its schedule.

It was partly the changes in editors as well as the complexity and diversity of the social sciences, from education and law to political science and economics, that proved challenging for Patricia. Before email or the Internet, she became skilled at persuading authors to write for us in long telephone conversations. No one refused her.

I faced an editorial uprising in the early months when I put the whole encyclopedia staff to work analyzing *Canadiana*, creating an index card for every article, noting its length, and assigning it a subject from a list I had compiled from the National Library of Canada's List of Subjects. It was tedious work but proved useful. It was my firm belief, not shared by the irritated editors in this instance, that the best way to build an encyclopedia was by looking at what existing encyclopedias had done, using *Canadiana* as a starting point and then making amendments to reflect the changing times. By comparing how the editors of *Canadiana* saw the world in the 1950s with how we viewed Canada in 1980, a new structure began to emerge in my mind. It was the best way of seeing who was missing from the worldview of the 1950s. For example, we found that *Canadiana* devoted virtually no words to urban themes, women's issues, Indigenous Peoples, the sciences, or politics. Some 150,000 words had been devoted to biographies of lieutenant-governors and only 10,000 words to visual artists—a world in other words that valued honourary appointees and bureaucrats above creativity. We would reverse that. Perhaps most deficient in *Canadiana* was the decision not to include biographies of living Canadians born after 1910. Yes, we knew that choosing among living subjects for biographies would be controversial, but I believed that we simply could not draw a convincing portrait of our generation without descriptions of living artists, musicians, politicians, and athletes, whatever their age.

A large contingent of scholarly consultants was invaluable as we developed the article lists, added and deleted topics, and suggested contributors. I filled dozens of notebooks with potential topics for articles by reading history books, textbooks, scholarly journals, high school curricula, and the daily press, and, within months, our revised article list bore little resemblance to that of *Canadiana*. As the senior editors each researched their article lists, suggestions flew back and forth, and the lists spread like fractals. Working closely with consultants (there were sixty in the sciences alone), we soon had working article lists ready for commissioning. In the 2020s critics would no doubt judge us deficient in our decisions from the 1980s, as we had of the editors of *Canadiana*. But my overall view has not changed: Canada was then and still is in progress, and each generation must try to make its own amends. It is the only way we can continue to be more inclusive—without feeling morally superior.

These days, with so much thought and talk about "information architecture," and with the databases and search engines available, a new encyclopedia would be planned in a completely different way. (In the case of Wikipedia, randomly, without authority.) I never thought that the process could be technical—computers and programmers were rare in 1980. Although an encyclopedia seems to be organized around the alphabet, you don't make one by casting out a net for As or Ds as you might with a dictionary. A coherent list of articles is revealed only after a manageable subject tree is nurtured and allowed to branch out, and we refined our drafts by meeting with professors at the University of Alberta and with groups of scholars at the Learned Society meetings in Halifax in 1981. Often the branches of the subject tree corresponded nicely with academic disciplines—for example, Social Science / Sociology / Demography led to Population Growth and Baby Boom. Other subjects such as sports, entertainment, and geographical features had no academic standing but clearly needed to be included. Some of the senior editors and many academics opposed the idea, but I overruled them. I could not conceive of a Canadian encyclopedia without entries on Gordie Howe, Neil Young, or Great Bear Lake.

It was during the process of building article lists that I completely changed the conception of The Canadian Encyclopedia from the one originally outlined by Wolfe, Owen, and Hurtig. Even in the proposal that won funding from the Alberta government, the encyclopedia was intended to be a single volume, like the Columbia Encyclopedia, useful for quick location of accurate information and essentially written by staff. We knew that short entries would have been completely inadequate to cover topics essential to the understanding of Canada, such as Federalism, Bilingualism, Multiculturalism, Parliamentary Democracy, Inuit Sculpture, Aboriginal Rights, and so many others. I decided that this plan would have been a terrible missed opportunity (worse than the one decried by

Owen in his review of *Canadiana*). With difficulty, I persuaded Hurtig to consider a multi-volume, fully illustrated version, written not by staff but by authorities from all over Canada. We would need over three million words for that version, not one million. I told him that only such a comprehensive work would be a true gift to Canada, but with creative marketing it would be an outstanding commercial success. I still believe that the value of any reference work depends on the participation of experts—not to write for one another, but to spread their knowledge to a general audience. Occasionally, articles would end up being collaborative—the supposed advantage of the later Wikipedia—but that method makes it virtually impossible to produce coherent, articulate entries. Hurtig bravely agreed to the greatly expanded encyclopedia, and his marketing plan grew to encompass the new vision.

Every prospective author received a basic outline for the commissioned articles, including instructions to begin with a clear definition, to use non-technical language, and to include a list of further readings. Above all, I determined that as far as possible every article would be signed by the expert who wrote it. Adherence to word counts was strict, not only because the overall length of the encyclopedia had been determined in advance but also because each topic had been rated in "significance" in relation to the others. Every article we received was read by three or more other experts in the field and fact checked by our staff. The senior editors added cross-references (which converted brilliantly to hypertext links in later electronic versions), incorporated readers' comments, and pruned and rewrote as needed.

To me, the tone of the encyclopedia was equally important to our commitment to expertise and the widest possible coverage of Canada's "limited identities." If we were to help form a common consciousness, I felt that we needed a restrained voice. We persuaded the fiery Robin Mathews, for example, to give an account of the politics found in literature that gave a clear sense of wrongs, without the wrath that often appeared in his work. In "Violence, Political," historian Kenneth McNaught strained

Our encyclopedia staff.
L to R, back row are Vivian Zenari, Kathryn Merrett, Gail Kudelik, Rob Wiznura and Susan Hutton. L to R, front row are Carol Woo, myself, Russell Bingham and Virginia Gillese.

to show that Canada does have a "torturous and little-examined history of collective violence." A reviewer in *Canadian Literature* later wrote that David P. Ross' discussion in "Poverty" had the virtues of Swift's "Modest Proposal." J.W. Mohr wrote about crime as a social creation in which Parliament, the police, and the courts "define" people into crime. The large percentage of "aboriginals" in prison get there, he wrote, because these institutions define the offences that result from native alcoholism differently for aboriginal offences than for "white" behaviour. Art Blue's discussion "Native People, Social Conditions" uncovered the source of Indigenous criminality in the weakening of Indigenous institutions by successive Canadian governments that have denied Native sovereignty.

Although these principles severely tested the mettle of our editors and our contributors, they are what made the printed encyclopedia of lasting value. It will forever provide a portrait of its time.

The sprouting article lists in each subject area were critical for judging coverage, length, and balance, but they soon took on lives of their own. Each senior editor and his or her consultants became vehement advocates of the importance of their domains. I was presented with five lists of articles, developed by senior editors with teams of consultants, each one of which would have consumed the entire three million words. While the work of the academic consultants was critical, their views were often narrowly focused. An encyclopedia based only on their approaches would have been far too specialized to be of much interest to general readers. For example, consultants did not want separate entries for ethnic groups, individual sports, towns, or specific plants, animals, or minerals. I could not conceive of a Canadian encyclopedia without articles on Ukrainians, Hockey, Glace Bay, Maple, Beaver, Birchbark Canoe, or Nickel. The interest of the general reader is in specifics, not in the abstract, though we tried our best to cover that too. What were the questions a student might ask researching an article on Confederation? What might answer a classroom question about the impacts of Treaty 11? What are the accurate, verified dates for events or spellings for names? In the end, even the Supreme Court of Canada found the encyclopedia a reliable source for details in several of its written decisions.

I needed advice and support in this critical balancing act between scholarship and popularity and got it from my generalist friends in the academic community, such as historian Norman Hillmer, political scientists Paul Fox and Norman Ward, and sociologist Wallace Clement. I had never foreseen that one of my greatest challenges would be managing the conflicts among an editorial staff, both among themselves and with me. It was a measure of their enthusiasm and devotion. For Frank and Mel, these quarrels raised the old spectre of my lack of managerial expertise, and I decided that I needed outside validation. I assembled a group of respected generalists in a Toronto hotel—they included journalist, critic, and writer Robert Fulford, historian Sydney Wise, and political scientist Paul Fox.

After a long day of reviewing article lists, the group supported my approach and stiffened my resolve to keep the encyclopedia focused on its generalist role. Some of the senior editors were not pleased, but Mel was reassured. I pruned the lists and returned them to the editors; they began assigning them to contributors from one end of Canada to the other. I wrote a 200-page style manual, which was also thrashed out in detail with the editors, and made it available to authors (clarity, concision, and lack of jargon figured prominently in the instructions, as well as usages and spellings). Some of the discussion with the senior editors about grammar and usage were far too enjoyable and had to be cut short. The letters to contributors included specific instructions as to length and content and, following a suggestion given to me by a computer scientist at U of A, included a contract with a clause retaining digital rights—of enormous, unforeseen benefit to a digital future.

Although I had determined from the very first that the encyclopedia would reflect the highest standards of accuracy—every article would be vetted by outside readers and thoroughly verified by internal researchers—we could not forget that for Hurtig it was a commercial publication that had to sell over 100,000 sets to make a profit. I personally revised every article list, inevitably recommending cuts. This process was most difficult for the first social science editor, who had created a scholarly list of interrelated subjects on "phenomenological" principles that was philosophically interesting but wholly discordant with the rest of the encyclopedia, and for science editor Adriana Davies, who, in assembling some of the country's most eminent scientists, produced a list that was not always "Canadian" in focus. One of the world's experts on black holes, Werner Israel, at the University of Alberta, for example, was enlisted to write about that mysterious subject but focusing on Canadian contributions. Cutting these worthy topics put me in a difficult position with the editors and consultants in whose hands I had put the encyclopedia, but my first responsibility was to Mel Hurtig, and he simply could not increase the length and make a profit.

My revision of that first social science article list, not so much for its length as for its discordant abstract approach, caused the most serious managerial issue of my tenure. I was warned by one of our secretaries that she had been forced to type outraged letters to all that editor's consultants, telling them

245

I was not intelligent enough to see the value of the lists they had prepared together. I fired the editor the next morning and made peace with the consultants, most of whom were puzzled by the episode. The severance led to a wasteful and very stressful lawsuit, which was resolved in our favour. In this difficult time I had the full support of both Mel Hurtig and Frank McGuire. When Frank and I handed the editor a severance cheque, we sat astonished as she ripped it to pieces and threw it in my face.

ONCE I HAD DONE what I saw as my primary job as editor in chief, laying down the broad lines of approach and the formulation of principles, the daily work of the encyclopedia was primarily in the hands of the senior editors, who had to find writers and consultants, persuade authors to write for a pittance, cajole and persuade, and then deal with the readers' reports and the editorial process. I never had a complaint after the process got rolling in the second year (with a new social science editor) from any contributor, and I received many compliments about how well treated they all felt. I knew that even with five senior editors, and several associate editors, we were still severely understaffed, so I undertook the commissioning and even the writing of several major subject areas, such as sports and geographical places, to relieve some of the pressure. I ended up writing several hundred thousand words, including the articles on book publishing, cultural policy, and hockey, all with the help of researchers and critical readers. The enthusiasm of the whole team was contagious, and we all felt that this project would be the most important of our lives. There was a shared relief when someone ripped open the mail and announced that the entry on the "Beaver," or "Ceramics," or "Cheese," or "Marriage and Divorce" had finally arrived. I spent eight to ten hours a day in the office managing the content and illustrations, and then four to five hours every night and every weekend day writing and editing. With the arrival of every entry, we felt that the project was exceeding our expectations—and that it might truly be completed on time.

The conflict between General Manager Frank McGuire and me, however, had never been resolved, and it remained a fruitless impediment. Disputes over authority are inevitable in any organization. McGuire had responded to Mel's ad for an editor in chief, though he had no editorial experience, describing himself as a "results-oriented manager." I wasted hours almost every day trying to justify to him why we needed editors, or proofreaders, or space, or resources. I had to fight with him over buying dictionaries or sending editors to the Learned Society meetings to discuss their areas with consultants. We even argued over what kind of bookcase I should have in my office: Ikea was too expensive, and he drove around town to find cheaper ones himself.

Mel invited me to his house to discuss the crisis. At his insistence, I told Mel honestly about McGuire's interference, the daily wasting of my time, and his lack of understanding, on condition that he not repeat what I said. I told him I was not raised in the streets of Toronto's Junction to become a snitch. Mel did not keep that promise.

This discontent and a heated shouting match Frank had with one of the senior editors leaked back to Hurtig (not through me), who decided to hire Harold Bohne, the director of University of Toronto Press, to make an independent evaluation of the crisis. In a letter to Bohne, Hurtig repeats McGuire's charge that I was a "hopeless manager." Hurtig always saw the differences between McGuire and me as matters of personality, or in his word "culture," but the senior editors and I saw his interference as a serious threat to our work and the principles of the encyclopedia—not to mention to the impossible schedule.

Bohne agreed to enter the hornet's nest and flew out from Toronto. McGuire insisted on picking him up at the airport and tried to keep him firmly in his sight, regaling him with complaints about me and insisting I should be fired. So we could meet alone, Bohne telephoned me late in the evening, told me he had finally escaped McGuire's grip, and asked me to meet him at the bar in the Macdonald Hotel. He told me I need not explain myself—that spending time with McGuire had told him all he needed to know about the problem. He arranged to meet the senior editors the next morning, before breakfast, to keep

McGuire at bay. Bohne's report, which Hurtig watered down in order not to offend McGuire (possibly fearful of his government connections), began with the words "I have every bit of confidence in Jim's 'management ability' based on my interview with him and comments made by his staff. Jim knows perfectly well what he is doing, and he will produce a fine encyclopedia, *if he is left alone to do so.*" (These italicized words and the following were omitted in Hurtig's version to McGuire.) He continued: "He works well with his staff and all of them are dedicated to him. ... That Jim ever had to justify the attendance of three people at the Learneds is quite unbelievable." Bohne told Hurtig that McGuire's comments about my lack of management skills were made strictly "to justify his excessive interference."

Hurtig made some administrative changes so that I would have more control over the budget, and while I knew that McGuire now resented me even more (he told me with savage bitterness that he knew "everything" I had said about him), I really felt that a new working relationship in which he provided the administrative support we needed, putting the goal of getting the work done above financial bickering, suited him better and relieved the main source of stress on me. I never retaliated by telling McGuire that he had seen only part of the contentious report, or that I knew everything that he said about me. Bohne's judgment ran against Mel's notion that he had been a mastermind in partnering such different individuals, and that Frank was there to save us from my management frailties. The encyclopedia was produced on time and under budget. The management of finances, payrolls, hiring, and production by McGuire were first class, but he never got over not being seen as the man in charge of the encyclopedia. His antipathy to Bohne was almost as great as his hostility to me.

CHAPTER 18

A Nation in a Nutshell

"They have shown us how Canadians as a collective mentality think, and how they understand their own being."

– Val Clery, Canadian Literature

MAKING A TRADITIONAL ENCYCLOPEDIA is a curious enterprise. No one set of books could possibly fulfill the many exalted demands made of these works. Perhaps it was possible in Diderot's time for an encyclopedia to represent all human knowledge or even to aspire to changing the world, but such claims had already become dubious when the legendary 11th edition of Britannica was published in 1911. Despite the explosion in information, I believed that an encyclopedia could still fulfill a role in attempting to present human knowledge in some semblance of coherence, a close approximation of accuracy, and some guidance of what was considered significant in its time. It could, in the words of H.G. Wells, present "the ruling concepts of our social order." A national encyclopedia such as ours might also achieve a more specific goal of displaying the rich diversity of its subject—Canada—and even of inspiring pride in its people. Truly, the aggregate of articles on our glorious land and resources and on the many unknown Canadians who contributed to every domain, presented a wonder to anyone who explored it.

This idea of a national encyclopedia seemed parochial to

many people, contradicting their notions of an increasingly globalized world. More than one professor at the University of Alberta asked me, derisively, who would possibly be interested in such a narrow-minded work? I agreed that national borders seemed arbitrary in discussions of physics or mathematics, but the whole point of our encyclopedia was to provide information on Canadian contributions to these subjects that never would appear in the general reference works emanating from the United States or Great Britain. Americans would never consider the need for a national encyclopedia, not just on the claim of parochialism, but because works such as Britannica and World Book and Encarta were produced in the US and presented American perspectives as universal. My most vehement hope for Canada was always that it could achieve a different, better North American destiny.

I was able to draw on my own publishing experience and some learning to evaluate what kind of portrait TCE would present of Canada and how that would differ from *Canadiana*. Some things would have changed very little since the 1950s. For example, there had to be heavy emphasis on articles about places, as Canadians remain very local in their focus. Failing to include separate articles on certain places, such as Waterloo and Burlington (based on the Statistics Canada's definition of the municipalities Kitchener-Waterloo and Hamilton-Burlington), from the first edition caused me serious grief.

While biography was of little interest to the academic consultants and a severe strain on the senior editors (until I hired Mary McDougall Maude to work on them exclusively), it is clearly of enormous interest to the public. Over the years, most of the comments or criticisms of the encyclopedia have concerned biography. It is a little dispiriting not to have had a single letter or email, among many thousands, comment on articles that caused the editors a great deal of editorial grief (for example, the 15,000-word article on "Philosophy in Canada" commissioned by James Ogilvy. Yes, Canadians have published books on the metaphysics of R.G. Collingwood, Whitehead's theory of reality, Paul Tillich's question of being, and the rational metaphysics of

A Nation in a Nutshell

Baruch Spinoza). Yet the shortest biography could inspire pages of corrections or vitriol.

While it was my intention that the engagement of literally thousands of consultants and authors would broaden the scope of the encyclopedia and enhance its objectivity, it was inevitable that my own biases would leave their mark. I valued creativity above all else. I determined that the encyclopedia would devote as many words to painters as to prime ministers. A poet such as Al Purdy might have a longer entry than popular historical figures such as William Lyon Mackenzie. To me, any sense of Canada exists by virtue of a shared culture as much as by a common history and geography. I tried to remain objective about contentious subjects such as abortion or federalism, and I understood that topics such as economic nationalism or Quebec separatism had to be written by fair but sympathetic authors. Whenever necessary or possible, we commissioned articles in French and had them translated. We were less successful in fulfilling my hope of including thoughtful or good-natured essays that might surprise a reader by revealing eccentric aspects of Canada or challenge principles, such as rights, that everyone took for granted. The severe word restrictions imposed by the commercial nature of the project left their scars on the truncated language and a text peppered with acronyms and abbreviations.

I worked hard to make sure that the encyclopedia avoided two influences that would have tarnished its credibility. It could not be, ironically, a "Mel Hurtig encyclopedia." Hurtig phoned me daily mid-morning, without fail, sometimes keeping me for hours, with suggestions drawn from his own broad interest in current affairs—many of which were anecdotal stories of American transgressions or failures of their health care system. He insisted relentlessly that I write down and then insert copious statistics that he lifted from Statistics Canada newsletters. I resisted peppering the text with meaningless statistics that would be glaringly out of date on the day the encyclopedia was published. Every conversation ended by him telling me that final decisions were mine (as my contract stated). The encyclopedia would not be imbued with Mel's vehement economic nationalism, nor could it be the mouthpiece of the Conservative Alberta government. After the right-wing periodical *Alberta Report* raised an alarm by accusing me in December 1983 of being a socialist, if not a communist, and of creating a left-wing screed with taxpayers' money, some Conservative Cabinet ministers demanded to see articles. I refused to respond to them, and Hurtig had to arrange for articles to be sent by McGuire. The government agreed to submit the entries to an intermediary, political scientist Peter Meekison, who was not only a well-respected academic but also a close associate of the premier.

Meekison's positive report on the objectivity and quality of the articles ended the crisis. While Jack McClelland had always taught me never to respond to negative press, Hurtig disagreed. He insisted that I respond to *Alberta Report*. I did so reluctantly in a letter to the editor, knowing that every word would be a new target, providing the publication's chief ideologue, Ted Byfield, with the opportunity to take a whole issue responding to "poor, pathetic Mr. Marsh." Though no one from *Alberta Report* had ever spoken to me or to any of my staff, Byfield predicted that the encyclopedia would be a disaster, and he wondered how I "ever got the job of editing an encyclopedia." It wasn't as bad as it sounded: being criticized by Byfield and his toxic conservatism provided me with a certain caché among my more liberal colleagues. Byfield proved to be wrong in his prediction that the encyclopedia would be a failure, but his attacks became an eerie forecast of the current bullying from both the right and the left that passes, almost universally now, for political discourse.

We were ambitious in asking the editors to hire a writer for every article, no matter how short. We ended up with some 2,500 writers for the first edition (more than Britannica had then for its forty-million words), which created an administrative and editorial trial. Nevertheless, the assembly of this broad-based community of respected writers from every part of Canada was our greatest accomplishment. They were paid a meager sum of eight cents per word, yet of the many we approached to write for the encyclopedia, only a few turned us down because of money. Many writers refused to take any payment at all, and everyone appreciated the offer of a free encyclopedia for their labours. The fact that we refereed the articles with several independent readers encouraged academics to write for us, as refereed articles gained them credit in their annual evaluations. We even persuaded high-profile writers such as Margaret Atwood, Pierre Berton, John Robert Columbo, George Woodcock, David Suzuki, and Peter C. Newman to make contributions. I was gratified also that the integrity of the work persuaded Quebec authors including Daniel Latouche, Marc Laurendeau, Fernand Ouellet, Paul-André Linteau, and Pierre Dansereau to contribute. I found that, despite the "two solitudes," there were often partnerships between English and French scholars, such as the one between Alan Artibise and Linteau, who shared their expertise in urban studies.

Once word of the encyclopedia's goals to represent all aspects of Canada was reported in the media, organizations, cults, religions, and advocates of all kinds lobbied us for inclusion or for control over our interpretations. My first visitor after I settled into my office in Ring House 4 at the University of Alberta was from a group called Technocracy. These ardent advocates of scientific and technical expertise urged me not only to represent them in the encyclopedia but also to step aside and allow them to organize the whole project. (They preached that they, and not elected representatives, should control the government, as well as the encyclopedia, since they could predict the future.) I played host to a Mensa group intent on showing me, with predictable condescension, that each of them was cleverer than me and far more worthy of being editor in chief. They fell into some disarray when I asked them if they had decided which one of them was the most qualified—would they choose simply by IQ? I had a television crew from a fundamentalist Christian television network arrive at our front door to challenge me on why the Bible and creationism, not science, would not be the guiding principles for the encyclopedia. (I escaped right by them without incident because they did not believe that someone so young looking could be the chief.)

The limited number of words (3 million, hardly more than *Canadiana* but triple the amount originally planned) meant rigid editing of the text and the casting off of hundreds of thousands of words. We had commissioned 3.2 million words and received well over ten million. Some authors submitted articles thousands of words over their allotment. This situation would have been impossible if we had stayed with the original plan for a one-volume encyclopedia. Having won over Hurtig to publish three illustrated volumes, our workload became even greater. I hired Carol Woo and Debra MacGregor to gather and clear permission for thousands of photographs. On many days they had hundreds of slides for me to view. The captions for these illustrations amounted to a sizeable book in themselves. We were able to negotiate reasonable terms, thanks to the editors' persuasions, with some of Canada's finest photographers, including Janis Kaulis, Tim Fitzharris, Richard Harrington, Freeman Patterson, Pat Morrow, and Yousuf Karsh. We commissioned a series of paintings from Quebec illustrator Claire Tremblay, who brilliantly and accurately depicted Canadian ecosystems, flora, and fauna. Many of our contributors worked hard identifying illustrations for their articles. The contributor writing our article on "Clouds," Professor Ed Lozowski, spent many hours in our office choosing the best cumulus or cirrus photographs. Stunning satellite photographs gave a unique portrait of Canada from space, common now but rare in those days. Hundreds of artists, architects, performers, and sculptors had their work illustrated, making The Canadian Encyclopedia the most comprehensive visual portrait of Canada ever published.

By summer 1982 we had commissioned some 9,000 articles from over 2,500 experts. How the editors managed to contact and persuade all those contributors, and to collect, evaluate, verify, and edit all those articles in such a short period of time is incredible. The schedule was a looming spectre in all our lives for those four or five years. We were ably supported by McGuire and the rest of the administrative staff as demands for space, supplies, phone lines, desks, filing cabinets, photocopiers, fax machines, typewriters, bookcases, and resources continued to grow. By mid-1984 we had some forty-seven editors, researchers, and proofreaders working out of two small university houses, including the attics, as well as secretarial and administrative staff. Fortunately, I discovered that the best way to surpass my "management deficiencies" was simply to hire great staff and to trust them.

The article list transformed itself from my ideal of a rational, logical progression to something more tangled and organic. I altered the alphabetical system to word-by-word so that the entry on our national motto, *A mari usque ad mare*, could appear first. Volume I proceeded with "Abalone" (which would have been first in a letter-by-letter arrangement), "Abbotsford," various Abbotts, and then "Abduction."

"Aboriginal Rights" was indicative of the kind of article that did not even appear in *Canadiana* but was extensively covered in TCE. The coverage of Indigenous culture, history, and art was the most comprehensive ever assembled to that time. One reviewer wrote that "Native culture receives extensive and intelligent coverage disproportionate to the number of native people in Canada." The article "Abortion" went through so many writers and readers (at least twelve) that it had to appear without a single author's name. As the articles migrated out of their subject areas, where they had been nurtured by the editors, into their destined places in the alphabet, they produced delightful juxtapositions on the pages for the reader. In the Bs, political activist "Buller, Annie" is followed by "Bunkhouse Men," "Bunting," "Bunyan, Paul," "Buoy," jurist "Burbidge, George," "Bureaucracy," "Burgeo," "Burgess Shale," and "Burglary." Thus, while the articles remained connected with tens of thousands of cross-references, they also shared serendipitous relations with their alphabetical neighbours. This phenomenon of juxtaposition and surprise is sadly lacking in electronic encyclopedias, robbing us of a certain associative curiosity. The appearance of each individual article was never looked at with lofty principles of unity, national pride, or even diversity—the overwhelming internal force was curiosity.

Because every small aspect of an encyclopedia is scrutinized, particularly by those lurking hedgehogs who know "one big thing," we set very high standards for editing and verification. Our in-house researchers checked every fact. Every entry was returned by the senior editors to the contributor for a final approval before passing through several stages of proofreading. We built a fantastic collection of index cards of facts that had been verified by researchers. I often saw an article at every one of these phases. Perfection, like completeness, is demanded of a reference work, but it is an elusive goal. So is "objectivity." It is useless to claim that such a thing exists in some pure form, as if we were the first generation to see all subjects with fairy-tale neutrality. We did our best to find sensible compromises in contentious entries without eliminating informed debate. Making the encyclopedia was part of a process towards these goals.

An even-more-vexing editorial problem than authority was a demand for currency. We had made so much of how badly out of date *Canadiana* was that being up to date became almost a fetish, particularly with Hurtig, who somehow saw the encyclopedia filled with statistics from the latest Statistics Canada reports he was mining for his speeches. I tried to explain to him that the primary role of an encyclopedia is to provide information of long-term, lasting interest, not to be as current as the daily newspaper—a chimera that would evaporate the day we went to press. Whenever possible we tried to provide consistent numbers from census data that could be used for comparison over time. (The issue of the population of cities was irksome. Cities conduct periodic counts, based on samples, and trumpet the results—either Calgary or Edmonton would loudly proclaim that they had passed each other, often by redefining their boundaries. But the only meaningful population statistics come from a census, which does not generalize from samples but counts every person.)

With only six months before the delivery date to the printers, only a fraction of the text had been processed, yet somehow the senior editors managed to get every single important entry delivered and edited. Where did the articles on "Masks,"

"Intellectual History," "Horseradish," "Fruits of the Earth," "U-Boat Landings," "Yew," "Ice Worm," and "Qaqaq Ashoona" come from? The answer is from everywhere. Some arrived on time; most did not. We eventually hired an additional staff member whose only job was tracking down overdue contributors. Her logbook included such esoteric explanations from delinquent authors as a vasectomy gone bad and a stroke that obliterated all memory of a half-written entry. One distraught author arrived on our front steps explaining that he had lost his article research when his house burned down. Another author, eighteen months overdue, claimed that he had a persistent cold. Of course, most of the entries arrived over length, as writers found it difficult to condense a lifelong interest into four hundred words. No one outdid the author who was asked to write a 500-word article on "Sheep and Goat Farming" in Canada. When it finally arrived, long overdue, it was some nine thousand words and had been retitled "Sheep and Goat Farming in Quebec." Thousands of articles had to be recommissioned or rewritten.

We were not aided in the editorial process, as we would be today, by computers or the Internet (though it is questionable how useful the web really is for accurate information). The general manager did manage to install cumbersome (to us now) Micron dedicated word processors part way through the editorial process to replace typewriters, and that greatly helped us to cope with endless editorial changes. We doubled the editorial staff and had proofreaders and researchers stationed in every corner and attic of our expanded offices and in offices in the Cameron Library. We tried to track the word count using the university's Spires database (designed at Stanford as a physics database management system), but when we were finally able to measure the typeset galleys accurately at the last minute, our designer David Shaw discovered to my dismay that we were some 300,000 words in excess. Hurtig could not add pages to a publication pre-sold at a set price without compromising his profits. This meant that I had to read the entire encyclopedia and cut great bleeding blocks of text from the galleys (much of which I was fortunately able to reinstall for the second edition in

KNOW IT ALL

1988). This was likely the worst editorial job that I ever had to do, made nastier by the bleeding nose and lung irritation I suffered from the constant smell of ammonia wafting off the galleys. For two months I sat ten to twelve hours a day reading and trimming, listening for some reason to Jean Sibelius' symphonies on my headphones, over and over in order. I am reminded of those days every time I visit my pulmonologist, or when I listen to Sibelius.

The pages of the first edition were made the traditional way, as I sat with renowned book designer David Shaw in his Toronto office on Eglinton Avenue for days, waxing and cutting the repro proofs and sizing and placing illustrations, captions, and tables. It might have been the last great example of that age-old method. It reminded me of the assembly of a gigantic scrapbook, as David and his assistant literally crawled about the floor with scissors and paste, assembling the yards of text, pictures, and captions into pages. "Jim, can you cut a few words from this sentence and save this page?" "We're going to have to crop this photo." From time to time, a missing line or two of waxed repro would show up on the sole of somebody's shoe. (Only three years later, I sat next to Sheila Birmingham as she made the pages of the second edition on a computer screen at the University of Alberta.)

The three volumes finally went to press in Montreal in the spring of 1985: 463,500 heavy volumes bound in navy blue, which was by far the largest printing job in Canadian history. It was a huge challenge for the printing company, Ronalds Printing, to deal with the thousands of pieces. At one point an exasperated manager flew from Montreal to Edmonton and tossed a negative of an abstract painting by Paul-Emile Borduas onto my desk, pleading, "Please. Show us which way up it goes!" "Every time we ask your staff on the phone it goes a different way." There was a barrage of corrections, all of which had to be conveyed by primitive fax machines rattling on at all hours of the day or night. While I have nostalgia for some primitive technologies, such as dedicated word processors or flip phones, I have an enduring hatred of the wretched fax machine. That device, with its error-prone sheet feeder, terrible scanning

With the senior editors of the First Edition, 1985, on the night of the launch. From left to right, Adriana Davies, Patricia Finlay, Mary McDougall Maude, me, James Ogilvy, and Rosemary Shipton.

element, and ancient modem running at a snail's pace grated on everyone's nerves and ran up staggering long-distance charges. When we received the blueline proofs (made from the negatives from which the plates for the press would be made, so named because the text and images all appear in dark blue on the light blue paper) with the pictures in place, we finally began to realize the scope of what we had done. I could barely bring myself to look, for I had a dread of seeing errors—it seemed almost better to pretend that there could be none.

The marketing campaign directed by Hurtig went brilliantly. Tens of thousands of sets were pre-sold, with orders for some 105,000 sets received by May 1984. Public interest was high because Hurtig was one of the most popular media figures in those days. While filming a segment on the encyclopedia for the CBC's public affairs show "The Fifth Estate," host Hanna Gartner asked me on camera if Mel Hurtig was the "greatest encyclopedia salesman in the world." But this was an encyclopedia like no other. Yes, it could be said the encyclopedia might make you smarter, inform you, help your kids with their homework, or settle an argument, but it was more than that. It was a bold statement about the country, an assertion of pride, and perhaps the closest thing we have ever had to an expression of a Canadian identity.

Hurtig threw a celebratory launching party for eleven hundred guests at the Citadel Theatre in Edmonton on September 6, 1985. Premier Peter Lougheed, Mel Hurtig, and I spoke before the Tommy Banks Band began to play the theme from *Superman*. The champagne began to flow down a tower of glasses. None of us had any idea how the critics would receive the encyclopedia. The last few months had been the most hectic of my life, and from the inside I could see only the seams and weaknesses. The first reaction that I heard, on the radio, was a pompous academic with an English accent from Carleton University condescending about how "The Canadian Encyclopedia was no work of genius." But my spirits soared when I got a phone call from the eminent historian John Saywell, who was reviewing the encyclopedia for *Saturday Night* magazine. He congratulated me and enquired just who I was to have created this "great work," when he had never even heard of me.

Mel handled most of the national media while I travelled from Halifax to Vancouver speaking on the radio and giving newspaper interviews. I tried to avoid playing the "know-it-all" who somehow was the encyclopedia, fearing that would only encourage guests to phone in and try to stump the editor. In Halifax, I got off to a confident start when I told a disappointed questioner that I knew the answer to his question about the family of fishes to which the mackerel belonged—"tuna." My confidence sank, however, when the next guest told me in detail that in the 1930s a man had been convicted of murder in a small town I had never heard of in Cape Breton. Could I please explain why this man was innocent and who, in fact, had committed the crime? I never again agreed to play trivia live, except on Peter Gzowski's radio show in Toronto, when I had him to help me.

The newspaper and media reviews ranged from complimentary to ecstatic. I had some odd requests from reviewers. One

A Nation in a Nutshell

Speaking from the podium, designed by David Shaw as a replica of the three-volume set of encyclopedias, at the launch of the First Edition, Citadel Theatre, Edmonton, September 6, 1985. The ovation I received from friends and supporters was deeply appreciated.

told me he had been hired to speed read the encyclopedia in a weekend. To make him look good, he asked, would I help him by pointing out in advance some errors? (I politely refused.) Reviewers naturally followed their own interests. Kenneth McGoogan, author of *How the Scots Invented Canada*, declared that "all things bookish and literary are blanketed." As examples he noted entries on "Authors and Their Milieus," "Autobiographical Writing" (in both languages), "Literary Prizes," and "the list goes on." "It is an intellectual triumph, uniquely Canadian in its approach and outlook," wrote editor and author Stephen Hume. "It is an adventure that Canadians who want to know more about their land should not miss," wrote humourist and columnist Eric Nichol. "On the scholarly side a magnificent accomplishment," wrote historian

261

Jack Granatstein, who also noted that it was easy to read (caveat that James Marsh wrote too many articles). A librarian said it "belongs just everywhere."

On a loftier plane, other reviewers wrote that the encyclopedia "helps us to see ourselves," and that the editor in chief "has made a noble effort to gather in a phenomenal number of subjects and put them in Canadian perspective." The *Toronto Star* noted that the encyclopedia was "a delight to browsers old and young, rich in detail and resourcefulness and perhaps best of all it incarnates a living sense of Canada's past and present." The well-respected book critic William French (who had provided a letter of support for the original proposal to the Canada Council) wrote that the encyclopedia captured "a nation in a nutshell" and was "an indispensable reference work for anyone with even the slightest interest in this improbable country of ours." When John Saywell's review appeared in *Saturday Night*, he called the encyclopedia a "superb accomplishment and an eloquent testimony to the scholarly maturation of a nation." (He had been a contributor to *Canadiana*.) What a rebuke to current postmodernist critics who claim either that we were pretentious even to try to represent the country or that we had gotten it wrong. For our time, we got it right.

One reviewer gave the encyclopedia his ultimate compliment that, "as someone who owns 4,129 reference works, this one will always have a special place in my heart." In *Books in Canada*, author and critic George Galt focused on how the encyclopedia reflected the efflorescence in the arts over the past thirty years. "I am left with the sense," he wrote, "that a vast and variegated land has met its match in print." Playwright and poet James Reaney stretched for a metaphor in *Saturday Night* comparing TCE to *Anne of Green Gables* and "Alouette," "in a very exciting way, a new communications satellite." With special music to my ears after my studies of L'Encyclopédie, John Hutcheson wrote in the *Canadian Forum*, "Diderot's Encyclopédie put the ideas of the Enlightenment on the map. James Marsh's The Canadian Encyclopedia will do the same for Canadian studies."

It was a great honour to receive the Order of Canada from the elegant Governor General Madame Jeanne Sauvé. She leaned towards me and said, "James, you are having far too much fun!"

On an even more literary note, freelance writer and broadcaster Val Cleary in *Canadian Literature* wrote that the encyclopedia had succeeded in its goal of describing and expressing Canadian consciousness. "They have done so in a way which fascinates because it shows us how Canadians as a collective mentality think, and how they understand their own being." Historian Viv Nelles in the *Canadian Historical Review* called TCE "a monument to the integrative power of culture, the myth of a fragile land, the limits of limited identities, and the waning of a useful past. James Marsh has bravely held up a mirror to his culture." All that work trying to represent the country now seemed to pay off. "The encyclopedia is probably the closest equivalent that we will have in this generation to an intellectual 'bee,'" Nelles wrote. The scientific content received a further appreciation of our work: scientist Richard A. Jarrell noted in his review in the *Canadian Journal of the History of Science, Technology and Medicine* that

> [the editors revealed] the history of science ... science and society, research and development, science policy, the Science Council, mechanical engineering, medical research ... entries on inventions such as Silver Dart, telegraph, telephone and the snowmobile to name a few. The encyclopaedia is the single most useful compendium of biographies of Canadian scientists, engineers and physicians anywhere.

In my contract with Hurtig, one of my duties as editor in chief was to deliver an encyclopedia that would garner "excellent reviews." Obviously, we succeeded.

Hurtig commanded media attention far beyond the scope of his modest publishing company. He attracted a special audience of nationalistic Canadians, who almost certainly purchased the encyclopedia as a gesture of national pride. By Christmas 1985, most of the 150,000 sets were sold. Premier Peter Lougheed and I travelled to Ottawa to present official copies to Prime Minister Brian Mulroney in his office on July 1, 1986. Mr. Mulroney clearly had great respect for Lougheed and asked him to stand close by as he showered in his office on Wellington Street so he could give him advice on some vexatious political issue. When Mr. Mulroney emerged, he opened the encyclopedia to the entry on himself, read to the end, and enquired about the author: "Who *is* Norman Hillmer?"

After our meeting with the Prime Minister, Peter Lougheed and I attended a dinner set on the outside grounds of Rideau Hall with Governor General Jeanne Sauvé and her husband Maurice Sauvé. A gang of bicyclists sped by us on the open lawn, pursued by a band of flat-footed RCMP. "Welcome to our world," the irritated governor general said. When the waiters left us, failing to deliver Peter Lougheed's beef dinner, he joked that they must have been too embarrassed to bring him Ontario beef. Madame Sauvé had to ask her reluctant husband to go and get it. "However did you, a Conservative, manage to partner with that radical gadfly Mel Hurtig to make this encyclopedia?" she asked Peter. "We both love Canada," he replied, "and we had Jim to sort it out."

CHAPTER 19

Who Is Powlisik?

"Love truth, but pardon error."

–Voltaire

IN 1985 the editorial team brought The Canadian Encyclopedia endeavour to a triumphant conclusion. It had taken five years of intense effort. The great commercial success put Hurtig Publishers well into the black, but it presented a dilemma for Mel. How could he build on this? He had me work on the possibility of an annual yearbook, which seemed to be the way Britannica and World Book kept themselves in business between editions. As for reprinting or revamping the first edition, we had to ask how many sets of encyclopedias could the market absorb and in what time frame? With the profits from the first edition and with financial assistance from Nova Corporation, the Canada Council, the federal Department of Communications and the National Research Council, Mel set me to work on a greatly expanded second edition. The first edition senior editors had moved on with their careers (two of whom, Adriana Davies and Rosemary Shipton, went on to earn the Order of Canada) James Ogilvy joined the federal government in Ottawa, and Barry Hicks, VP of Hurtig Publishers, replaced Frank McGuire in finance and production. Editors Nancy Brown Foulds, Carlotta Lemieux, Co-ordinator Sheila Birmingham, Debra MacGregor, and my assistant Carol Woo provided continuity, along with numerous researchers and proofreaders.

The great deficiency of our "national" encyclopedia lacking a French version was at the same time being resolved. The promise of Hurtig Publishers to the Alberta government that the French rights would be given without charge was kept when a deal was made with a Montreal based publisher. We had submissions from several well-known publishers, but one stuck out dramatically. Born in Lithuania, Alain Stanké was deported to a German concentration camp when he was only ten years old. He moved to France at the end of the Second War and took a degree in Paris before emigrating to Quebec in 1951. He became a prominent broadcaster and journalist and in 1975, he founded his own publishing house, Les Éditions Internationales Alain Stanké. In addition to publishing over two thousand works, Stanké wrote twenty-seven books, including *J'aime encore mieux le jus de betterave* (1969), an account of his childhood during the war.

The project began with a complex movement of materials in two directions, handled by Debra MacGregor. We sent our English files for translation into French and Stanké sent French language articles that they newly commissioned to us for translation into English and inclusion in our new edition. I felt a great satisfaction with the process, as I felt that this was how the original encyclopedia should have been made. The production, editing, and co-ordination was handled seamlessly by Louise Loiselle, whom Stanké called his *"pivot central de l'encyclopédie."*

Stanké published *L'encyclopédie du Canada* in 1987 with great pride, he wrote in his introduction, calling it "a unique work which examines the country, its history, its people, its institutions and presents a rigorous inventory of all that represents Canada."

The editorial process of our own, second edition was quite different from the first edition. The first edition was now in the world and a community of readers, critics and supporters came to life.

I was astonished by the thousands of letters we received commenting on the published encyclopedia. My assistant, Carol

Woo, brought me a new pile every morning, patiently awaiting my replies. Most began with a compliment before going on to point out some grievous omission or error. An elderly lady in Regina wrote to comment on the small biography of one of her relatives, the politician Hazen Argue. Why, she implored, did I pick that man from the entire Argue clan? She provided potted biographies of dozens of Argues far more worthy than "that wretch" for inclusion in the encyclopedia. Another reader commented on the biography of explorer Samuel Hearne, correcting the direction that the explorer took on some obscure little river. The reason he knew, he wrote, was that he had recently paddled that river himself. Another reader pointed out that our statement that an all-weather road between Jasper and Edmonton was built in 1927 must be wrong. "I remember well," he continued, "trying to get from Edmonton west in September 1929, got stuck in a mud hole at Wolf Creek east of Edsen [sic] and had to spend the night in a barn." Here were the piranhas pecking away at the fringes of that myth of complete accuracy.

Some of the most unpredictable correspondence concerned the illustrated endpapers that Hurtig commissioned (he considered the endpapers and the cover to be in his marketing domain). The purpose was to show the diversity of the contents with a representative array of Canadian personalities and symbols—an old-fashion montage, which I hated. It violated my principle of inclusion, impossible to show with such a small sample of clichés. While the encyclopedia itself might have been too rich and varied a source to criticize, everybody had an opinion about the endpapers. Why depict Wayne Gretzky but not Gordie Howe? We were able to explain away the Golden Boy, the salmon and the astrolabe, Captain Cook, Glenn Gould and Laura Secord. All that was fine, except for Powlisik. I had no idea where the artist had found this Inuit face or why he gave it that name—he could never tell us. We got hundreds of letters about Powlisik. Who was he? Why did we have a picture of him but no biography? It was no good saying we were portraying diversity because we really had no idea who he was. Even reviewers got into the act. My apologetic letters seemed to many an admission

Who Is Powlisik?

The launch of the French edition in Montreal, 15 April 1987. On the left Alain Stanké and Louise Loiselle who co-ordinated the massive translation as well as the commissioning of many new articles.

that the encyclopedia was not all it was cracked up to be in its authority. I was greatly relieved when Hurtig agreed to scrap the endpapers in the second edition. I replaced them with a map of Canada.

Carol Woo or I patiently responded to every letter. Many complaints spun on those exquisite distinctions you must learn to love if you are an editor of a reference work. "I realize the difficulty that such a comprehensive work as the Encyclopedia presents," wrote E.D. Lane. "However, in future editions it might be useful to avoid words like 'sea trout' (although I don't know how) as they usually lead to more questions than answers." A school principal corrected us about the date for Canada's first kindergarten (1882 at Jeremiah Suddaby School). Almost always the letters began well. "I hope that you will not consider the comments in this letter to detract in any way from that well-deserved sense of achievement," began J.A. Robertson before correcting some spelling errors and attacking our entry on Nuclear Safety as "journalistic." Valerie Haig-Brown responded to the article on

Launch party of The Junior Encyclopedia surrounded by students at my old school, Davenport (at that time called Carleton), Toronto. It was my birthday September 10, 1990, and the school presented me with a beautiful birthday cake.

her famous father Roderick by pointing out the missed distinction between "fly fishing" and "sportfishing."

The encyclopedia spurred some readers to go rooting through their family tree. Mary Burles thought that the assassin of Thomas D'Arcy McGee might have been related to her late stepfather. "Your illustrations are superb," she wrote, "but I want some information on Darcy McGee's murder. One of my Irish aunts before she died a summer or two ago said, 'As far as we know none of the family hung. Maybe some of them should have.'" The poet Ralph Gustafson, and others, wrote to ask, "Please let me know why there is no separate entry on my work." "It is all very well for us to say that any list can only be representative, never complete and always contestable," I replied, "but when you are the person omitted, I know it still irks." We added an entry on Gustafson in the second edition.

*Carol Woo was an enduring presence
at the encyclopedia from 1984 as Illustrations Editor
and Assistant to the Editor in Chief.
Here tending a booth at a teachers' conference.*

The encyclopedia brought out the champion nitpickers. Barbara K. Whistler wrote me a three-page letter showing me that our use of quotation marks was "distracting and sometimes irritating." Some letter writers overstated their case. A group wrote me to regret that "our community, Chemainus, now becoming known worldwide as 'the Little Town That Did,' did not receive its own entry." No place harassed me so much as Waterloo, Ontario, enraged at being lumped in the encyclopedia as "Kitchener-Waterloo" (following Statistics Canada's metropolitan definitions). The campaign to get Waterloo separated in the next edition was spearheaded by Betty Gardner, who involved the mayor, school children, and storeowners. To prove the justification of her cause, she invited Carol Woo ("Not James Marsh, please!") to visit and not to worry too much about the city's beer and sausage image. "Poultry and fish are more to our taste," she said reassuringly. Students were encouraged to hang the editor in chief in effigy. I added a separate entry on Waterloo to the second edition.

Whenever possible we tried to involve our authors in the responses. A sheep farmer from White Rock, British Columbia, W.J. Harper, objected to our claim that coyotes are not a threat to livestock. "Coyotes are a serious and on-going threat to livestock," he claimed, "in spite of continuous poisoning." We tracked down our author, C.S. Churcher, then living in South Africa, and he responded, "Coyotes seldom hunt in packs and usually take prey much smaller than themselves (sheep are larger!)." A onetime farmer himself, he wrote, "I have lost sheep to feral dogs and (in Africa) to leopards but never to coyotes."

I was surprised at the number of young people who sent us letters. Eldon Grant wrote, "I just turned 16 and bought these books out of my birthday money. They are the best encyclopedias I have ever read." A nine-year-old boy told us how useful the article on owls was, but he wondered why we used no periods in our abbreviation BC for British Columbia.

By responding to these comments, verifying the facts, and adding articles whenever I thought appropriate, I felt we were making the second edition of the encyclopedia, published in September 1988, even more a part of the Canadian community. However, it was not a "wiki" approach: every suggested correction was thoroughly vetted by our editors and consultant experts and cleared finally with the authors.

From a marketing standpoint, this second edition, appearing only three years after the first, turned out to be premature. Hurtig was a small, regional publisher who could not afford to keep a large editorial staff together for another five or ten years. The idea of publishing interim yearbooks, like Britannica or World Book, did not make economic sense, and Hurtig believed that only a successful new edition could keep the enterprise alive. This set, comprising four volumes bound in red with an added 750,000 words, was launched with considerable fanfare at the St. Lawrence Centre in Toronto.

Presenting the new Second Edition set of the encyclopedia to then Minister of Canadian Heritage Sheila Copps. We laughed at our ability to hold the weight of two full sets.

Because there was less immediate demand for the second edition, Hurtig gave in to the bookstore chains' demand for large discounts, and, in response, many of the angry independent booksellers returned their sets and refused to stock them. The chains then passed the discount on to the public, lowering the price to $99—a figure the small bookstores couldn't match. Hurtig claimed to have written $685,000 in refund cheques to booksellers. The second edition sold well enough, but, clearly, the market was saturated with some 250,000 sets now in the market.

The Junior Encyclopedia of Canada (I always hated the name but could not think of a better one) was an attempt to reach a different market. Britannica and World Book had success with their scaled-down products aimed at younger students. Funded by the federal Department of Communications and a grant from the CRB Foundation of Montreal, The Junior Encyclopedia was a noble adventure in trying to produce a Canadian reference for younger readers. The editors, who included Rosemary Shipton,

Carlotta Lemieux, Nancy Foulds, Sean McCuthcheon, and Daniel Francis, approached this encyclopedia as a writing rather than a research exercise, attempting to describe the topics in clear, concise language. It was not a watered-down version of TCE but an entirely new work. The contributing editors, unable to assume any level of knowledge among their readers, had to explain the most basic concepts and, simultaneously, make the entries interesting and informative to children and youth.

Editorial manager Debra MacGregor field-tested over a thousand articles with students and teachers in classrooms from Alberta to Nova Scotia. The process was extremely valuable as we found that young readers were very specific and concrete in their comments, often going straight to the heart of the matter. The five volumes were attractively laid out and beautifully illustrated with over 3,000 photographs, drawings, and maps, but the whole project was in a commercial sense overly hopeful. Once again, the reviews were positive. *Quill and Quire* called it "unquestionably an impressive achievement."

The negative aura around the marketing and sales of the second edition led Hurtig to make the fatal decision to market The Junior Encyclopedia by direct mail. I tried to dissuade him and told him the booksellers would get over their pique at being mistreated during the second edition of The Canadian Encyclopedia if they thought they could sell the new product. By the time the misguided direct marketing campaign was abandoned and reluctant bookstores began to accept the sets, Hurtig was in the financial crisis that, soon, would cost him his company. He eventually made a unique arrangement with the booksellers: rather than purchasing the books from the publisher at a given discount and reselling them at a suggested price, booksellers were paid a fixed commission of $20 for each set they sold. Bookstores were not asked to stock copies but took orders, which were then fulfilled from a warehouse in Toronto. Chains such as Coles, however, refused to take part.

On the verge of bankruptcy, Hurtig dismissed the staff, including me, with one month's severance, and in 1991 sold the company to McClelland & Stewart. He was in a crisis of his own making, and after the first edition had made him wealthy, I felt betrayed. During that final month he insisted I sit among his secretarial staff, humiliatingly clipping useless newspaper articles. Avie Bennett, the chairman and owner of M&S, told me that his main incentive to purchase Hurtig Publishers was the encyclopedia, and me; he had no interest in the rest of the business. As for Hurtig, he continued to remake himself in a remarkable way, forming a new political party, running for Parliament, and becoming a bestselling author.

Bennett hired me to continue my role as editor in chief, updating material in the encyclopedia and exploring the possibilities of bringing this unique reference work into the electronic age. He wanted me to move to Toronto but agreed it would be difficult to duplicate our standard of living, surrounded by green space in the river valley of Edmonton, in the Toronto real estate market. I set up a home office and ran a successful virtual operation until I retired in 2013.

CHAPTER 20

Into the Digital Age

"Where is the Life we have lost in living?
Where is the wisdom we have lost in knowledge?
Where is the knowledge we have lost in information?"

– *"The Rock," T.S. Eliot*

THE TIME from the appearance of the first print edition of the encyclopedia in 1985 to the sale of Hurtig Publishers to M&S in 1991 saw momentous changes in the technology, not just of typesetting, printing, and editing, but in the actual delivery of information. In 1981 Ron Senda, a programmer from University of Alberta Computing Science, paid me a visit. He shook his head in amusement when he saw the bank of walnut cabinets containing drawers filled with thousands of index cards, alphabetically organizing article titles and authors. He invited me to his office across campus and showed me the magic of a "database program" called Spires, which ran on the University of Alberta's then-legendary Amdahl mainframe (it was said that only the US military had one, but today even the cheapest laptop is more powerful). With Ron's guidance and several programmers, our handwritten index cards were tapped into Spires. Soon we could print out lists of articles, authors, and schedules in a flash, calculating the numbers of words commissioned so far. We were the first encyclopedia in the world to use a computer to organize a reference work. It saved us an enormous amount of time and helped to make possible an otherwise intolerable deadline. It was another example of the fortuitous partnership between the encyclopedia and the University of Alberta. The university ultimately rented us two larger houses and more office space, and our employees had free academic access to the libraries. The faculty of almost every department were co-operative in providing advice and in contributing articles.

The first articles that arrived, by mail, by hand, or by delivery service, were typed on IBM typewriters, edited, and filed for delivery to typesetters where they had to be entered again. Around 1982-83 we began to use dedicated Micron word processors to enter and correct text; by the second edition in the late 1980s, we were using university computers to typeset and make pages. (The office manager vehemently opposed allowing editors anywhere near a computer. We had one terminal in our offices on which a typist made entries and corrections.) These advances were moderately revolutionary, but the real transformation came not with the use of computers as tools to produce the encyclopedia but with using electronic technology to deliver it. When in November 1985 Fraser Sutherland, managing editor of *Books in Canada*, wrote to me to enquire when TCE would "be going on-line in a computer data base," I naively wrote back saying I thought it was in a database but had no notion of how it would ever be going "online."

The idea of delivering as well as organizing an encyclopedia electronically arose from the spread and evolution of the personal computer throughout the 1980s. Barry Hicks of Hurtig Publishers, who replaced Frank McGuire and shared my enthusiasm for the editorial possibilities of the PC, had taken some initial steps before the company was sold to McClelland & Stewart. George Goodwin, a VP at M&S, initiated the first real electronic version of the encyclopedia, on CD-ROM. Goodwin introduced me to typesetting consultant Kate Hamilton, who was working with the M&S editors in electronically formatting the text of their books. She in turn initiated me into the arcane language of SGML. I read the book of codes she sent me before spending a weekend with her in Toronto explaining my process in structuring the encyclopedia; from the information tree that we nurtured, she compiled a set of codes that would not only make the encyclopedia text easy to format and organize for any database program but also make every transition from one electronic medium to the next extremely easy. For example, the move to the Internet was simple, as HTML is merely a subset of SGML. Other reference works, such as the Dictionary of Canadian Biography, went through the nightmare of having to strip codes from Microsoft Word or WordPerfect documents and then manually code them in SGML.

The first CD-ROM disk that we produced was predictably flawed as the developers struggled with the complexities of the new medium. The challenges of creating a CD-ROM for both Microsoft DOS and Apple platforms, neither of which were sufficiently advanced to deliver multimedia, proved costly, but there was enough interest, particularly among educators, to persist. Those were the days when some of the most intense relationships were between perplexed and frustrated purchasers of the CD-ROM and our full-time support staff.

After a bizarre sidestep in which M&S produced a version of the text on twenty-one floppy disks, a saner and more usable CD-ROM was produced with KCSL (Kaufman Consulting) in Toronto. Kaufman adapted his own search engine and produced a professional disk that eventually proved almost as popular as the printed books. The encyclopedia text was a natural on CD-ROM; it offered advantages over the printed versions, with hypertext hot links to related articles (easily adapted from the print cross-references already marked), swift and sophisticated searches, and, increasingly, multimedia. (Kaufman was naturally most interested in using the encyclopedia to showcase his proprietary search engine, and he resisted my plans to integrate more multimedia and later my insistence that we provide online updates—something I discovered at a multimedia conference in San Francisco.) We were also able to integrate the *Gage Canadian Dictionary* with the text of the encyclopedia, along with some 3,000 pictures, maps, drawings, and videos. Any word in the encyclopedia could be double clicked to provide a

Showing students all the books contained on the CD-ROM of the encyclopedia when I was invited to open the new Children's Library in Toronto.

dictionary definition. In an ever-more-frustrating attempt to keep up with competing international encyclopedias, particularly Microsoft's *Encarta*, we added *Roget's Thesaurus* and integrated the text of the Columbia Encyclopedia—the original inspiration for TCE.

The 1998–99 Canadian Encyclopedia on CD-ROM featured three separate versions, including an updated World Edition with a new interactive quiz called Canucklehead, which I had written to raise money for a charity, and introducing a Student Edition with the updated and revised text of the Junior Encyclopedia of Canada. This version of the Junior Encyclopedia was a disappointment to me: I had wanted to create an interactive disk entirely redesigned for younger users, but M&S decided for financial reasons simply to use the same interface as the World

Edition. It was a failure. A Deluxe version included all the material on "World" and five additional disks. An extensive project to translate the text into French was completed with the help of a grant from the Department of Canadian Heritage. The text of The Canadian Encyclopedia was now finally bilingual on a single disk. An adept user could search an article in TCE, jump to a definition of any word, switch to French, then follow a trail to international sources.

By the year 2000, marketing and the attempt to outflank *Encarta* had gotten out of hand and there were now four electronic versions: World, Student, Deluxe, and "National." The production and marketing of electronic products proved perplexing to a traditional book publisher. While the launch of the print versions sparked hundreds of reviews in newspapers and magazines and dozens of interviews coast to coast, the appearance of electronic versions did not interest newspapers, magazines, or television at all. We were competing not with other struggling publishers for book reviews but with the billion-dollar software and gaming industries. We got mentions in the giveaway computer papers, but no air play on the daily broadcast computer shows in Toronto and Vancouver, which were focused on their advertising money from Microsoft. The Vancouver tech show repeatedly referred to *Encarta* and ignored our Canadian CD-ROMs—the show's advertiser was Microsoft. In the late 1990s a young woman approached me with a letter. Claire Citeau had recently arrived from France and was studying marketing at the University of Alberta. She learned about the encyclopedia from one of my staff and, as she explained in her letter, we had a great product in our electronic encyclopedia but no idea how to market it. Over the next several years, she designed brochures, spoke to teachers, and helped me to host conferences across Canada. Claire was simply another example of how luck played such an important role in our success.

The digital world put another nail in the coffin of nationalism, even on "Canadian-owned" educational networks. The digitization of the encyclopedia and its integration, willy-nilly, with other reference works destroyed the image of coherence and authority we had worked so diligently to create. The information was intact, expanded, and easier to access, but the image of a national representation was lost.

While the tensions in developing the print versions had generally been confined to internal editorial spats, relations between editors and programmers and between programmers and graphic designers proved a greater challenge in the new electronic world. Software developers treated the content as a mere showcase for technology or software design, and they rightly considered that most editors were technologically naive. In any event, the CD-ROM era, which seemed so promising, was fleeting. The little disk that seemed to contain so much could not keep up with increasing expectations for video and sound. DVD, which for a while proved a very successful technology in the delivery of video, never succeeded as a delivery platform for multimedia. In any event, it was quickly obliterated by the Internet, not only in the delivery of content, including dictionaries and encyclopedias, but by streaming video as well.

In a last, nostalgic *fin de siècle* gesture, McClelland & Stewart produced a single-volume print edition of the encyclopedia in 1999. The move back into print provided a great opportunity for a thorough edit and verification, long overdue, but this chunky door-stopper volume was not a commercial success. Despite its bulk, it seemed somehow smaller and less imposing than the multi-volume sets, especially because it lacked any of the strikingly beautiful illustrations. Dutifully, the Quebec publisher Stanké brought out its own single-volume version in French a year later. Although we generated much greater interest in the press than we had enjoyed in the CD-ROM years, and I undertook yet another cross-country press tour, we were never able to recreate the marketing fervour of the mid-1980s. The nationalistic ardour in the country had been cooled by years of bickering with Quebec and Alberta, exhausting constitutional squabbles, and the relentless domination of American media. Almost overnight, the world found its information in a completely new way. The Internet began delivering databases of information and, with increased bandwidth, more and more multimedia.

For all its revolutionary character, the CD-ROM business still followed the old book-publishing paradigm, selling individual units to customers through retail or in bulk to departments of education or to computer companies such as Dell to bundle with their hardware. The Internet changed all that. Unfortunately, the idea that money would now be generated by people paying to access information on the Internet did not prove successful in the encyclopedia or the dictionary businesses. There is too much "free" information online, and Internet users do not expect to pay, unless they are playing games or being entertained. The paradigm shifted towards that of television, whereby "free" content is accompanied by advertising and more insidious means of generating revenue. The Canadian Encyclopedia was not a viable commercial online operation on its own. It existed only with support from Canadian Heritage.

The Internet version of TCE was programmed by Netcentrics in Edmonton, with an interface designed by 7th Floor Media in Vancouver. It was launched in Edmonton in October 2001— only a few months after Wikipedia—and remains free of charge and free of advertising for the use of all Canadians and people worldwide. Despite the ease with which information can now be found by using either Google's indexing or the internal search engine, the encyclopedia online has inevitably lost its caché as a coherent expression of a Canadian identity. The advent of Wikipedia, made universal by its number-one ranking in Google for any search, without any consideration of its reliability or authority, has eroded the use of references such as The Canadian Encyclopedia or the Dictionary of Canadian Biography. The idea that a popular mass, levelled into cultural entropy, can cobble together collective wisdom by denigrating expertise and authority is either a symptom or a cause, or both, of the current deterioration of our education system, our collective intellect, and the worldwide decline of democracy.

The publication and success of The Canadian Encyclopedia in print now seem as far away in the past as Diderot. It simply would not be possible in today's fractious intellectual environment and contentious political climate. No politician in Canada

Helping Prime Minister Jean Chrétien find the article on himself in the CD-ROM version of The Canadian Encyclopedia. Avie Bennett looks on.

today has anything approaching the public spirit of Peter Lougheed. The editorial principles of veracity and authority on which TCE was compiled were still accepted, at least by a large part of the population, when we put it online in 2001, in stark contrast to the impending groundswell of Wikipedia.

IN THE LATE 1990S several organizational changes occurred behind the scenes that had an impact on The Canadian Encyclopedia and on my working life. The future of the encyclopedia seemed secure after Avie Bennett and George Goodwin arranged for financial support, $1 million per year from Canadian Heritage through a licensing agreement for the online encyclopedia. Then came a shock. In 2000, Avie Bennett announced that he had sold 25 percent of McClelland & Stewart to Random House and had donated the other 75 percent to the University of Toronto. Bennett had been in a real quandary about M&S's future. He had owned the company for seventeen years and had never turned a profit. The returns system after Indigo and Chapters came on the scene was bleeding the industry dry. The sudden bankruptcies of Jack Stoddart and General Publishing only two years later in 2002 was another indication of that gross imbalance in commercial power.

Bennett was at first extolled for his generosity for the donation and was rewarded with the Companion of the Order of Canada. However, the Association of Canadian Publishers was skeptical and expressed dismay that "Canada's most-storied book publisher, McClelland & Stewart, will be downgraded to an imprint of a foreign-owned multinational corporation. Today's announcement marks the end of a long and illustrious history of a Canadian cultural institution."

The agreement was rubber stamped by the Conservative Harper government despite the *Investment Canada Act*, which forbade such a sale. Within a few years the deception of University of Toronto's stewardship was exposed, and Random House had complete ownership of M&S. While the University of Toronto held 75 percent of M&S shares, Elaine Dewar wrote in her revealing book on the whole affair, *The Handover*, the fine print of the secret agreement gave Random House effective control of M&S from the start and made its future absorption into the multinational inevitable.

Bennett had, despite all this, saved The Canadian Encyclopedia once again, exempting it from the sale to Random House. In November 2000 he transferred it to the Historica Foundation, which had been formed in 1999 by Lynton "Red" Wilson, former chairman of Nortel Networks, with a large donation from Charles Bronfman and support of Bennett, Peter Lougheed, John Cleghorn, Yves Fortier, Antonio Lamer, and others. Wilson expressed concern that historians were not "encouraging loyalty, national pride, and citizenship." He had formed this view after reading Jack Granatstein's controversial book *Who Killed Canadian History*. I was in an uneasy position now in Historica, since I had written a newspaper review of Granatstein's book. I wrote that his determination "to save history" was to be applauded. But I did not accept his dismissal of the new generation of historians focused on women, labour, the environment, minorities, immigrants, and Indigenous Peoples—narratives that had gone untouched by older historians—topics that I had insisted be included in The Canadian Encyclopedia. Granatsteins' book gained attention because of the alarms set off by the endless surveys done by the conservative Dominion Institute, wringing their hands over the ignorance of Canadian history among Canadian students. From my own education in Canadian history and in the creation of The Canadian Encyclopedia, I believed that history is not just a series of dates, wars, and prime ministers to be memorized. Though it is not quantum physics, the study of history is difficult and multifaceted. It deals with conflict, paradox and change, and complex relationships among a bewildering array of factors, all within the context of time.

Fortunately, no one noticed or cared about my views, though I expressed them to blank stares in speeches at the annual council meetings. In fact, the move to Historica provided my staff and me with brilliant new opportunities. Its first president, Tom Axworthy, respected the encyclopedia and he appointed me Director of Content for the whole foundation. Not only were my staff able to bring The Canadian Encyclopedia online for present and future generations, but we also produced, over the next few years, major new websites on Youth Voting, Champlain in Acadia, Asia Canada, a Black History Portal, War of 1812 (in partnership with *Canadian Geographic*), Historywire, the Department of Canadian Citizenship website on Refugees, a social studies teaching database Access.ca, and a youth engagement site FYICanada. All these websites were researched and edited by my staff and designed by 7th Floor Media in Vancouver. We believed that we contributed significantly to the web presence of Canadian information.

We also reached out to hundreds of thousands of Canadians when George Goodwin raised sponsors for several beautiful historical calendars, with Canadian events displayed day by day. I was also involved with two of the organization's programs, Youthlinks and Encounters with Canada, in which I met hundreds of students from all over Canada studying Acadia, exploration, Indigenous issues, democracy, and several other topics. I acted as the host to gatherings of students brought together in Moncton, Quebec City, Kingston, Lethbridge, Halifax, and elsewhere. It was a highlight of my life to speak to and converse with these young students. I attended but was not involved with the excellent Historica Fairs program, which sponsored Canadian history projects in junior and middle schools in twelve hundred communities across Canada. I had many unforgettable conversations with young students who explained their projects on Ojibwa Culture, Louis Riel, an amazing family tree on How I Came to Canada, Komagata Maru, the banning of the Potlatch, and Japantown, Forgotten Streets. These proud, and always excited, young students were not ignorant of Canadian history.

The staff I assembled in the late 1990s and beyond were in the vanguard of the home office revolution set off by the worldwide pandemic that started in 2019. Editors worked from home in Edmonton, Vancouver, Toronto, Ottawa, Montreal, Quebec City, and a village in Saskatchewan. Most of our communication was by telephone before email became ubiquitous. Every few months I flew to different parts of the country to meet staff, web designers, printers, funders, authors, and others. Over the next ten years or more, the skills and professionalism of these editors and researchers would enable us to continue to update the encyclopedia through its various electronic iterations and also to provide content for numerous other major web projects: a social studies teaching database and search tool called Access.ca, a youth engagement site FYICanada, "Voices" (Youth Voting), Champlain in Acadia, Asia Canada, Black History Portal, War of 1812, Asia-Canada, Historywire, and the Department of Canadian Citizenship website and mobile display on Refugees. All these online contributions to Canadian knowledge were produced with the same professionalism as the encyclopedias. They were designed by consultants, written by experts, and vetted by editors. None of this work would have been possible without my associate Laura Bonikowsky, who

With the two Alberta pillars of The Canadian Encyclopedia, Peter Lougheed (left) and Mel Hurtig, at the 25th anniversary of the publication, held at the Conference Centre in Ottawa. A school choir sang "Un Canadien errant" *in my honour.*

encouraged and connected our far-flung staff, and Trish Lyon, based in Toronto, who flawlessly entered every word, as she had for the updates and new entries of The Canadian Encyclopedia.

In all these web projects I worked closely with 7th Floor Media at Simon Fraser University and its director Noni Mate. For me, at least, it was a beautiful, creative friendship, in which 7th Floor not only read my mind but inevitably improved the ideas that initiated these projects.

When I served on the federal Information Highway Advisory Council in 1994, I found it dominated by the giant telecoms. I served on a fringe committee arguing for as much funding for Canadian content as for commercial profits, with little effect. We felt strongly that the electronic encyclopedia and the websites we produced for schools made a major contribution to Canadian education.

In the last two years of my tenure as editor in chief, I had a vision that we could remake the online encyclopedia to be more interactive, more thematic, more thought promoting, more connected to both curricula and to multimedia—in short to be something much greater than information packed in a database and accessed only through a search engine. 7th Floor Media made several promising designs, but I was unable to secure funding for these plans. However, we were able to advance one last initiative by developing Cities in Time apps, beginning with Vancouver in Time and Toronto in Time. Lorraine Snyder researched historical views of prominent places such as Kensington Market, Palace Pier, Casa Loma, Gibraltar Point Lighthouse, and the Lion's Gate Bridge, over a hundred for each city. With these photos as guides, my associate Davina Choy, while toting a huge binder, found the identical angle for me to shoot the "now" photographs. We walked both cities for hours and days on end and 7th Floor Media programmed the apps. It was an enjoyable *schwanengesang* to my career, absorbed in history, working closely with my staff, and testing the technological edge.

The transition across the world from a print-based culture to the Internet and social media began as a dream of a connected, transnational world, an information utopia. But as with every technological revolution, this change has drowned us in unintended consequences. The online community can become a mob. Facebook, Twitter, and Google have become tools of propaganda, consumerism, and lies; they pose serious threats to our privacy, freedom, and political systems. How have we devolved from a world of literacy and been seized by something so addictive, cynically exploiting a vulnerability in human psychology? Social media's values have triumphed in an extremely short period of world history. Any search for information on Google is analyzed, stored, and monetized.

There will be no return to the reflective print culture of books, with its editorial gatekeepers and its philosophers who were among the progenitors of democracy. There was briefly a vain hope that social media, with its ability to spontaneously bring millions into the streets, might be lethal to oppressive regimes, but these mobilizations come without leadership and easily dissipate. The opponents of change or progress in governments and corporations have far greater access to the use of software, as the invasive use of facial recognition in China and elsewhere has proven. I hear from even my Canadian friends, "Why do you need privacy if you have nothing to hide?" Facebook or Twitter could never produce a Martin Luther King. Instead, they created Donald Trump.

I used to lecture at the University of Alberta about the values of authority and objective truth in creating knowledge, but I would be ridiculed as an "elitist" for such views these days. This breakdown in respect and tolerance, and the disappearance of gatekeepers from publishing and politics, erodes our democracy from within. It may not survive this threat.

CHAPTER 21

Bookends

"I have no more made my book than my book has made me..."

– Michel de Montaigne in his essay "On Giving the Lie"

THE MOST POWERFUL LIGHT throughout my writing of this memoir has shone on the role friends have played as the bookends of my life. "Each friend represents a world in us, a world possibly not born until they arrive," wrote Anaïs Nin. I felt indeed that my friend Joan already occupied part of my heart when she first looked directly into my eyes when I arrived at the door of my new apartment, on First Avenue, in Ottawa in 1970. She asked me in a conspiratorial whisper, "Are we going to be lovers, or friends?" She was a beautiful free spirit, generous and gregarious, and she became an intimate, thoughtful friend. She had long brown hair and an angelic singing voice. We ate meals together, took long walks along the canal in Ottawa; we talked, about love, our partners, our desires, her experiences as a child decamped from one military base to another, of her experiences singing in coffee houses in Ottawa and Montreal, and about her unhappy marriage. Over the years our friendship deepened.

When Joan moved with her children and her new partner John to live in a remote shack at the edges of Algonquin Park, near Barry's Bay, I braved the discomfort and mosquitoes to visit her. She managed in these modest conditions to bake amazing bread and one of her specialties, *kugelhopf,* in a wood-burning stove. When she and her family and other friends shipped in from their little commune at Barry's Bay for Thanksgiving or Christmas or for other celebrations, they all stayed with me, bunked on sleeping bags and mattresses throughout my apartment on Springhurst Avenue. We swarmed the Byward Market together and feasted on fish, scallops, turkey, vegetables, and pies. Joan and John brought thick cream from their Jersey cow, wild berries from the meadows, and honey from their hives. Their friends were American draft dodgers, hippies, recluses, copped out poets and professors, weavers, and carvers. Joan was the hub of this disparate community, the hostess, the mother figure, the matchmaker and a generous provider of food, love, and emotional encouragement. One day Joan and I drove to the Ottawa Byward market and picked up Louise, who was standing on the sidewalk. "My God," said Joan. "Look at her! She is so beautiful. What are you waiting for?"

When we were forty, Joan fell seriously ill with leukemia. A few days before she died in Ottawa, she phoned me in Edmonton and asked me if I would come to say goodbye to her; she asked me to deliver her eulogy. "You were always my most literate friend," she told me. "We talked so well; we had our own language." I tried to catch a plane in time, but I was stricken on the way to the airport with what was later diagnosed as sarcoidosis. I did not know if it was the stress of her dying that triggered the illness, but it coincided fatefully. Irritating, ugly blue bumps swelled on my body; my joints became so painful that I could not walk; my heart was skipping beats and cysts formed on my bones. Joan died two days later in the arms of her many friends.

How can we express our thoughts in such desperate times, infused with remorse and grief? Can the books we read help us when we need to share our burdens? Does grief develop the powers of the mind, as the cliché claims? Is there true consolation in music, poetry, art? I returned home from the airport that night I was to fly to Ottawa, sat down, my body dwindling, scanning my bookshelves for help with the greatest writing challenge that I have ever faced: that eulogy. How could I find words that might express my love for a dying friend? Guided by a book of poems by Rainer Maria Rilke, I sketched a draft. I dictated it through tears over the phone to Louise, who bravely delivered it at the memorial. "How sweetly she drew us together and shone light on our darkest fear. It comforts us to know that she was not snatched away, but tenderly unloosened in our sight, caressed by those she loved," Louise read.

Joan's last words to me, on the telephone the day before she died, were "Jim, I want to show you that it is not so hard to die. This is my final gift to you." I have thought about her words, if not every day, at least in all the transitions, in all the accomplishments, the failures, the awards, the disappointments, the illnesses, and the longings. Her words colour them all as she speaks to me every time I think of her. I have not however approached the equanimity about dying that she tried to encourage in me. I picked up Louise at the airport on her return to Edmonton from Joan's funeral; she drove me straight to the hospital, where I spent the next week being diagnosed and treated. The disease remained misdiagnosed until a medical intern swept in one day and told me that she had heard about my purple bumps and that she knew what ailed me; she was researching that very disease—sarcoidosis. She asked me if she could delay treatment so that a professional photographer could photograph those miserable blue swellings for her thesis. She seemed excited so, of course, I agreed.

I suppose that there is irony in the fact that my mother's sarcastic nickname for me when I was a kid was "Know It All," in that I became an encyclopedist (from the Greek *enkuklios paideia* "all-round knowledge"). Of course, no one knows the all of anything. These days, claiming to have an all-around education or some appreciation of the perplexity of the human condition, of contradiction or paradox, is considered simply arrogant elitism; claiming that you know one thing absolutely, no matter how false, is the current obsession, particularly if you can express it in a tweet or on Facebook.

As a lifelong editor, I believed what every other one in my vanishing profession believed, that the books we shepherded

My friend Joan shortly after she got her diagnosis of fatal leukemia.

were an integral part of our culture: explaining it, celebrating it, and at their best, creating it. I have been so thoroughly involved with Canadian authors and manuscripts in my day jobs that I deliberately spent my nonworking hours reading the poets and novelists of the world. Canadian authors such Alice Munro, Margaret Atwood, Leonard Cohen, John Newlove, Margaret Laurence (whose letter of support for my nomination into the Order of Canada I treasure), and Robertson Davies provide guidance and insight into deeper human concerns, but I have gravitated repeatedly to Shakespeare, Chekov, and Proust for broader perspectives.

Books infiltrated my life from my earliest days. No one guided me there. No one in my family ever read to me, or to themselves for that matter, except for Annie Radford, who read the Bible by her bed every night. As a small boy, I pulled volumes from behind the glass doors of the barrister bookcase on Norfolk Street. I pretended to read, turning the pages, staring at the pictures and mumbling random words. "We read to show we are not alone," wrote C.S. Lewis. I somehow sensed that there was a brighter life to be lived in books that meant so much more than the messy, abject realm in which I dwelt. At school I was spellbound by teachers reading *Mill on the Floss, Prester John*, the poems of Keats and the plays of Shakespeare. At Perth Avenue, I was raised from bed in the middle of the night by my father and told to choose words randomly from a dictionary, testing him in a bizarre and dangerous spelling bee. He was proud that he had carried that small dictionary in his pocket as a soldier during the war in Holland and he bragged, wrongly (as I found out questioning him), that he had memorized it all. I spent hours with a one-volume world encyclopedia, the sole other book in our house on Perth, learning facts that I dared not display for fear of my mother's sarcasm. Ironically, that encyclopedia was so out of date that much of what I thought I learned was indeed, by then, wrong. Later there were the novels, poems and philosophy books in which I searched for meaning, for ideas and for images that might nurse a nascent consciousness, for romantic ideas of the other world that I longed for. I was not a diligent reader. I skipped, backtracked, or tossed the book aside when it became to my mind predictable or boring.

My reputation for loving books, as opposed to actually reading them, got me hired in publishing, sight unseen, and culminated in guiding my career as an editor, making, altering, adapting, designing, and writing books, and finally creating that ultimate set of books, an encyclopedia. One of the greatest pleasures I had during the years I directed The Canadian Encyclopedia was my friendship with my French tutor, Irene Blum, who introduced me in depth to Marcel Proust. I regretted being the editor of a national encyclopedia who could not speak French. Determined to overcome this language deficiency, I enrolled at Berlitz, where I met Irene. After one lesson, she gave me her phone number and told me that she would tutor me personally, as I was too smart to benefit from the Berlitz method. (*"Les américains aiment le jus d'orange,"* I still remember from that first Berlitz lesson.) We began the lessons at my office and continued in my home for years afterwards. At the end of the workday every Friday, we sat at my dining room table and after *dictée*, read aloud in French. We read Flaubert, Racine, Molière, articles from *Le Monde* and art gallery catalogues, in which the endless recounting of the measurements of paintings supposedly reinforced my knowledge of numbers. Repeatedly, we returned to Proust. I read the text out loud and then tried to translate excerpts from A *la recherche du temps perdu*. Irene patiently corrected my pronunciations and my translations. I still have difficulty reading Proust in French—the extraordinary length of the sentences and the innumerable characters—but I have read the great work in English more than once and have listened to it on audiobook, each time transported to Proust's world, more tangible than my own, filled not only with the portrayals of the Baron de Charlus, Oriane de Guermantes, Charles Swann, Odette de Crécy, Albertine, the elusive narrator, and so many others, but with deep insights into the human condition, slipped effortlessly into the narrative.

Irene's family was born in Chernowitz, that multilingual city throughout history ruled in turn by Romania, Hungary, Austria, Russia, Germany, and now Ukraine. Some of the greatest writers in German (for example Paul Celan) and Yiddish writers, were born there. Roughly half the population, like the Blums, were Jewish. Irene's mother spent time in a labour camp and fled to Israel with her husband Richard, then France and finally to Canada, where Richard established an international reputation as a mathematician. Irene spoke fluent German, Romanian, French, and English. Headed for a brilliant academic career, her life was derailed by her brother's suicide. She desperately claimed that his disappearance from a ferry in the English Channel was an accident (he was pursuing a career in opera but had his heart broken in love), but she knew in her heart that he had jumped. Irene dropped out of her PhD studies at the University of Toronto and took refuge in an abortive acting career and, to pay the bills, in language tutoring. Her mother, Martha Blum, followed her Chernowitz destiny and published her first novel, *The Walnut Tree*, with great critical success, at the age of 86. When Irene was dying of throat cancer in a palliative care ward, I sat by her bed discussing Flaubert with her. Proust was too painful for her. I told her that she was the smartest person that I had ever met. She told me that she had never experienced love. Sadly, the books were no consolation. I didn't know that she had slipped away, until one day I arrived at her empty hospital room. Irene's gifts to me last: the correct pronunciation of the French "u," the frequent laughter we shared over our lessons, and above all the hours we spent in another world of books, in French.

When I was age 14, staying on Norfolk with Annie Radford for the summer, my mother Ada phoned and told me that she had finally succeeded in having my father Harry committed to the 999 Queen Street mental hospital. "You're going to end up in 999!" was an expression we used as kids in Toronto to taunt our antagonists. "Don't bother coming back here," she told me. It was strangely anticlimactic, after all my yearning to live with Annie Radford. Her husband Charlie's understandable objections to a fractious, ungrateful teenager living in his house placed a dark cloud over us. My years with Annie were difficult because I resented being told by everyone, by her and particularly by her daughters Grace and Jean, that I was ungrateful. It only reinforced how insignificant I was. One day in front of number 4 Norfolk, Annie's granddaughter informed me cruelly that I was not part of their family no matter long I squatted at her grandmother's house. Unfortunately, fuelled by guilt, I was disrespectful and dismissive of Annie. I regret it, but she persevered. Her patience and love slowly built confidence in me and support for my fantasy world of literature and art, no matter how rude I may have been. "I loved you more than any of my own children," were the last words she spoke to me. I wish that I had told her what she meant to me, in saving my life. "There is no man, however wise, who has not at some period of his youth said things, or lived in a way the consciousness of which is so unpleasant to him in later life that he would gladly, if he could, expunge it from his memory," wrote Proust. Patiently, Annie's love laid a level of mortar on the emptiness of Ada's neglect. You cannot just replace the absence of one person's love with

*Trevi Fountain, Rome, with daughter Dr. Rebeccah Marsh in 1999.
I went to hear her give an address to
an international conference of physicists.*

another. Ada was, as Annie had told me, my real mother, and the one whose abandonment and resentment I still feel.

So, the nightly panoramas of ruins, humiliations, plummets into elevator shafts, loss and fire that began very early continued, and echo in my dreams to this day. Though many of the nights were lost, the days became happier. Friends and mentors continued to fulfil what a real mother and father did not, introducing me to art, poetry, photography, music, and humour. I feel fortunate that art enabled me to escape my troubled self, that I could see the world multiplied and enriched by Cezanne, Van Gogh, Bach, Hafez, Ozu, Eliot, Li Bai, or Mozart. Most of this treasure is to be found, of course, outside our schools. In my brief time at university in Waterloo, I learned more reading and discussing

Marx, Freud, and Tillich with my roommate Al McIntyre, as we drifted off to sleep in our apartment, than I learned in classes. I failed numerous times to experience the hope that I had learned in Eric Fromm's *Art of Loving,* in finding love with a girl. When I met Lesya, the intense emotions of loving her, being loved (I thought) and being rejected by her, changed my life, and deepened my expectations and understanding of love. I am grateful to her, as I am to the girl with the multicoloured eyes who introduced me to Teilhard de Chardin, to that stranger who swept into my arms and kissed me in a gas station in Hull, to Susan who gave birth to our daughter Rebeccah, whom I embraced within the first minute of her birth, and to Louise, who restarted my heart and has shared a lifetime with me.

Pausing and looking back on a life enforces an ultimately imaginary narrative of connections and causes and a deceptive sense that there is a single conscious self, lodged inside our brain, sealed in our memories. Because a writer follows one chapter with another, he or she implies that the sequence was coherent, or inevitable, whether by chance or by design— and that it is accessible through memory. "I begged of you, O Memory, / to be my best assistant," wrote the modern Greek poet Constantine Cavafy. My account has at least partly been determined by my will to find how I might overcome trauma, unhappiness, or even mental volatility to achieve meaning and personal happiness. I recognize how as a child I prepared defences to survive and how difficult it has been to tear them down when they became impediments. Ultimately, any sense of identity is a deposit of experiences that have been layered over a sense of self that began with the loneliness, emptiness, and anger into which I awoke that day Ada snatched me from the love and security of my life with Annie.

The struggle of a self in the hostile environment of childhood seems in retrospect a series of disconnected experiences: a mother's sarcasm and blows, the stench of liquor and tobacco, the appearance of multiple ghostly selves in the mirror, readings of Thomas Hardy and Dylan Thomas, the first sight of a Shakespeare play, the first hearing of the opening bars of Beethoven's *Symphony No. 5*, a violin searching for death's presence in Bach's *Chaconne*, the intimate closeness standing next to a first love as Sviatoslav Richter held us mesmerized at Massey Hall, playing the lilting cadenza in the first movement of Beethoven's *Piano Concerto No. 5*, the silence and the pauses in Wagner's redemptive *Prelude to Parsifal* drawing tears from me as I sit with Louise in the Seattle Opera House, the power outage and the glittering tropical fish suspended in the darkness of Dr. Szatmari's office. Whether all this amounts to a life, or just a dream, or even reliable memories is impossible to say.

I know that there were hundreds who applied for the job of editor in chief of our national encyclopedia. I have no doubt that many of them were better choices than me. Yet, once chosen in an almost random chain of circumstances, I think that it was unknown to anyone, even myself, that I was perhaps uniquely qualified. Not especially in my editorial expertise. Many had edited more and better books than I had. But being hired to create a work that would, as historian Viv Nelles expressed it for me in a newspaper review, hold up a mirror to our culture, I felt at every turn challenged by my staff, by academics and critics, in ways that ever deepened my understanding of this impossible country that we were portraying. I started with a philosophical base from my studies and from necessity I had to read and study the great Canadian historians of the day to combat my ignorance. The interpretations of Donald Creighton, Harold Innis, Guy Frégault, Arthur Lower, Ramsay Cook, John Saywell, W.L. Morton, Jean Hamelin, Blair Neatby, Mason Wade and others—with all their opposing views—provided a rich tapestry that was an antidote to the (enjoyable) mythologies of popular historians. The first time that I met Pierre Berton, once again an encounter with a great Canadian at the Château Laurier in Ottawa, he learned who I might be. He loomed over me menacingly and told me to stop reprinting those "fucking" nineteeth century history books in the Carleton Library Series, particularly those of J.C. Dent, from which, I later discovered, he derived not only some of his narratives, but so many of his vivid personal characterizations in his gripping, heroic myth of the building of the Canadian Pacific Railway. Among the history students whom I met at Carleton were several who would, to make their young careers, savagely attack that "idiot" Donald Creighton. I told them that I did not agree with his centrist, perhaps anti-French ideology, but that with his great literary style and lifelong devotion to John A. Macdonald, they had a long way to go before they had the right to dismiss him. Now of course it is Macdonald himself who is dismissed for his flaws, by those who project their presentist righteousness backwards over time. As Eric Fromm wrote: "There is perhaps no phenomenon which contains so much destructive feeling as 'moral indignation,' which permits envy or hate to be acted out under the guise of virtue."

One powerful book in my life that was outside the historical narrative, for its ideas as well as its literary impact, was George Grant's *Lament for a Nation*. It was the first volume of the Carleton Library Series that I dealt with, not as an editor of the text, as it was a reprint, but in co-ordinating a new edition and new introduction by the author. I was not only moved by Grant's melancholy outlook but also by my conversations with Grant himself, who was recovering from a terrible car collision. Though I could not accept his deep conservatism, or his dismissal of liberal individualism, or his religious imperatives, I remain persuaded by his lament for the impossibility of true nationhood for Canada, even more so in an era of authoritarian bullying, globalization, social media, increasing inequality, and regional particularisms. There is an ever-diminishing appreciation of what democracy and freedom have given us, driven out by rampant resentment and anguished victimhood. There is so little appreciation for what our history has accomplished, eroded by the judgments of present-day critics of the failures of our ancestors to live up to their lofty, presentist moralities.

Modern multicultural Canada, while presenting a progressive and open face to the world, does not offer its citizens a collective, shared desire to build a unique society north of the United States. None of the Committee for an Independent

Canada nationalists ever really defined the national project that they advocated. They had no cultural ideals. In the end their goals were ownership, profits, and government subventions. The great Canadian critic Northrup Frye called the Canadian identity "an eminently exhaustible subject." That thought was always in my mind in the making of The Canadian Encyclopedia. I tried to spread the "know what Canada is" as far as possible, asking contributors in every part of Canada to ask that question and to respond to it in every possible way. I wanted TCE to be a great communal, not nationalistic, endeavour. If it could not present an illusion of a coherent northern destiny, distinct from the failures of our menacing southern neighbour, at least it was a wide-ranging expression of the local identities to which Canadians are devoted.

I HAD A STARK REMINDER of Canadian parochialism when the encyclopedia was published in 1985. I had through my years in Edmonton defended and promoted my birth city of Toronto as remarkable in ways deprecated in the West. I was warned in 1980 to get rid of my Ontario licence plates as soon as possible, or to get run off the road. Today Edmonton pick-up trucks boast "Fuck Trudeau" banners. When I returned to Toronto to promote the encyclopedia, I went as I always did first, to my favourite bookstore, Albert Britnell Book Shop on Yonge Street. I told the manager that I wanted to tell her about The Canadian Encyclopedia. She looked at me and said derisively, "Why on Earth would we be interested in a Canadian encyclopedia produced in Edmonton?" I never set foot in that store again. It is now ironically the location of an American-owned Starbuck's coffee shop. Fortunately, other booksellers in Toronto stocked the encyclopedia sets and the entire print run of 150,000 sets (450,000 volumes) was sold out across Canada in only five months. My friend Ed Borins, whose bookstore was located at the Park Plaza Hotel on the corner of Bloor

Street and University Avenue, was particularly supportive, though he and Mel Hurtig got into a terrible squabble over price cutting. I ended up arbitrating with a determined Ed on one phone line from Toronto and an angry Mel from Edmonton on another line.

In my daily reading I have always had a biography on the go amidst my other books. I am fascinated with other lives, of the great composers, artists, writers, military leaders, scientists, politicians, philosophers. How did they start? How did they change? At what point does a coherent being enter into and conquer (or succumb to) the real world? I have loved memoirs and autobiographies from the first day that I started to read *Speak, Memory* by Vladimir Nabokov, when its extended version appeared in 1966. It remains the most evocative autobiography I will ever read.

Nabokov called it "a scientific attempt to unravel and trace back all the tangled threads of one's personality." I would have loved to have done that. Its vivid descriptions and haunting spell of resurrecting time are gifts to a reader but intimidating to a writer. Among other memoirs, I was deeply engaged by J.R, Ackerley's droll and regretful *My Father and Myself*, Frank McCourt's *Angela's Ashes*, Mary Karr's *The Liars' Club*, Yiyun Li's, *Dear Friend, from My Life I Write to You in Your Life*, Laurie Lee's, *Cider with Rosie*, James Salter's, *Burning the Days* (the best sentences, ever) and John McGahern's, *All Will be Well*. Any of these masterpieces present challenges to any mere scribbler's aspirations to write. One day at an historical conference in Toronto, Denise Chong, the author of the superb memoir *The Concubine's Children*, spoke to a small seminar about her work. She told us that everyone should research their family and tell their stories. I replied, "What if you don't like what you find?" She answered with a wordless, sidelong gaze, and I began to assemble the notes about my life that have led to this volume.

ACKNOWLEDGMENTS

For the life I have tried to convey, this is an incomplete list of the friends whom I have walked with, for however brief a span, on a journey that would have been impossible to accomplish on my own. John Hunter, Jon McKee, Phil Balsam, Lorna Macewan, Tony Brace, Al McIntyre, Al Hand, Dan Francis, Joan Evoy, Michel Boyer, Sandra Weber, Irene Blum, Bill Beard, Scott Brinsmead, Stephanie Goodman, Suzanne and Kevin Polkosnik, Mark Caplan and Isabelle Chanoine (and our goddaughters Lea and Louise).

For both their friendship and their encouragement of this book, Norman Hillmer stands out for his endurance in supporting me through the encyclopedia years. This volume would never had appeared without his kindness and encouragement. My beloved friend Patricia Finlay provided a key insight into a fragment of the text I imposed on her. Dinah Forbes read a very early draft, saved me from numerous structural flaws and instructed me not to let anyone talk me out of that title. Denise Chong sparked this project many years ago and has patiently asked, "When will I see it?" My friendship with Dominique Ritter and our discussions about life and writing endured when she left the encyclopedia and moved back to Montreal. Jan Novotny helped clarify my mind in our discussions of writing and philosophy on our many fine walks. Adriana

Davies read and helped refine the text on making the encyclopedia. Rosemary Shipton generously applied her editorial skills and memories to the encyclopedia chapters.

I am thankful to my colleagues in my publishing career. Peter West was a true mentor to me. Anna Porter presented me with an opportunity at Carleton University without which the rest would not have happened. Douglas Gibson believed in The Canadian Encyclopedia and encouraged me to tell its story. George Goodwin steered me into the world of McClelland & Stewart, raised funds for the encyclopedia and multiple other projects and guided us into the digital world. Noni Mate of 7th Floor Media was a friend and vital, creative partner. Jim Burant and I were friends all the way back to our art history days at Carleton and he was a great help to the encyclopedia from his management position at the National Archives. My neighbour Yves Sauvé connected me with my publisher/editor/designer Lorene Shyba and buttressed my sometimes-shaky confidence at his always open door. In embracing this manuscript, Lorene Shyba has, with her professionalism, passion, and inspiration, helped me to relive the years of excitement and rewards of my long publishing career. I am grateful to our proofreader Jennifer Theroux for her diligence and eagle eyes.

I could never be diligent enough in acknowledging the contributions of my staff, in every iteration of The Canadian Encyclopedia, every one of them with deep care and devotion, many of whom have told me it was the time of their

Acknowledgments

lives. Arlene Birmingham, Sheila Birmingham, Russell Bingham, Laura Bonikowsky, Claire Citeau, Davina Choy, Adriana Davies, Derek Drager, Mélanie Fafard, Patricia Finlay, Myriam Fontaine, Nancy Foulds, Virginia Gillese, Flo Hayes, Susan Hutton, Valerie Jacobs, Kate Johnson, Gail Kudelik, Christina Lanteigne, Marshall Letcher, Carlotta Lemieux, Trish Lyon, Debra MacGregor, Susanne Marshall, Mary McDougall Maude, Kathryn Merrett, James Ogilvy, Anne-Marie Pederson, John Rasmussen, Dominique Ritter, Robyn Ross, Susan Schroder, Rosemary Shipton, Lorraine Snyder, Susan Spier, Claire Tremblay, Rob Wiznura, Carol Woo, Sasha Yusufali.

Our daughter Rebeccah has filled our lives with laughter, love, and intelligence and with a gift to relive it all with our granddaughter Charlotte. When she was only nine years old, Charlotte urged me, "Grandpa, you better finish that book you are writing, or I will have to finish it for you!"

I did not spend much time with my sisters Marian and Sally or my brother John when we were young, but we connected later in our lives with love, far from the memories of the family maelstrom. Sally has helped patiently with refining our memories.

Lastly, for my partner Louise Mary Edwards, who patiently shared the stress and endless questions radiating from the saga of both my life and this memoir: I am thankful to have lived with her enduring beauty, grace, and kindness.

DV

REFLECTIONS
SERIES